Top Secret Executive Resumes, Second Edition:

Create the Perfect Resume for the Best Top-Level Positions

Steven Provenzano, CPRW/CEIP

COURSE TECHNOLOGY
CENGAGE Learning

Australia, Brazil, Japan, Korea, Mexico, Singapore, Spain, United Kingdom, United States

COURSE TECHNOLOGY
CENGAGE Learning™

Top Secret Executive Resumes, Second Edition: Create the Perfect Resume for the Best Top-Level Positions

Steven Provenzano

Publisher and General Manager, Course Technology PTR:
Stacy L. Hiquet

Associate Director of Marketing:
Sarah Panella

Manager of Editorial Services:
Heather Talbot

Senior Acquisitions Editor:
Mitzi Koontz

Marketing Manager: Mark Hughes

Project Editor: Cathleen D. Small

Copy Editor: Cathleen D. Small

Interior Layout: Jill Flores

Cover Designer: Luke Fletcher

Indexer: Larry Sweazy

Proofreader: Gene Redding

For product information and technology assistance, contact us at
Cengage Learning Customer & Sales Support, 1-800-354-9706

For permission to use material from this text or product, submit all requests online at **cengage.com/permissions**
Further permissions questions can be emailed to
permissionrequest@cengage.com

All trademarks are the property of their respective owners.

All images © Cengage Learning unless otherwise noted.

Library of Congress Control Number: 2011933244

ISBN-13: 978-1-4354-6040-9

ISBN-10: 1-4354-6040-5

Course Technology, a part of Cengage Learning
20 Channel Center Street
Boston, MA 02210
USA

Cengage Learning is a leading provider of customized learning solutions with office locations around the globe, including Singapore, the United Kingdom, Australia, Mexico, Brazil, and Japan. Locate your local office at: **international. cengage.com/region**

Cengage Learning products are represented in Canada by Nelson Education, Ltd.

For your lifelong learning solutions, visit **courseptr.com**

Visit our corporate website at **cengage.com**

Printed in the United States of America
1 2 3 4 5 6 7 13 12 11

To my friends, family and business associates,
the finest in the world.

Acknowledgments

This book would not have been possible without the trust and feedback of thousands of executives, recruiters, HR managers and career experts over the years. I'd also like to acknowledge all those at Cengage Learning who helped to create this new edition, especially Stacy, Jill and Mark for their creativity and input. Special thanks to my parents, Tony and Doris; brothers Randy, Jim and Bill; and sister Grace Marie. And of course, Max the Cat. I'd also like to thank some great friends, who've always been there for me: Karen Evertsen, Joan Magic, Steve Harbaugh, Dean Gladwin and Jeff Burns.

About the Author

Steven Provenzano is president of ECS: Executive Career Services & DTP, Inc. A former corporate recruiter and author of eight career-related books, he has written more than 4,000 resumes. Steven has appeared on CNBC several times, CNNfn, WGN, ABC/NBC in Chicago, and numerous radio programs. He has also been featured in major newspapers, such as *The Wall Street Journal*, *Crain's*, and the *Chicago Tribune*. He is a Certified Professional Resume Writer (CPRW) and Certified Employment Interview Professional (CEIP). His work is endorsed by *Chicago Tribune* Career Columnist Lindsey Novak and top executives at firms such as Motorola. Website: www.Execareers.com. For a free resume analysis, send your resume in confidence to Careers@Execareers.com, or call toll-free 877-610-6810 or 630-289-6222.

Contents

Contents

Contents

Contents

Introduction

Welcome to the second edition of *Top Secret Executive Resumes*—the secrets of professional resume writers. I wrote this for executives, managers, professionals and leaders from all industries seeking new and better opportunities. If you're one of those, then congratulations, because there's no better time to create a better future for yourself.

At my career marketing firm, I get calls all the time from top executives looking for feedback on their resume or for someone to write it for them. These talented people head large companies; others are vice presidents, directors or sole proprietors. Even with unemployment around 9 percent at the time of this writing, we still find that high-quality people are always in demand. With the explosion of e-commerce, LinkedIn, Twitter, texting and of course, that old standby, email, business decisions are made with lightning speed. Competition in all industries is intense, and smart executives are constantly on the lookout for highly qualified people just like you.

Given the huge pool of unemployed workers, employers now look for executives with wider skill sets to work longer hours, and they expect higher-quality work and devotion to their companies. Just like their customers, they want more bang for their buck. They expect a focused, hardworking team player with well-rounded skills in team training and communications, maybe even finance, marketing or the latest computer systems. At least one of these, communication skills, will be directly reflected in your resume and will give a first impression to someone you may want to work with—so it better be good.

With intense competition for the best positions, the need for an excellent, mind-blowing resume has never been greater. Even those still employed are looking for better work: more money, more challenge, a better geographic location or all of the above. That's why it's essential to create a high-impact resume that markets you and your skills—your personal brand—with impact and precision, so you can stand above the crowd.

Fred Wackerle is a recruiter who only fulfills CEO and Board searches. Here's his top 10 list of leadership skills. How do you stack up?

1. Unquestioned integrity
2. High work ethic
3. Ability to handle failure (and quickly learn from it, I say)
4. Leadership and motivational skills
5. High personal values and an ability to motivate yourself
6. Appropriate balance between work and family
7. Ability to focus and prioritize
8. Straight talker
9. Self-confidence
10. Willingness to make tough and unpopular decisions

Yet when all is said and done, remember that you don't need to be "perfect" to be hired for a new position, you just need to appear less imperfect, trainable and more likable than most other candidates seeking the same position. If you doubt this, take a look at bosses or co-workers you thought weren't qualified to hold their position. How did they get their job? They marketed themselves into that position, and they won over the interviewer by making a personal connection. They came across as likable, trainable and professional. How did they keep their job? They kept learning and growing within the company, day after day.

A New Philosophy

After writing more than 4,000 resumes for executives and professionals worldwide, I've found they all have three things in common: They want a better position, they can't get that position without an interview and they often can't get an interview without a great resume.

People still walk into my office with a basic history of where and when they worked and a short outline of their daily duties. I tell them that's a start, and then I ask "The Question":

What do you really want to DO in your next position?

This is the most basic question I can ask of a new client, and some are surprised by it. You'd be amazed at the answers I get. Many people assume they will keep doing the same exact work they were doing for their previous or current employers (which, of course, they don't have to), until they really start to think about the question.

But no two jobs, even if they have the same job title, are exactly the same. That's why it's essential to look at the types of skills you would like to use and then create a resume that targets a position that uses them—with the right kind of product or service, whenever possible.

Fortunately, the content and design of your resume is one of the few aspects of your job search over which you have complete control, and it is one of your most valuable assets. During my career seminars, I tell people that their resume can be the most important document they will ever have—more important than their driver's license, their passport or even their birth certificate. No other document can have such an impact on their income and, most importantly, on where and how they spend 40 to 50 hours of their life each week.

A New Approach

Some of the most qualified executives think a resume is just an outline of old jobs and educational background (that's what I call a "job list," a history of your working life). To some extent that's true, because your work history is an essential part of your resume (more on this later). But done correctly, expert resume writing can help open doors to the really good positions, increase your income and help you enjoy what you're doing every day. To do this, your resume must:

Develop and market your skills and abilities.

This may sound like a simple concept, but think about it: Does the average "job list" resume really develop and market the skills and talents you walk in the door with, and really explain what *you* can bring to your next position? Usually not, and for one important reason: When you send out a "job list" resume, you're stating what you've done for previous employers, but not what you can do for your next employer.

And that's really what this book is all about—helping you identify and sell, on paper, your most relevant skills, knowledge and training. With so many people looking for new jobs, competition for the best executive jobs is tough: Most jobs aren't advertised, and of course, many companies first hire from within and then look externally.

Simple and basic? Or ineffective?

From time to time, I get top executives calling my office who say they want a "simple" or "basic" resume, and I cringe. They think there's something magical about those words, bringing me brief descriptions of their work history and education.

But when I hear the words "simple" or "basic," I stop them in their tracks and tell them: "We'll make it effective." Never underestimate the power of a few "basic" words.

What You're Up Against

With the advent of the Internet, job postings can be viewed by thousands of executives all over the world, generating hundreds of responses the very same day. Web sites such as CareerPath.com offer high-speed access to job advertisements nationwide. A single display advertisement in the Sunday paper can draw hundreds of resumes, and that was before the Internet took off. Listings on large job boards such as Monster.com or CareerBuilder can draw thousands of resumes in a single day. Research tells us that most resumes have only a few seconds to grab the reader's attention, so yours must rise quickly above the rest.

Here's a chilling statistic: A survey of 150 executives from the nation's 1,000 largest companies was conducted by Accountemps/Robert Half. Can you believe that 70 percent said they spend two minutes or less reviewing an applicant's resume? Years of hard work and training, and you may get just a few seconds to market yourself. That's why your resume must become less historical and more of an attention-getting advertisement, a billboard, a marketing piece.

Avoid the Resume-Screening Process

As a former corporate recruiter, I quickly learned that resumes are typically used to weed out potential candidates. If you've ever been in the position to hire new employees, you know how this goes. No matter how many job openings a company may have, it simply doesn't have the time or staff to interview every single applicant. I did what many of my peers did—I sifted through the day's resumes and made three piles: "Great," "Possible," and "Never." I called people from the "Great" stack for interviews. Eventually, we threw out or filed the "Possible" and "Never" resumes.

With the advent of resume-screening software, or Applicant Tracking Systems (ATS), your executive resume may be scanned as quickly as any other resume, either by a screener in the human resources department (who may pass it on to the hiring executive) or electronically by a computer.

In both situations, employers are looking for essential keywords that relate to their job requirements, including, but certainly not limited to, project management, budgeting, international marketing, team leadership, staff training, finance, CEO, COO, CFO and so on. Computers and people may also be searching for particular certifications, software brand names or keywords specific to certain industries. Assuming this is found, readers may then check for a steady work history (little or no job-hopping, or too many jobs in too short a time), educational background or training.

If the initial glance passes muster, the HR representative may pass along your resume, with several others, to the hiring executive. Typically, that manager is the direct supervisor over the position and will make the final decision about whom to call for interviews. The initial interview is usually conducted by HR department staff (many of whom may not have a detailed understanding of the position at hand), and a short list of candidates is created.

Finally, three to five candidates will be interviewed by the hiring manager (sometimes with other department managers present), and a decision is made to offer the position to the candidate who best suits their needs, corporate environment, payroll budget and, most importantly, who is most liked among that group of hiring managers.

Clearly, there are plenty of opportunities throughout the process to eliminate resumes and candidates. Your job search isn't about having every possible degree or certificate or qualification—it's about making the best of what you have and what you can offer, right now. It's about winning the confidence of others and about not being eliminated by someone else who may technically be less qualified than you.

The Need for Accuracy

As noted earlier, research shows that the average resume has only a few seconds to catch the reader's interest. For the same reason, brevity, accuracy and overall appearance are key to a successful resume. If you're not sure how to spell a word, look it up. If you don't know how to type accurately, hire a professional typist or CPRW.

Job Search Facts

Proofread, proofread, proofread!!! OfficeTeam conducted a survey of 150 managers from the nation's 1,000 largest companies. The survey revealed that 76 percent said they would not hire candidates who have one or two typographical errors on their resume, and 45 percent said it would take only one typo to eliminate a candidate from consideration. Be careful what you send—have family and friends proofread your resume from top to bottom, and bottom to top.

Accuracy and clarity are essential. I've seen thousands of resumes from top executives, many of which had basic typing and spelling errors. Nothing turns off an employer more quickly. Did you know that a common misspelling of the word manager—as manger—won't be found by most spell-checking software? I've found this typo on numerous resumes, and I didn't rely on my software to find it. The impression is, "If this person can't even produce a decent resume, how could she possibly perform this job well?" Later on, I'll offer proofreading suggestions and tips for designing and creating a high-impact masterpiece.

Remember, you can choose to present yourself through your resume in an average way—or in an outstanding way. The difference between a good resume and a great resume may just be the foot in the door you need to land the best interviews—which will lead to more opportunities for *better* job offers.

Interview Yourself

Before you start writing anything, conduct a full, honest inventory of the skills and talents you can—and want to—bring to your next position. This requires honesty and objectivity. Are you really proficient at everything you do? Of course not. On the other hand, don't take any of your applicable experience for granted. It can be a mistake to assume that an employer knows what you can do simply because he is already in that particular business.

I truly believe that writing an effective resume is a process of self-discovery, so I try to create personal advertisements for my clients. I assume they have certain abilities, skills and training that will be useful in their next position. It's my job to identify their best talents and then develop those talents on paper—otherwise, they're not much use in the job-hunt process.

You must take stock of your knowledge and achievements in your chosen field and decide what to develop, what to downplay and what to leave out.

This discovery process will prove even more valuable when you go on job interviews. It can help prepare you for interview questions (tips on those later) and actually create new career choices, when you see that your skills may be applicable to entirely new industries.

Job Search Facts

Market studies show that about 70 percent of professionals get their jobs through informal referrals—that is, *networking*. Another 12 percent are filled through search firms, 9 percent through mass mailings, and only about 9 percent through published advertisements, including the large Internet job boards. Although it may be who you know that matters, you will always need a great resume to pass on, even through a personal contact.

Some New Perspectives

Remember, your resume will not get you a job—only you can do that—but it can certainly *prevent* you from getting one. If your resume doesn't effectively sell your skills and showcase your experience and achievements, you can bet there are plenty of others on the hiring manager's desk that do.

Opinions, Opinions

Everyone defines a great resume differently. That's why there are very few hard-and-fast rules about the "perfect" resume. In fact, top executives may appear overqualified (that is, overpriced) for certain positions. What's perfect is what will work best for you given your situation and the income level of the position you seek. Just because a resume style or format seems to work for someone you know, that doesn't mean it'll work for you.

Tips on Professional Services

Throughout the resume-writing process, consider a free resume analysis by a Certified Professional Resume Writer (CPRW). There are only a few hundred CPRWs nationwide, and they must pass a challenging test and meet rigid criteria before receiving certification from the Professional Association of Resume Writers (PARW). Not all CPRWs offer a free resume review, but most will be glad to oblige.

A good CPRW may be able to write better about you simply because he is not you. The best ones know what employers want to see and may have experience as CEOs or corporate recruiters with major businesses. They can take an objective look at your background, ask you numerous in-depth questions and create a high-impact marketing piece. The writer should offer a free resume analysis and not even try to quote prices without seeing what kind of work is involved for your resume. For a free resume review by me or my staff, send your resume to: Careers@Execareers.com. You may also visit our website at Execareers.com or call me personally at (630) 289-6222, or toll-free at (877) 610-6810.

Making the Most of This Book

This book was designed to help you identify, develop and market your skills and abilities, with the goal of landing interviews. I'll try to outline the entire process we use for the top executives we write for, including evaluating past work experience, education and skills and then translating and developing them into powerful selling points. I'll discuss essential points of format and organization for your achievements, as well as layout and design, writing and using a cover letter, making job contacts and acing the interview.

Additionally, this book includes three before-and-after resume examples, a military conversion resume and more than 70 executive resumes that produced calls, interviews and/or new positions for my clients. Their names and company names have been changed, but the circumstances of each resume represented in this book are real life. Study the different formats, designs and phrasings. I've tried to include a good cross-section of resumes from our executive clients. Make notes in the margins, fill out the worksheets and circle phrases and ideas that apply to you—as long as this isn't a library book.

The more you involve yourself in the writing process, the better you'll understand what makes a successful resume—and the better your final results will be.

The Power of Now: Determine and Market Your Career Potential

Your resume is part of a cohesive, high-impact career-marketing program, and when written correctly, it can pay huge dividends. We've all heard that the average resume gets about one to two minutes of attention by employers—if you're lucky. In fact, it may never be seen by human eyes if it's first screened out by an ATS (*applicant tracking system*), such as RESUMate, PeopleClick or Sendouts. Thousands of employers nationwide now use some type of ATS, especially with hundreds of resumes pouring in each day via direct email or through CareerBuilder, Monster.com and many other such sites. That's why a strong Profile/Keyword section at the top of your resume is essential and why virtually every resume in this book has one.

When you understand how resumes are sorted and viewed these days, you can leverage the latest technology to your advantage, rather than let it block your career advancement. Yet when all is said and done, and the computers and software have their way, I've learned there's one common question that runs through the mind of virtually every employer:

What Can You Do For Me?

Let's say your resume makes it past the electronic screening software and finally lands on the desk (or computer screen) of the hiring manager. In the first few seconds, he's looking for:

1. Reasons to keep reading

2. Reasons to consider you specifically for the position at hand

3. Reasons to stop reading and move on to the next resume—saving himself time and effort

All three of these items need to be addressed from the very first sentence of your Profile/Skills section, right through to the end of your resume. Obviously, the more reasons you give, the better. Put yourself in his shoes and pretend you're reading your own resume: Is it enough to write that you're skilled in new business development? Or do you need to be specific? (For example, "Skilled in the hiring, training and motivation of high-impact sales teams in product lines, executive sales and the acquisition/management of Fortune 500 accounts in major national markets.")

Every line you write on your resume must answer the question: Why should I interview this candidate?

In the following pages, you'll find worksheets to help you identify your transferable skills, hands-on experience and achievements with employers. This will become the content, the "meat," of your resume and is the most important step in developing your executive marketing piece. Not only will this exercise help you extract the accomplishments that will answer questions of prospective employers, it will help *you* learn more about yourself and make you more confident as you pursue new opportunities and walk into job interviews.

If necessary, review performance evaluations from previous jobs and ask co-workers what they think of your skills and strengths. Take the time to consider which aspects of work you're best at and, most importantly, what you really enjoy doing.

What would be the ideal position for you? What turns you on at work? For many executives, it's being in charge of a wide range of functions: from staffing and budget planning to writing procedures, developing products or creative marketing. It's time to choose any or all of these areas and then develop and market the skills you have in each of them.

Begin with the personal inventory on page 4 and then use the skills assessment to brainstorm your favorite skill areas for the Profile at the top of your resume, where you interpret and develop your most relevant skills for the reader and highlight the knowledge you would most like to leverage in your next position. Without a strong development of your best talents right up front, you're asking readers to figure out what you can do for them simply by reading about your work history—you're even expecting them to read your entire resume—*and it's very possible they can't or won't do this.*

The skills-assessment sheet is really your wish list. Here's where you can write about and develop your most important skills and abilities, extracted from your entire work, education, volunteer or personal life. I'll talk more about how to write your Profile in the next few chapters, so you may want to skip completing the skills-assessment page until then.

Perhaps most important: Never try to describe the type of person you are in your Profile/Skills section. I still see this every day in homemade resumes or those written by other "professional" resume firms. That's because it's the easy way out: Writing about someone's subjective attributes is easy—and ultimately less refutable—than developing and marketing someone's hardcore business knowledge, talents, skills and abilities. Stating that you're self-motivated, professional, seasoned, energetic, and so on can't be proven, and this can, in fact, be said about anyone.

Why use this type of wording? Don't fall into this trap! The farthest I'll go here is something like "personal, yet professional communication skills…hire, train and motivate teams to peak performance," and so on. If you really want to develop more of your personal attributes, do so in the cover letter and customize that document for each employer and each position; check Chapter 13, "Cover Letter Essentials and Examples."

Getting Started: Your Personal Inventory

The personal inventory includes the standard nuts and bolts about your work history and education: company names, job titles, achievements and so on.

Name

First Name _____

Middle Name _____

Last Name _____

Address _____

Street _____

City _____ State _____ Zip _____

Telephone with Area Code _____

Email Address: _____

Desired Position or Industry: _____

Employment (List most relevant jobs first)

From Company _____

City/State _____

To _____ Type of Business _____

Product or Service _____

Positions or Titles _____

Responsibilities and Duties _____

Supervisory Duties _____

Accomplishments or Major Achievements _____

_____

From Company _____

City/State _____

To _____ Type of Business _____

Product or Service _____

Positions or Titles _____

Responsibilities and Duties _____

Supervisory Duties _____

Accomplishments or Major Achievements _____

_____

Education (Most recent first)

College _____

City/State _____

Degree _____ Year _____

Major _____ Minor _____ GPA _____

Coursework _____

Achievements/Activities _____

_____

College _____

City/State _____

Degree _____ Year _____

Major _____ Minor _____ GPA _____

Coursework _____

Achievements/Activities _____

_____

Awards/Scholarships _____

Seminars and Special Training _____

Vocational/Trade School

City/State_____

Certificate _____ Dates Attended _____

Awards/Achievements _____

Special Jobs/Equipment _____

Vocational/Trade School

City/State_____

Certificate _____ Dates Attended _____

Awards/Achievements _____

Special Jobs/Equipment _____

High School _____

Dates Attended _____

City/State _____

Achievements/Activities _____

Military Service _____

Dates Enlisted _____

Special Skills/Training _____

Awards/Achievements _____

Honorable Discharge? _____ Rank _____

Professional Memberships

Organization _____ Dates _____

Offices Held _____

Duties/Responsibilities _____

Skills Acquired _____

Organization _____ Dates _____

Offices Held _____

Duties/Responsibilities _____

Skills Acquired _____

Organization _____ Dates _____

Offices Held _____

Duties/Responsibilities _____

Skills Acquired _____

Organization _____ Dates _____

Offices Held _____

Duties/Responsibilities _____

Skills Acquired _____

Community Services and Volunteer Activities

Organization _____

Offices/Titles Held _____

City/State _____ Dates _____

Specific activities in which you were involved and skills utilized

_____

_____

Organization _____

Offices/Titles Held _____

City/State _____ Dates _____

Specific activities in which you were involved and skills utilized

_____

_____

Organization _____

Offices/Titles Held _____

City/State _____ Dates _____

Specific activities in which you were involved and skills utilized

_____

_____

Personal Interests, Sports and Hobbies _____

_____

References

Business

Name _____ Title _____

Company Name _____

Company Address _____

Telephone: Office _____Home (optional) _____

Name _____ Title _____

Company Name _____

Company Address _____

Telephone: Office _____Home (optional) _____

Name _____ Title _____

Company Name _____

Company Address _____

Telephone: Office _____Home (optional) _____

Personal

Name _____ Profession _____

Telephone: Office _____ Home (optional) _____

Name _____ Profession _____

Telephone: Office _____ Home (optional) _____

Name _____ Profession _____

Telephone: Office _____ Home (optional) _____

Name _____ Profession _____

Telephone: Office _____ Home (optional) _____

Skills Assessment

Transferable/Marketable Skills and Abilities	Specific Job Duties and Achievements
Write down the specific skills you'd like to use most in the ideal position. This is the basis for the Profile bullets at the top of your resume.	Write about daily duties at positions, beginning with your most recent or relevant position.

1. Skill Group: A big picture of talents in general areas, such as research and development, production, etc.

   _____

   _____

   _____

   _____

   _____

2. Skill Group: Expand on the first group, such as loan acquisition (for M&As), strategic planning, more specific types of operations, etc.

   _____

   _____

   _____

   _____

   _____

1. Duties and achievements at present or most recent company, such as type and size of operation supervised (products, operations, or finance, etc.) and services produced, etc.:

   _____

   _____

   _____

   _____

2. Duties and achievements at previous position:

   _____

   _____

   _____

   _____

   _____

3. Skill Group: Expand on the second group: types of leadership skill, such as staff hiring, training program development, procedure planning, etc.

_____

_____

_____

_____

_____

4. Skill Group: Expand on entirely different areas: technical skills in your industry and/or specific, related hardware and software knowledge, used for what purpose?

_____

_____

_____

_____

_____

5. Skill Group: This can be a final wrap-up bullet, with items such as knowledge of specific foreign markets, foreign languages or other unique talents.

_____

_____

_____

_____

_____

3. Duties and achievements at previous position:

_____

_____

_____

_____

4. Duties and achievements at previous position:

_____

_____

_____

_____

5. Duties and achievements at previous position:

_____

_____

_____

_____

Organizing a High-Impact Resume

In a market where job postings appear and disappear at the speed of light, it's easy to feel overwhelmed. Fortunately, a resume is the one part of your job search over which you have total control. It's your chance to sell yourself and create a positive first impression.

Because each of us has different experiences, skills and achievements, there isn't one perfect way to organize a resume. In this chapter, we'll take a look at the three most common resume formats to determine which may work best for you.

Chronological Format

The Chronological format is one of the most commonly used resume formats (although it's my least favorite). It emphasizes your work history, positioning it either first on the resume or following the Job Objective or Title. The Employment History is typically listed in order of the most recent job first, but that's not always the case. If your most relevant work history was long ago, you may list that first and continue in reverse chronological order.

Many people use this format because it's simple to write, and its main emphasis is work history. If you've had a steady work history and you've gained skills and achievements as you have progressed, this may work for you.

The main problem with this format, however, is that it doesn't *interpret* your work history for the reader. If you're applying for a position that's very different from your most recent one, your resume might be rejected before the reader learns more about your most relevant, most marketable skills and abilities.

The Chronological format may also be troublesome if you've had an erratic job history—gaps in employment are made apparent by the chronological listing of jobs and may raise questions in the reader's mind. Most troublesome: This resume puts the entire emphasis on your past and is therefore not a future-oriented document. In essence, the Chronological resume makes it easier for the reader to take you out of the running for a position, saving him time and effort.

Functional Format

A Functional format consists of a summary of job-related information (past information). It emphasizes essential skills and certain job-specific achievements out of context. This summary actually replaces specific job descriptions under company names and job titles. The Employment section is then reduced to only company name, city/state, dates of employment, and job title. Although I've seen people actually omit any company names or dates, I don't recommend this unless you've really got something to hide about your past that you think will immediately knock you out of consideration.

For example, if you were seeking a CEO position, you might list in your Functional summary that you had full P&L responsibility for a $500 million operation with more than 200 employees. However, you would omit that this was six years ago and that you've been a director of marketing since that company closed down.

Job seekers may use this format to downplay gaps in work history or the fact that they're jumping into a new career or type of position. But many recruiters and hiring executives are aware of this (hey, they have resumes, too). Now you see why I rarely recommend this format. A Functional resume can send up red flags to readers who may suspect that you're hiding something. Remember that many employers don't enjoy reading resumes and see it as a weeding-out process. Any perceived negative may be all they need to not call you in. Avoid as many potential negatives as possible and, in most cases, use my favorite format, the Combination, instead.

Combination Format

Here's the format I like the most, and the one we use most often for our executive clients. Just about all of the resume samples in this book are in Combination format. It combines the best of a modified Functional summary and a Chronological format. It usually begins with a short Title or Objective (explained later) followed by a strong Profile/Skills section to sell your most relevant and marketable skills, abilities, knowledge and training acquired throughout your career. The Profile is the heart of your resume, consisting of the most relevant keywords applicable to your position or industry at any given time. It's your transferable skills, what you can and really want to do for the employer, and what you want the employer to notice about you.

After a hard-hitting Profile section (drawn from items and keywords listed in your Skills Assessment sheet), you'll need a high-impact Employment (chronological) section. Here's where you emphasize how you've applied your skills: daily duties and achievements—*in context*—at specific companies. Notice I used italics to emphasize that your daily duties and accomplishments are in context. That's because it's essential that employers know where, when and how you applied your skills and what you achieved at specific jobs.

This format develops and markets your applicable skills and reassures the reader that you have nothing to hide by offering details about work history and job-specific accomplishments. You may also incorporate volunteer jobs and non-paid experience into your Employment section. This is fine, but label them as such—don't try to lead the reader into thinking they were paid positions.

You may leave out shorter jobs in certain cases, provided they don't show long gaps between employment. Consider leaving out months and using only years to hide short gaps. For example, you could place a job dated 2007–2008 beneath a position dated 2008–Present. Never mind that you left the older job in February of 2008, had a meaningless temporary assignment for two months, and didn't begin your current job until May of 2008.

Remember that you don't want to lie on your resume, but there are instances when we feel it's okay to omit irrelevant positions. In this type of situation, be prepared to tell interviewers, in person or over the phone, that you didn't think listing that short assignment was relevant to your job search—or give other reasons, as appropriate. I'm giving you some options here, but when all is said and done, *you* must be able to back up everything you include in or leave out of your resume. *You* must feel comfortable answering questions about how you've developed—or downplayed—items about your prior employment, education or transferable skills.

Potential Results

Many of our clients have said they received a 20- to 30-percent positive response rate (requests for interviews). Of course, the exact response rate you'll get depends on a variety of factors: relevant skills, recent training on new systems or procedures, how you customize your cover letter, whether you call and/or research the company, and whether you follow up your resume with a phone call or letter.

Distinguishing Yourself

Because time is tight during a job search, and the competition can be intense, the trick is to get as much relevant information across to the reader as quickly as possible. As an HR manager reviewing resumes, my requirements were simple—the candidate had to do what most applicants fail to do:

1. Demonstrate on paper that he had truly considered at least some of the essential requirements of the position.

2. Identify his most relevant and transferable skills and abilities.

3. Effectively pre-sort experience and information in terms of relevance to my needs.

4. Match his skills and abilities in the Profile/Skills section to those demanded by the job.

5. Clearly develop those skills and abilities in an objectively written (as opposed to subjectively written) Profile/Skills section up front, ahead of work history.

6. Back this up with evidence: job-specific duties, achievements and accomplishments.

Job Search Facts

Starting to feel underqualified? Don't worry, because here are four more reasons why your Profile section is so useful. According to a survey by the American Society of Training and Development, the top four qualities employers are looking for today are:

1. The ability to learn

2. The ability to listen and convey information

3. The ability to solve problems in innovative ways

4. The knowledge of how to get things done

I would add to this several intangibles they'll notice about you at the interview, and to some extent on the phone:

1. A positive attitude

2. Confidence, including eye contact, handshake, body language, and so on

3. Professional demeanor: cool, calm and collected

4. Clear, professional communication skills

These are qualities they can't train you for on the job. If you feel you need work in these areas, I highly recommend you consult a career coach. You must consistently demonstrate all of them in the writing of your resume, in your phone conversations, while networking and most importantly, at the interview.

Keeping Your Resume Honest

Remember that hiring managers may be in a rush to get someone on the job. When they come across too many adjectives or get a sense that the applicant is trying too hard to sound perfect (rather than communicating tangible skills and qualifications), they may just assume you don't have relevant skills. They'll go on to the next resume in the stack and look for essential items.

If you find yourself embellishing too much, look closely at what your talents really are. When employers come across too many fluff words, such as "self-motivated," "computer literate," or "hardworking," they may simply not read the Profile section and just quickly scan your jobs. Then all that expensive paper, time and effort was for nothing. That's why I always remind people that content matters most.

There's another reason for leaving out the fluff: If employers think you're trying to embellish too much in your writing, they may wonder, "What is this person trying to cover up? A lack of genuine skill? A rocky job history?"

Never lie on your resume. Someday, your boss may ask you to do something you can't, and there goes your credibility and possibly your job. You must be able to back up everything on your resume during an interview. It's easier to develop your most important skills for the work you're seeking when you give yourself credit for your real talents, spell them out simply and then position them to your (and the employer's) best advantage.

Resume Essentials

I know most of us don't like to fill out forms, but by now you should have filled out the worksheets in the previous chapter. If you haven't done this yet, do so now, because those sheets will provide the primary content for your resume.

Let's review the definitions and importance of the different pieces of information your resume may include.

Name, Address, Phone Number and Email Address

It's hard to believe, but I've actually received resumes without phone numbers! Needless to say, those applicants didn't get far with our company. Be sure you've listed your contact information correctly, and include a LinkedIn address if you have one.

Job Titles

You can change job titles to be understood by as many employers as possible. For instance, "Marketing Manager: Northeast Sector" can become "Marketing Manager" followed by an explanation that you were "responsible for a team of 12 in the marketing of X products throughout the Northeastern United States." However, don't give yourself a promotion, listing a title that implies more responsibility than you actually had, such as Director of Marketing.

Company Names and Dates

Unless you've had four or five jobs shorter than one year and you are writing a purely Functional resume, include company names and locations (city *and* state, unless they're local). Use months as well as years or, as mentioned previously, omit months if it helps you leave out jobs or cover your tracks. However, be consistent and be able to back everything up in an interview. Note different ways of listing dates throughout the resume samples in this book.

Job Duties

Identify key duties in your jobs and then develop and highlight your achievements and how you exceeded job expectations. Include part-time employment when it applies to the position desired. You may also include part-time jobs or volunteer work that shows initiative, self-motivation, leadership and organizational or communication skills.

Licenses and Certifications

Obviously, include licenses and certifications, such as ISO 9001 certification. Be sure to include civil service or government agency licenses, grades and classifications when appropriate for the type of job you're seeking—for example, Series 6 and 63 license holder, CPA or CFP. You should also spell out these acronyms if you think there's a chance they won't be understood—for example, MCSE: Microsoft Certified Systems Engineer, and so on.

Education

List the highest level of education reached first. Avoid listing high school if you have a college degree. Education becomes less important as work experience and abilities expand. Place your Education section following Employment when you have several years of applicable work history.

You should also include college attendance and course completions, even if you didn't earn a degree.

Include additional professional training, especially if it was sponsored by an employer—it shows the firm had confidence in your ability to learn and succeed. List which firms sponsored the seminars or college courses.

If you have no applicable work experience, develop any relevant education or training in your Profile/Skills section, qualified with sentence starters such as "Trained in…," "Familiar with…," or "Knowledge of…." You need to get your most relevant keywords—your value in the job market—right up front and be clear about your level of knowledge or expertise. Check the Profile/Skills sections in the resume examples that follow.

Languages

Knowledge of a foreign language can be extremely valuable. List your level of proficiency: "Speak conversational French," "Fluent in Spanish," "Read and write Italian," "Familiar with Russian" and so on. You can mention these in a communications bullet in your Profile section or near the bottom in a Personal section, as shown in some of the resume examples.

Professional Memberships

You should list trade and professional groups if they're relevant to your future position. This demonstrates an active interest in industry developments and that you're up to date in the latest concepts and technologies with your peers. These affiliations can prove very valuable in personal networking.

Eliminate from Your Resume

The following sections cover information that you should eliminate from your resume.

Salary Requirements/History

When employers want to know your salary requirements, they generally want to know whether they can afford you—or how cheaply they can get you. They also want to make sure they don't end up paying more than they need to fill the position. If this is requested in the job posting or advertisement, you may include it, but on a separate salary history sheet and never on the resume itself. On the other hand, consider the following survey, and you may wish to omit salary information all together.

In a survey of more than 200 employers who posted job openings stating, "Resumes without salary history will not be considered," a full 94 percent of respondents said they would *still* call a candidate if they thought he was right for the job, even if salary history or requirements were not included.

If salary information is not requested, then do not offer it; you could be knocked out of consideration for being over- or underpriced. Another option is to mention a salary range in a cover letter. ("Although I am seeking an income in the range of $95,000, this number is negotiables depending on the potential for advancement, benefits, type of position and geographic location.")

It's best, however, to avoid discussion of salary until you've hooked the employer. Once you get an offer, or at least have a phone conversation, *then* you can negotiate compensation, including benefits, insurance, stock options, bonuses, geographic considerations and potential for career advancement.

"Resume" at the Top of the Page or "References Available Upon Request" at the End

If the person reading your resume can't tell it's a resume, do you really want to work for her? As for references, create a separate References sheet with three or four names, titles, and phone numbers of previous supervisors and personal contacts, if you're sure they will give you a positive reference. (See the example after the cover letters in Chapter 13, "Cover Letter Essentials and Examples.")

Print these on the same paper stock as your resume and bring this page along with your resume to the interview to complete job applications if necessary.

The personnel representative or hiring manager may want to contact a former employer, but usually someone will check with you before doing so. Double-check this at the interview if you are concerned about keeping your job search confidential.

Reasons for Leaving a Job

For the most part, don't include this information on your resume—you want to highlight positives, not negatives. The only exception to this is if you were promoted or transferred within a company. Why? Because this shows continuity and growth—*positive* reasons.

During the interview you may be asked why you left a particular position—and you should be prepared to answer such a question then. Rehearse a concise response with a positive spin. Until you're confident about this, check your library or bookstore for books on interviewing, or consult recruiters. We work with several top career coaches and counselors, so feel free to call for referrals.

Religious or Political Groups

This type of information has a chance of working against you, so don't offer it unless you know it will be perceived in a positive manner. Try to put business considerations first. What do these associations have to do with the position you're seeking? Like anything else, if it won't help you get in the door, leave it out.

If you have volunteer experience with schools or service groups (Kiwanis, the Rotary Club, Boy Scouts, and so on), then you should develop and include this experience on your resume in a Personal or Volunteer section. You may also leverage the communication, organizational, and leadership skills acquired with these groups and paraphrase them in your Profile section with those qualifying sentence starters: "Trained in…," "Familiar with…" and so on.

Any Negative Information

Remember that resume reading is a process of elimination, so don't give the reader any reason to take you out of the running. Never mention lawsuits or a bad experience with a former supervisor, and avoid including any item that could be seen as affecting your performance on the job—for example, the fact that you were unemployed for two years because of an illness. You may disclose this to the employer, if asked, when you get the chance to explain yourself directly, but no one's asking you to spill your guts up front in your resume.

A Photograph

Unless you're applying for a job as a model, don't include a picture or other physical description of yourself. You may briefly list excellent health in a short Personal section, but when you provide a photo, you open yourself up to being considered based on your appearance. Don't subject yourself to the personal biases of an HR department or hiring executive.

Optional Items

The following sections cover some optional items you can include in your resume.

Title

Titles are further explained in Chapter 3, "The Proactive Executive Resume." If you're applying at a large company that may be hiring for many positions at the same time, this component will help readers quickly match you and your resume to the job you're seeking. Whenever possible, modify the title to match the actual job description: "Chief Financial Officer," "Director of Marketing," and so on. If you don't have the time or resources to constantly update the title; simply rely on the first paragraph of your Profile/Experience section to show readers what you can do for them and where, in general, you're coming from.

Objective

Also explained in Chapter 3, you may use an Objective in place of a Title. This element helps define and summarize your job goals so the reader can quickly determine what type of position you're seeking. It also focuses on what *you* want, which is fine as long as you know it's in sync with what the employer wants. Always keep this to one sentence or less. Objectives are best when they're specific and focused rather than broad and vague. Just like titles, they may also be omitted completely, in which case the first paragraph of the Profile section takes over.

Military Service

You may include any positive experience in the military, especially leadership experience. If you're seeking a position with a firm involved in defense contracting that hires former military personnel, then your military background may prove invaluable. Include highest rank attained, supervisory experience and applicable training. For technical positions, include systems and equipment operated, repaired or maintained.

If your only applicable work experience was in the military, then it must be developed like any other job. On the other hand, if you're looking for work that's completely unrelated to skills gained during your time in the military, it may be best to list only the highest rank attained and the city and state of deployment.

A Personal or Interests Section

If you need to fill room at the bottom of the page, include two to three lines outlining your interests. But make sure the interests you choose can help lead to interview discussions or are related to responsibilities demanded by the job. You could mention that you're an avid golfer or that you subscribe to certain trade journals in your industry.

The interests you list may also represent indirect skills that can reflect positively on your potential. For example, playing on a recreational sports team may indicate that you work well with others—you're a team player. Your involvement in a Big Brother or Big Sister program shows you can be a good role model and that you have leadership potential.

Of course, omit items that have no connection to tackling the job—especially pastimes that might be considered controversial or in conflict with the company's goals.

Age and Marital Status

Legally, these two items have no bearing on whether you're called in for an interview. But let's face it; some employers still discriminate based on age and marital status. Revealing your age can label you as too young or too old. What if you're twice as old as the president of the company or half as old as the average manager? You may be perfect for the job, but prejudice can run deep. Leave out your age altogether and get the reader to focus on your relevant skills and abilities.

One Page or Two?

Contrary to popular belief, one page is not always best. Two-page resumes earned a bad reputation years ago because people were including too much useless information. They were writing long, irrelevant job histories or expanding too much on their personal likes and dislikes, hobbies and so on.

Try to think in terms of *relevance* rather than number of pages. About 90 percent of my clients require two- and even three-page resumes. Unless you have an extensive *and relevant* work history or a detailed technical background of more than five years, try to keep your resume to two pages—but don't leave out important skills simply to force your resume into two pages.

Once again, it's *content* that drives the length of your resume. Imagine that you're writing a proactive advertisement of you as a person and of your most relevant skills. The Profile/Skills section lets you make sense of your background for the reader, even before he picks up your resume. Grab that person's attention by spotlighting the skill and talent you'll bring him. Whether that takes two pages or three of course depends on how many benefits you have to offer.

Job Search Facts

An Accountemps survey polled 150 executives from the nation's 1,000 largest companies. A full 64 percent of respondents said they prefer two-page resumes from candidates for executive positions, and 73 percent said staff-level applicants should stick with one page.

3

Chapter

The Proactive Executive Resume

To pack the most punch into your executive resume, think like an advertiser. You are the product, and as such, you must interpret and market your benefits to the reader in a present-day, proactive manner. Again, the Profile section gives you complete freedom and space to determine how you want to be perceived by the reader.

It's always tempting to focus too much on the history of your work experience, of which you may be proud, rather than interpreting the value of that history (your marketable skills and abilities) to the reader.

The language you use must add strength to your descriptions of work experience, skills and training, but it should not be so businesslike as to seem like just another memo, business letter or outplacement-style resume. As advertising executives would say, "Don't just talk about the steak; make it sizzle." Avoid run-on sentences; use semicolons, commas and periods to let the reader breathe between phrases. We live in a sound-bite world, and your statements and listings should be written in short, concise, digestible sentences.

Go for strong, action-oriented words when describing your experiences. Avoid passive-sounding verbs, such as "did," "was" and "used." And employ more powerful descriptors, such as "exceed," "increase," "perform" and "direct" (or the past tense of such words at former positions) whenever possible. Try to vary your use of words; while "achieved" is a terrific word to describe your accomplishments, it loses its impact if repeated in every bulleted listing.

A Professional Resume Writer's Tip

It's okay to use sentences that take "I," "we," "he," "she" and other pronouns for granted. Omit these words altogether. Use the abbreviated third-person form shown in the Profile sections in this book. This is more direct. It helps you get straight to your qualifications and sell them. When space is tight, however, or if you must have all of your qualifications on two pages, you can reduce the Profile section to two or three short paragraphs with bullets.

When developing your resume, keep a dictionary and perhaps a thesaurus by your side. A thesaurus will help you find synonyms for commonly used words when you're searching for a fresh way to describe a skill or experience. Another flaw I've been seeing lately is too many sentences starting with "responsible for." Avoid doing this more than once per page, although you can sprinkle it lightly within text. Alternative sentence starters for job descriptions include: manage(d), direct(ed), in charge of, supervise(d), control(led) and so on.

The following list features some powerful, high-impact words you may find helpful, used before or after the keywords specific to your position or industry.

Power Words

Achieved	Demonstrated	Introduced	Reinforced
Adapted	Designed	Investigated	Reorganized
Administered	Developed	Maintained	Researched
Advised	Drafted	Managed	Restructured
Amended	Eliminated	Modified	Reversed
Analyzed	Established	Monitored	Reviewed
Approved	Evaluated	Motivated	Revised
Assigned	Expanded	Organized	Saved
Assisted	Expedited	Participated	Scheduled
Budgeted	Focused	Performed	Screened
Built	Forecasted	Planned	Solved
Collected	Formulated	Prepared	Spearheaded
Compiled	Generated	Processed	Streamlined
Computed	Guided	Produced	Strengthened
Conducted	Implemented	Promoted	Structured
Controlled	Improved	Proposed	Supervised
Coordinated	Increased	Provided	Supported
Created	Initiated	Purchased	Taught
Cut	Innovated	Recommended	Trained
Decreased	Instituted	Recruited	Trimmed
Delegated	Interpreted	Reduced	Updated

Title or Objective?

Resume-writing professionals argue about the value of including job objectives or titles in resumes. Some claim the two elements are unnecessary and only take up space. Others believe they add focus to the resume and quickly tell a busy employer exactly what type of position you are seeking. I lean toward the second school of thought. Let's define each element and then examine its merits and its weaknesses.

The Title

The more straightforward of the two elements is the Title, and its purpose is pretty self-explanatory. It's two to four words defining the exact position—or overall type of position—you're seeking, centered at the top of your resume, typically presented in all caps, bold and/or italics.

When applying for a specific position, the Title should read exactly the same as the job title used in the job advertisement or posting.

If you are willing to work for a company in any capacity and would be interested in other job openings, then you may omit the Title completely and let the first bullet of your Profile section do the talking. You also have a chance to personalize and target your presentation in your cover letter, discussed in Chapter 13, "Cover Letter Essentials and Examples."

If it's not possible to constantly change your Title as you come across new job listings, simply use an overall Title that describes your area—or level—of expertise. Some examples are:

- EXECUTIVE LEADERSHIP
- EXECUTIVE MANAGEMENT
- MARKETING / MANAGEMENT
- SALES / MARKETING or SALES REPRESENTATIVE
- DIRECTOR: NETWORK ENGINEERING
- HUMAN RESOURCES
- MANAGEMENT / OPERATIONS
- DIRECTOR: MARKETING / SALES
- PRESIDENT / CEO

The Title is easily changed with every resume you send out. However, because it stands alone at the top of your resume, a Title should never consist of just one word, but of two to four words.

The Objective

The Objective is a short statement that comes directly after your name and contact information; it describes the job you want. It may even work in tandem with a Title as a one-line expansion of the type of person you are or the type of work you're seeking.

As you read this definition, you may already see what the weakness of such a statement might be. Remember that a resume is supposed to focus on what the prospective employer wants. The Objective tends to focus on what you want.

Still, there are times when the Objective can enhance your resume. For example, if you know exactly what you want to do, and it matches perfectly with the position you're applying for, then by all means introduce your resume with a targeted Objective that zeroes in on the job.

However, if you're not sure about the job responsibilities of the position you're applying for—or you're applying at a company where you'd be willing to consider other openings just to get in—then don't waste resume space by including an Objective. Instead, rely on a Title and the first paragraph of your Profile section to develop relevant skills and abilities pulled from your education, training, volunteer background and, of course, work experience.

It's best to customize the Objective for each resume you send. Short and sweet, the best Objectives are specific and indicate a clear focus.

Here's an example for someone who's very sure about what she wants:

> **OBJECTIVE:** A position as president or CEO where profit-building skills with a Fortune 500 firm would be utilized.

Note the open-ended approach of this finance professional:

> **OBJECTIVE:** A position in finance where proven abilities as controller and CPA would be of value.

Also open-ended, but more demanding:

> **OBJECTIVE:** A position utilizing comprehensive experience in marketing and new-business development and offering the potential for career advancement.

Completely open-ended, and only to be used as a last resort:

> **OBJECTIVE:** A position where solid leadership skills would be utilized in challenging new business environments.

You may also use the above without the word "Objective," and right after a Title:

> ### *MANAGEMENT/OPERATIONS*
> A position where solid leadership skills would be utilized in challenging new business environments.

Again, if you are interested in a broad range of jobs within a given company, you may consider omitting these components. That's when a Combination resume format works especially well: The first Profile bullet gives the reader a big picture of the types of skills and knowledge you can bring to the job. This puts even greater importance on the Profile section of your resume, discussed in the next chapter.

Market Your Skills
in the Profile

In the Profile section, you develop your most relevant skills, abilities, knowledge and qualifications. Although I sometimes use the word "summary" to describe a Profile section, I use it only as shorthand. (To me, a summary implies a weak overview or re-hash of your past.) A Profile section should fit you, like a key into a lock, into the ideal position you're seeking right now.

The Profile gives you control over marketing yourself. You choose which skills to emphasize, which to downplay and which keywords to include. Without a Profile, you're at the mercy of your job history. Here's where you actively interpret and sell your most transferable and relevant qualifications. It's what you can really bring to the table and why the reader should call you in. You can and should use elements of your Profile in your 30-second "elevator speech," when you must quickly describe your value proposition to a potential employer or network contact. It's an essential component of the Combination format; other sections, such as Employment / Experience or Education, support it with job-specific details.

Pack It In

Even if you're having trouble fitting all your relevant work history on two or three pages, you should still try to include a shortened, two- to three-sentence Profile section at the top of your job chronology. You should always give the reader a solid context: how to think about you, reasons to keep reading, the meaning behind your work history and how you'll fit into his organization. Remember, they're hiring you and your skills—not your last job.

The Functional resume may include dollar amounts, percentages, numbers of people supervised and so on. However, because this is out of context for the reader, surveys of recruiters have shown that it's their least favorite format.

Here's an example of how effective the Profile can be: I once wrote a short Profile section —only six lines of text—for a client of mine. He sent out 20 resumes and received four job offers in just the first two weeks. He also received compliments on the writing and design of his resume from employers. I told him to act as if he wrote it himself.

It's important to note that your Profile section may contain marketable skills and abilities, regardless of whether you've used them on the job. You can list almost any skill, aptitude or training with the right qualifying words. Start with the skills that are most valued by the prospective employer and that are your strongest. You can then follow those with weaker skills, as long as they're still relevant.

Using data from the worksheets in Chapter 1, think about how best to extract your skills and abilities from your actual work experience and training, and how to present them as transferable.

Keep your Profile to two to five bulleted paragraphs for a two- or three-page resume. A one-page resume is fine with one to three bulleted paragraphs or sentences, depending on space considerations.

A Professional Resume Writer's Tip

The first bullet or paragraph of your Profile section acts as an umbrella over the other items. It provides a big picture of where you're coming from and gives the reader reasons to keep reading.

Start with the type and level of skills you have that would best match the job, keeping in mind what you really like to do. These might include three or four top executive items, such as experience in startup operations, new business development, market penetration, and/or mergers and acquisitions.

In the next paragraph, begin to break down and expand upon the major areas mentioned in the first paragraph. Which skills can you leverage to give you success in your key areas? These might include strategic planning, market research, competitive analysis, budget development and/or forecasting for multiple locations (or international or Fortune 500 accounts).

In the paragraphs that follow, get more specific: Proficient in (or knowledgeable in) the setup and management of multiple operations, the management of multimillion-dollar budgets, ISO 9002 standards, OSHA or EPA requirements (in what industry?), production-line setup and/or scheduling, CAD/CAM systems, Windows 7, NT and so on.

Following is a list of present-tense sentence starters to get you going on your Profile. Note that the "I am" or "I have" at the beginning of each section is not included, only implied. I normally keep these items present tense because you still have the skills, don't you?

For your Profile section:

- Proficient in...
- Experience in...
- Skilled in...
- Perform...
- Plan and implement...
- Utilize...
- Familiar with...

- Comprehensive experience in...
- Extensive knowledge of...
- Proven abilities in...
- Plan and conduct...
- Train and supervise staff in...
- Knowledge of...
- Trained in...

For your Experience / Employment section:

- In charge of...
- Direct...
- Coordinate...
- Effectively lead...

- Manage...
- Control...
- Supervise...
- Responsible for...

Develop your qualifications into phrases your prospective employer would appreciate. Leave out the fluff and imagine yourself already in the position; think of the actual, hands-on skills you would need on a daily basis. Write down everything you think of on a blank sheet of paper or on the Personal Assessment sheet; then narrow it down and make a short list of items you feel would be most useful in your dream job.

Keep It Relevant

The main goal here is to keep your Profile section relevant to both your needs and the employer's. This section is about overall ability, and it's one of the best ways to take control of your resume and your future.

If you're still having trouble starting this section, think of the type of work you've done that would be useful or relevant or that shows an aptitude for the next job—then extract, develop and market the skills you used to do that work.

Here are some examples:

- Skilled in long- and short-term strategic planning and business development in major national markets.

- Coordinate logistics, inventory control and vendor relations, as well as contract negotiation and cost-reduction in the "X" industry (if desired).

- Plan and conduct training programs for staff and managers in new product lines, sales presentations and account tracking procedures.

Combined with your education and knowledge of the field, these skill sets will help project you as able to walk in, tackle the responsibilities and succeed in your new position.

The First Paragraph = The First Impression

Avoid beginning with heavy adjectives. Give employers at least three strong, no-nonsense reasons to keep reading. Don't start this important section with subjective phrases, such as "highly motivated executive" (I hope so) or "seasoned executive." What are you, a salad?

Rather than stating that you're great, motivated or professional, tell them why you think you are, using specific, honest business language. The one to four paragraphs that follow should expand on that first bullet. Group like skills together. Check out these examples of first paragraphs and notice how each paragraph works to build on the previous one:

Emphasis on M&A activity, banking and finance:

- Skilled in mergers and acquisitions with Fortune 500 companies; coordinate banking procedures, loan acquisition and effective, long-term business relationships.

Emphasis on major aspects of new startups:

- Comprehensive experience in startup operations, including long- and short-term planning, staffing, budget administration and international marketing.

Emphasis on the creative:

- Proficient in team leadership and the direction of major national organizations, with a proven ability to penetrate international markets through high-impact advertising and promotions.

Take a look at these examples of corresponding supporting paragraphs:

- Effectively hire, train and supervise accounting staff and management in accounts payable/receivable, payroll and general ledgers for multiple operations.

- Plan and implement procedures for production-line setup, assembly operations, quality control, packaging and import/export activities.

- Coordinate market research, strategic planning and competitive analysis for new product introduction, with successful experience in European and Asian markets.

Get the idea? Once again, avoid overused, general statements, such as, "Excellent communication skills" and instead explain why that's true—give the reader specifics. Without details and tangible skills backed up elsewhere in your resume, your statements could read as fluff. For instance, in the following example, the writer offers specific applications for good communication skills, both written and oral:

Communication skills:

- Plan and conduct written and oral presentations in a professional manner.

- Manage staff training, performance reviews and written documentation.

- Compile (or oversee the preparation of) financial statements and annual reports to the SEC and IRS, as well as other federal and state agencies.

- Proficient in cost reduction through detailed monitoring and reporting on quantities, parts, components, component/finished good prices, labor cost and quality.

Still think communication skills aren't so important? An Accountemps survey of more than 1,400 CFOs found that 96 percent of those who responded believe communication abilities are a major success factor for accountants—a position not always associated with the need to communicate well. In other words, if you're a genius but you can't communicate your knowledge and work well with others, why would anyone hire you?

Be careful not to oversell yourself. At executive levels, you may come across as too much for a small company to handle; you may have twice the experience of the company's president.

A Constantly Changing Document

If you're not satisfied with response rates from the first draft of your resume, don't be afraid to downplay or omit some higher-level leadership skills from your Profile section. Readers need just enough to pick up the phone (or send an email) and ask more about you. That's when you can have a personal, interactive conversation about mutual interests.

Save several versions of your resume, emphasizing or downplaying top leadership skills to suit different positions. Just like customizing your cover letter, this takes extra time and effort, but in the long run your career is worth it.

Developing Your Career History

L et's briefly review the three most common resume formats. In the traditional Chronological format, the Employment or Experience section is the focal point of the resume. Your career history comes right up front, following the name and contact information and the Objective or Title, if used.

In a purely Functional resume, the Employment section may be absent, replaced by an expanded section that summarizes experience, including job-specific duties and achievements out of context. Most Functional resumes include a brief listing/skeleton of your work history—usually just company names, job titles and years employed. However, according to surveys, the Functional resume is the *least* liked among recruiters. They sense you're trying to hide dates and specific information about your job history, and they're usually right. That's why I never advocate using a Functional resume—there's too much potential for confusion, and confusion means they won't call you.

My definition of a modified, Combination format includes the best of both worlds: a Profile section of transferable skills (what you can and want to do for the new employer, extracted from work, education, and so on) followed by the Employment/Experience section (what you have done or are doing for past or present employers, including quantified achievements), followed by your Education section (college degrees and so on). Throughout my career in resume writing, and from feedback from hundreds of recruiters and employers, resumes that use a Combination style can be very effective if written with impact and clarity, even for those with a rocky work history.

In any case, the Employment/Experience section is a development of actual work events and is a fairly structured element. Tell the reader what you've done or achieved at other companies, and back up and verify the statements about skills and abilities in your Profile section. Almost always, your previous jobs are listed in reverse chronological order—that is, your most recent work experience is listed first, followed by the previous job, and so forth.

A Professional Resume Writer's Tip

Here's a great little excerpt from an article that appeared in *National Business Employment Weekly* (NBEW): "An easy method of quantifying your experience in a resume is to follow the SMART approach: Results need to be Specific, Measurable, Action-oriented, Realistic, and Time-based. When a result includes each point, it will have impact, say recruiters."

Each job listing in the Employment section of your resume should include the following components:

Company name. Use the complete name, avoiding nicknames or abbreviations that may not be familiar to the reader. You may omit this in rare cases where confidentiality may be compromised, as when posting your resume on large, non-exclusive Internet databases.

Company location. Use city and state only, and don't list the company phone number—you want the employer to call *you* first. If you think the company's name won't be easily recognized, include a short description, in italics, on its own line, such as: *A national distributor of circuit board equipment and supplies.*

Your job title. You might consider translating your title to a more universal title if the internal label is unusual or unfamiliar to other work environments. Just don't promote yourself to a job level you didn't really have.

Dates of employment. Typically, use year *and* month. However, you may omit the month, particularly if you have a history of longevity—staying with employers for many years. In this case, as long as the years are correct for the jobs you're listing, you could leave out or combine irrelevant jobs lasting only a few months.

Job descriptions. Most employers will have some idea about your responsibilities by your job title, but spell them out anyway. That's because a CEO at a $1 million company has far different responsibilities from a CEO at a $1 billion firm. What are the size and scope of the company (if you want to stay with that size company)? What departments do you oversee, if any? Check the resume samples for ideas. Develop or downplay product lines and daily duties to match future career goals. In other words, if you really want to get out of the service sector and into managing tangible products, you may want to spare the details about the types of services your company provides.

Try to include specifics. If you supervise people, indicate how many employees report to you directly and how many indirectly. If you're in charge of a budget, include the amount (if you think it's substantial and will interest readers at the size and types of companies you're shooting for; otherwise, omit this or write "multimillion dollar budget").

If there is anything unique or unusual about the job that the title or general description doesn't reveal, mention that as well. For example: "Travel to offices in Canada six times annually."

Also, consider whether your general management skills include researching and writing (or producing) status reports. If so, on what topics: product or material costs, finished goods, labor cost or quality? Do you think this will be a valuable talent at the position level you're targeting or too menial a function?

Even after years of resume writing, I've found there are few hard and fast rules for what to include in an Employment section, except this one: Include any and all information that you feel is most relevant to your current career goals and that will present you in the best light at the size and type of company you would like to work for.

Keep this in mind, and you will avoid appearing like a $200,000 executive going for a $75,000 job, and vice versa.

Achievements at each position. Employers love to see achievements, accomplishments, and results that demonstrate excellence on the job. Here you can list awards, percentage increases, and any other raw data to support your image of success. Typically, this information will appear in a list or bullet format, which sets it off and catches the eye of the reader. For example:

- Ranked #1 in quality control since promoted to this position.

- Analyzed and streamlined sales and marketing efforts; expanded annual sales from $500,000 to $750,000 in the first six months since joining the company.

- Increased profit margin from 18 percent to 25 percent through cost reduction and more effective staff training.

Check the resumes in this book for achievements and quantifiable, verifiable results. Did you increase the efficiency of operations? Reduce downtime? Speed turnaround or inventory turns? How much money did you save the company by introducing a new maintenance procedure, operation, computer system (what type?) or other piece of equipment? Of what value was this to your past or present employers? Did you win awards? Get promotions? How did you improve conditions?

Try to give the reader a scope and perspective to understand your achievements: What percentage of overall revenues? How many others were you competing with for the top sales award? Again, try to do this without misrepresenting yourself or using generic language or vague wording.

When you proofread your resume, ask yourself whether your descriptions of achievements could apply to anyone or only to you. Step back and look deeper into your skill sets. What measurable results did you bring about in your previous jobs—in terms of dollars saved or earned, time saved or production increased?

If you find yourself trying to stretch the truth, then maybe you're not right for the position you're shooting for, or it's not right for you. It's time to reassess and look at yourself more objectively.

Are your talents transferable to other fields or markets? Someone with strong marketing or leadership skills should be able to apply them to a wide range of products, markets and industries. That same person could leave actual sales and marketing behind and be very effective in training and developing staff and management. We've all heard of top executives entering academia and conducting MBA courses or specialized training programs, seminars and workshops or breaking out on their own.

Following is an example of a high-impact job description. Note the overall layout, including placement of dates off to the right (to deemphasize) and the company name emphasized with an underline. This creates an "umbrella" effect over the job title and description. Also note that bullets are used sparingly and only for emphasis of major achievements or unique responsibilities you'd like to emphasize. The first sentence gives an overall big picture of daily duties, followed by a more specific breakdown of those duties:

EXPERIENCE: <u>Strong Brothers Health System, Inc,</u> National HQ, New York, NY

Chief Administrative Officer/Executive Vice President   6/04–Present

In charge of virtually all operations for this $259 million, multi-institutional healthcare system with multiple sites, including two hospitals and four elder-care facilities.
Plan and implement national polices in tandem with the Corporate Compliance Officer and VP of Mission Services.
Design, implement or oversee virtually all policies for legal services, human resources, treasury functions and financial planning.
Directly supervise three hospital CEOs and three VPs; indirectly responsible for more than 2,800 employees.

⇨ Established all strategic direction and financial structures.

⇨ Maintained performance levels that achieved an A2 Moody's rating.

⇨ Determined all strategic, financial and operating objectives for this tax-exempt corporation.

⇨ Effectively centralized strategic planning, while decentralizing operations.

⇨ Involved in selecting facility and system trustees, as well as agenda design, resulting in a professional board process.

Remember that bullets add white space; they give the eye a focal point and help break up gray blocks of type. You may repeat some skills that appear in the Profile section, but here you'll show exactly how those skills were applied and what they produced.

A note about dates: I sometimes recommend moving descriptions of jobs that occurred 18 or more years ago into a section labeled "Prior Experience." Employers are most interested in your most recent experience anyway, and if your "ancient" work history is irrelevant or adds nothing to your credentials, you may want to leave it off entirely. If those experiences enhance your overall value, you may still mention them, but minimize them so you have space to focus on more recent experience.

At this point, I've focused on skills and abilities and where you've applied them, but employers will also want to know about your education, special training, certifications and other credentials. Let's move on to the Education section, covered in the next chapter.

Education:
Market Your Best Credentials

Just as with skills and work history, how you list your formal education, training, special courses and required certifications depends on their relevance. Because this is your personal advertisement, begin with the information that will put you in the best light *right now* and play up your strengths. In fact, in rare cases when education is both very recent and your strongest suit, you may place it right under the Profile section and just above the Employment/Experience section. However, I usually reserve this technique for those with MBAs or PhDs from prestigious schools.

For example, if you just earned an MBA in finance, and you're seeking a position in that arena, you may list that degree above your current position (let's say, Director of Marketing) if it's less relevant to your career goals.

For most executives, however, work history will be more relevant or recent than education. That's why most samples in this book place the Education section toward the end of the resume.

Here are some examples of Education sections developed for our clients. Note that the layout is consistent with the Employment sections illustrated in the previous chapter in that the name of the institution is underlined and acts as an umbrella over titles of degrees and coursework. Whatever format you choose to present your work history and education, consistency is essential.

EDUCATION: <u>Judson College,</u> Elgin, IL   Graduated 12/06

Bachelor's Degree: Marketing Minor: Accounting

Studies included market research, strategic planning, creative product development and business-to-business selling.

Even if you didn't earn a degree at a certain college, it may still be to your advantage to indicate that you have taken or are taking courses, perhaps listing the specific classes that may be relevant to your job goals.

<u>Elgin University,</u> Elgin, IL   Spring 2005
Completed various Liberal Arts courses.

<u>Bergen Community College,</u> Paramus, NJ   1/03
Completed courses related to Business Management.

<u>Plaza School of Technology,</u> Paramus, NJ   7/02
Trained in CAD (Computer-Aided Drafting) versions 11 and 12

<u>National Education Center,</u> Rets Campus, Nutley, NJ   4/00
Associate Degree: Electronics Engineering

CERTIFICATE: HAZMAT Certified by the State of Illinois   2009

Some clients ask me, "Should I include my high school information?" I tell them yes, if there's no other indication that you've graduated from high school. In other words, if you list that you've earned a bachelor's or an associate's degree, it's assumed that you graduated from high school.

As for dates, I sometimes advise leaving off the date of graduation—whether for high school or college. Age discrimination still exists, and often older workers are the targets of this bias. But remember, if you omit the dates for one listing under Education, then leave them off for all. If you choose to list that you earned an associate's degree but leave off the fact that you did so in 1972, then you should also leave off the date for your recent completion of a certification program.

I recommend listing certifications and training programs following such formal education listings as college. However, you may also highlight your most relevant certifications in the Profile section.

If you have a minimal amount of formal education, your certifications, as well as workshops, seminars and other professional training experiences you've gathered, become more important. When you list these, be sure to point out any pertinent subjects covered, and note that you completed or graduated from the course.

> **EDUCATION:** Successful completion of an Executive Leadership seminar by Hewlett-Packard Corporation.
>
> Completed seminars by Anthony Robbins and Zig Ziglar on communication, sales and self-motivation.

Give yourself credit for any kind of training, formal or informal. This communicates much more than the fact that you have acquired a certain knowledge. It also conveys to the reader that you are self-motivated, have a desire to keep informed about changes in your field and are eager to grow and advance—traits that all savvy employers are looking for.

Designing an Executive Resume

If you ask a dozen people about resume design and layout, you'll get a dozen different responses. Here are some key points on resume design, culled from what works best for our clients. Check the resume examples for a variety of ideas to personalize your layout.

The initial appearance of your resume—or any advertisement for that matter—is of course very important. Whether or not we know it, we all make snap judgments about everything we see or choose to read. Is it attractive, does it draw the eye, do you feel good about reading further? There must be something about your resume that makes the reader want to continue reading.

Just like an Armani suit or a pair of blue jeans, the appearance of your resume will create, or at least slant, the first impression you'll make on the hiring authority. Because you have only 20 to 60 seconds to grab the reader's attention, according to some estimates, your resume must appear inviting, lightweight and clean. It must prod readers to pay attention to you long after the first few seconds, when their attention is at its peak.

Resume formatting is easier and more fun than content development. Be creative, but sparingly use a variety of elements, including type (sizes and styles), white space, margins and such special treatments as bullets, indenting and boldface type.

What Typeface? What Size?

Typefaces used for text are either serif or sans serif. Serifs are the "hands" and "feet" at the top and bottom of letters. Serif typefaces include fonts such as the one you're reading now, while sans serif typefaces include those without these items.

This is an example of a sans serif typeface. (Arial, 11.5 pt.)

This is a sample of a very common serif typeface. (Times New Roman, 11 pt.)

Serif types are recommended for most printed materials. Almost every major newspaper and book uses serif type. Serif is easy to read; the theory is that serifs help the eye move along more easily from word to word. If you're in a creative or high-tech field, such as advertising or leading-edge package design, or your resume copy is sparse, you might consider a sans serif face, such as Arial, Helvetica, Kent or New Gothic. For a more conservative, executive approach, stick with Times New Roman or Bookman.

Keep your type size between 10 and 12 points—11- or 11.5-point type is best. Anything smaller is hard for the eye to scan, and anything bigger can seem excessive. Fill the page with essential information and then adjust the size of type, margins and tabs to make it all fit.

Bullet Points and White Space

One of the best ways to make your resume attractive and readable is to use white space— space without type. Break up blocks of text, add white space with bulleted text, and use healthy margins and indents. Compare the block-style of the page you're reading right now to the much lighter look of the resume samples in this book. Which would you rather read at first glance? White space gives readers a break and helps them quickly scan the page for key points.

Bullet points of many shapes are common in resumes. When not used on every line, they're a great way to make achievements, or anything else you want to highlight, jump out at the reader. I usually indent (tab) after each bullet. Most word processing software will give you a wide selection of arrows, large circles, diamonds or boxes to choose from.

Another method of adding white space, used in almost every resume in this book, is to indent each paragraph after the appropriate heading (such as Experience, Employment and so on). I prefer an indent of 1.5 to 2 inches from the left margin.

Yet another trick we use is to leave blank spaces between groups of text, as seen in the following resume examples:

PROFILE: Comprehensive experience in information technology and management systems, including full responsibility for projects, schedules and performance for a multibillion-dollar organization.

⇨ Skilled in needs assessment, problem identification/resolution, process reengineering and cost analysis, as well as price structuring, order expediting, inventory tracking and budget administration.

⇨ Analyze and interpret financial and statistical data to facilitate critical decision-making; well versed in import/export procedures and distribution logistics; hire, train and supervise teams to meet project goals.

You may also use a simple dash or asterisk for a more subdued, conservative look. These don't stand out as well as the computer-generated bullets, though:

* Successfully implement innovative programs to increase profits, enhance market position, reduce operating costs, meet strategic goals and ensure client satisfaction.

* Skilled in departmental/facility startup, call center management, process re-engineering, staff mentoring and information technology transfer.

Use frills such as boldfacing, underlining, italics, bullets or dashes for emphasis, but not on every line. They quickly lose their impact when overused. They should be used only to make major points stand out or to set items apart and break up type. Avoid using all the elements—boldfacing, underlining and italics—on the same line of type. Choose a combination of any two. My personal favorites are bolding and underlining, but pick whichever you like.

Some of these techniques may seem trivial, but it's the little things that make a great resume. Without attention to detail, you end up with yet another data-sheet resume like those sent out every day by the thousands. These techniques will help distance you from the pack and win the resume game.

Line Length

The resumes we design for our clients follow a simple format. The body copy is usually indented about 1.5 inches from the left margin, which creates shorter lines and makes the resume easier for the eye to scan. (That's why newspaper columns are so narrow.) This provides white space and an excellent place to put your section headings (Objective and Profile, for example). Outside margins should be 1 inch all around, but they may be shortened to .75

inch or widened up to 1.5 inches as needed to fit your information on one or two pages. Again, don't be afraid to use three pages if that's what it really takes to develop and market your skills.

If you still need more or less space than margin shifting allows, change your type size by one-half point, but try to keep it within half a point of 11 points.

Avoid violating your margins or hyphenating words at the end of a line. You can make an exception to this rule for compound words, such as self-employed, when the line ends after "self."

Don't worry about squaring off (fully justifying) your lines unless space is really tight. Note that if space is a concern, you may also use the entire width of the page, as seen in many of the examples here.

Most resumes in this guide are fully justified, to pack more information on each page, but we almost always place a return at the end of each individual sentence. This automatically adds white space between lines, and your resume avoids that "tombstone" look, with big blocks of gray type.

Placement of Dates

I recommend placing dates directly across from the job title or company name, flush right. However, an assistant director for alumni career services at a major university said she liked to see dates placed immediately after the company location: "Chicago, IL, 8/93–1/94." I agree with this if you'd like to hide or mask dates of shorter positions.

Printing Your Resume

Be sure to use a high-quality laser or inkjet printer. Whenever possible, customize and print each resume as needed for specific positions. As for photocopying your resume, remember that no copy machine can reproduce the print quality of a genuine laser-typeset original. Avoid printing more than 10 resumes at a time, because your resume should remain flexible— you may want to make updates and changes to it the very next day.

What Color Paper?

I advise my clients to stick to white, off-white, or ivory paper—these are good, easy-to-read colors. Avoid grays or beiges, as they reduce contrast between paper and ink. Lighter paper works much better when the resume is faxed or scanned into a database. Avoid splotchy parchment papers or those with unusual textures. If you want your resume to stand out on a desk of white papers, use a natural or ivory color. Avoid linen paper, as the toner from some printers won't adhere to their uneven finish and may even break off if the document is folded or mailed.

We email resume documents to our clients so they can modify and print their own copies one at a time for each new opportunity. As mentioned, this is by far the best way to go.

Proofread, Proofread, Proofread!

Before you print or send out a single resume, always proofread slowly and carefully. I find typos, grammar mistakes or format problems in virtually every resume I see—even those from writers, authors, editors and CEOs. Be sure to check *everything*, including dates of employment, the spelling of company names and your name and address.

Don't trust the spellchecker in your word processing program. One trick that helps catch typos is reading your resume backwards. Start with the very last word and read to the first. This forces you to focus on the words individually. Have relatives and friends read over your resume, too. You might be too close to it to catch errors obvious to a more objective reader.

You'd be surprised at what can slip by in the finished version. This is your life, your career, your future on paper—it must be as close to perfect as possible. You're welcome to send your resume directly to me for free proofreading and feedback; see the contact information at the end of this book.

Now let's talk about distributing and using your resume effectively.

Electronic Resumes
and the Internet

Your resume most likely will be screened by an HR representative and then by the hiring manager—that's *if* it gets past the resume-scanning software used by thousands of companies these days. Two such companies in the Midwest that use resume scanning and sorting software are Motorola and FirstCard, one of the largest credit-card processing companies.

If received via email or the company's website, your resume may be added to the company's pool of hundreds, even thousands of resumes and sorted by keyword. If it's faxed or mailed, it may be placed on a scanner and loaded onto their database, becoming an electronic—or digital—resume. Employers then use the system to find certain keywords for a match. When written correctly, the Profile section will contain all of your most important keywords.

Examples of keywords used in an executive search include:

- Mergers
- Strategic planning
- Acquisitions
- Marketing or market research
- Profit/loss or P&L
- Team training or leadership
- Budgeting or forecasting
- Financial and/or analysis

Examples of keywords for computer systems include:

- ISO 9001, ISO 9002
- iSeries 250, IBM 570
- Windows NT
- Windows 7
- Macintosh
- Excel or Lotus
- MS Office, Word, PowerPoint, Outlook

Keywords may include such operational skills as:

- Accounting
- Cost reduction or cost analysis
- Inventory control
- Distribution and/or networking

Keywords may include such industry-specific terms as:

- Automotive
- Electronics or computers
- Food and beverage
- Chemical
- Mechanical
- Finance or consumer finance

Keywords may identify level of employment:

- Executive
- Supervisor
- Manager
- Assistant
- Director

Formatting Tips for Electronic Resumes

Of course, nothing is perfect, and document scanners can make mistakes. If your resume is scanned from paper into a computer system, letters and sometimes entire words may be read incorrectly. Underlining, italics, and certain typefaces can be misinterpreted, and essential keywords may not be picked up.

That's why emailing has become the most popular way to send your resume to employers, recruiters and large job boards, such as CareerBuilder.com and Monster.com. Depending on the requirements of the website, you can send your resume as a fully formatted, MS Word attachment, as part of an email. However, if you're on a site that asks you to complete an online form, then save your resume in stripped-down text format (a.k.a. Plain Text), with no graphics except asterisks (*) for bullets, and all the copy flush left. That way, there's very little chance of words being misread.

Note that many of the guidelines for designing traditional paper resumes (discussed in Chapter 8) will not apply to preparing an electronic resume.

Electronic Resumes: The Wave of the Future
by Wayne Gonyea

Wayne Gonyea is an electronic-career strategist and developer of numerous career-related websites. He is co-author of *Electronic Resumes and Selling on the Internet*, and he holds a master's degree in counseling. He offers the following advice regarding electronic resumes:

Computerized resume scanning requires a major re-engineering of resumes for job hunting. We emphasize the importance of OCR (*Optical Character Recognition*) in the entire process. OCR comes into play initially when the paper resume is scanned into computers. Although resumes can be received by companies electronically via email and diskette, many of them are still received on paper, thus requiring scanning.

Resume-management systems scan resumes into databases, search the databases on command, and rank the resumes according to the number of resulting "hits" they receive. At times, such searches utilize multiple (10 to 20) criteria. Resume-management systems are usually utilized by major corporations and recruitment firms. The reliance on these systems, coupled with the downsizing of human resource departments in many corporations, has resulted in a situation whereby many resumes are never seen by human eyes after they enter the electronic systems!

A resume must be as computer- and scanner-friendly as possible so its life in a database will be extended and its likelihood of producing hits is enhanced. To satisfy the idiosyncrasies of the scanning process, keywords are essential. Keywords tend to be the nouns or noun-phrases (Total Quality Management, UNIX, Biochemist), as opposed to the verbs often found in traditional resumes (developed, coordinated, empowered, organized).

Another way to look at keyword phrases is to think in terms of job duties. Detailing your job duties may require a modified mindset for those accustomed to traditional resume writing. However, the words and phrases that detail your job duties are the phrases—the keywords—that get your resume noticed.

Describe characteristics and industry-specific experience in keywords to accommodate the electronic/computer search process. Use these guidelines to enhance the processing of text-formatted, keyword resumes through the electronic system:

- Left-justify the entire document.

- Utilize a basic, Courier font, about 10 or 11 points. Most software will default to Courier when you save a file in text format—it's the most basic, generic typeface.

- Avoid tabs.

- Avoid hard returns whenever possible.

- Avoid italics, script, underlining, graphics, bold, or shading.

- Avoid horizontal and vertical lines.

- Avoid parentheses and brackets.

- Avoid compressed lines of print. (Typesetting and proportional spacing may cram too much into one line if there's a long word near the end of the sentence.)

- Avoid faxed copies, which become fuzzy.

I suggest that successful job-seekers prepare two versions of their resume. Traditional market-driven resumes will continue to be designed for the eyes of real people, to be viewed in 20 seconds or less. They will follow the formats presented by resume writers and resume-writing programs. The keyword resume, however, should be used in any situation where computer scanning might be involved.

Having noted Mr. Gonyea's advice, take a look at this survey:

Job Search Facts

Let's hear it for snail mail. An OfficeTeam survey of 150 executives who responded from the nation's largest 1,000 companies found that they would prefer to get your resume the old-fashioned way—through the mail. That method ranked first, at 21 percent, while fax and email lagged far behind, at 8 percent and 4 percent, respectively. On the other hand, some companies prefer to receive resumes by fax or email, as this speeds the process—you may jump ahead of the crowd if you can deliver your resume the day of, or the day after, a job posting.

Diane Domeyer, executive director of OfficeTeam, said of her preference for traditional paper resumes received in the mail: "It shows a candidate has extended a greater effort to personalize the information. In addition, such elements as the choice of paper, quality of printing, and layout of the document give insight to overall professionalism."

If you wish to send your resume via email because you know a particular employer prefers to receive and store resumes electronically, then you should modify your basic resume as recommended by Gonyea. Your fully formatted resume will probably be an MS Word or WordPerfect file. All you need to do is click "Save As" and save a second version (perhaps under the name "yourname.txt") as a text-only file and then keep it as a separate file on your computer.

When you want to respond to different job openings via email, you can modify the resume, cut and paste it, and send it simply and quickly. If the recruiter (or database) prefers to receive MS Word files, send your fully formatted version as an attachment—but *only* one file at a time, to avoid compression of two or more files. It can be difficult for some recipients to decompress multiple files from a single attachment. Remember that you can use this cut-and-paste technique only with a text-only (.TXT) file.

The Best Employment Websites

Some basic online research will reveal the most popular employment-search sites. Of course, don't rely solely on these sites in your search; just because millions of other job-seekers are using them, that doesn't mean they're a productive use of your time. In fact, many believe that's a great reason to avoid them all together. Post your resume on these sites if you wish, but continue calling companies directly, networking, and talking to friends, family and business connections as much as possible. Check the Appendix , "Job Search Resources," for more sites and resources.

According to ConsumerSearch.com, the top five sites for various uses are:

1. Best job search engine: SimplyHired.com

2. Best networking site: LinkedIn.com

3. Best for media types: MediaBistro.com

4. Most popular job site: Monster.com

5. Best online classifieds: Craigslist.org

6. I'm personally adding one more to this list: Hound.com

Keep Job Boards in Perspective

Even with all the hype about Internet job boards, such as CareerBuilder and TheLadders.com, only about 5 to 7 percent of all jobs are filled through such websites. The vast majority—60 to 70 percent—are filled through personal networking: communication with those in a position to hire you or with people who know hiring managers and tell them about you—or tell you about them. It's been this way for years, and it's not likely to change. Still, an expertly written resume is essential even after you've talked with a hiring manager; he needs to see a document that develops and verifies your most important skills, work history, achievements and education—if only for his files.

The Importance of Your LinkedIn Profile

Our in-house career coach and former corporate recruiter, Karen Evertsen, swears by LinkedIn as the best choice for recruiters in virtually all industries to quickly find the candidates they seek. Rapidly expanding as the business (rather than social) network site of choice, LinkedIn provides a quick, easy source of potential candidates, along with profiles of their best talents. That's why Karen and I recommend using a condensed version of your resume—especially the Profile section at the top—on your LinkedIn page. This can greatly increase your response from recruiters and shorten your job search.

Perhaps the best aspect of LinkedIn is that it's okay to present the essence of your resume on it even if you're not looking for a position. There's no assumption that you're seeking a new job—your boss won't care, and he probably has his resume posted there too. Do a quick search for his name—I bet it's there.

Job Search Tip

When mailing your resume for a more personalized presentation, be sure to use large, 9×12 envelopes, preferably the type that open on the long side. This creates an executive impact and keeps your resume flat, avoiding the accordion look of folded resumes. More importantly, folding along a line of text can actually crack the type off certain papers, and the reader can get black toner all over the place—not a very good first impression. Unfolded, your resume will stand out even before it's opened. Next to a stack of #10 envelopes, which would you open first?

Don't forget the extra postage: Two first-class stamps should do it for a two-page resume and a cover letter.

One other tip: Always keep two or three copies of your resume in the back seat (or trunk) of your car in a firm, cardboard postal envelope. You never know when you might meet a valuable contact at a social function or drive by a new facility under construction with the sign "Now accepting applications." Don't laugh—I got my first HR job this way.

Now that your resume has been created, you need a plan   a job-hunting strategy to market your skills and abilities. I'll cover that in the next two chapters.

Networking and Using Your Resume Effectively

Imagine you're employed in a top consulting position and your client is you. Your short- and long-term goals are clear: to find yourself a new and better position. Treat the job search as another position requiring motivation, common sense, diligence and positive interaction with others. This can be hard work, but the payoffs are well worth it. What's the best way to find out about career opportunities? Consider the options in the following sections.

Most Important: Build Your Network

Sometimes, what you've heard over the years is true: It's not what you know but who you know that leads you to a job. This is the best, if least common, use of your resume: getting it into the hands of the right people—people with connections at companies or organizations who might (someday, if not today) need someone like you.

A network is a collection of people with whom you have relationships; it can include co-workers, colleagues, industry connections, friends and relatives, any of whom may connect you to your next opportunity.

Some people think networking is meeting strangers in social circumstances, shoving a business card in their hand and then calling them to ask for a job. Networking should never be a forceful action, but rather a building of relationships. As you build these relationships, you'll share information about yourself, help your contacts when you can and turn to them for advice and help when you need it. The same core concept of resume writing applies to networking: *What can you do for me?* Upon first contact, most people don't want to hear your life story or entire work history; they want you to quickly summarize your skills, abilities, industry and career goals most important for their situation, all in about 30 seconds. This is also known as your "elevator speech," a clear, concise advertisement about who you are and what value you can bring, right here and now, to another person. See the Appendix, "Job Search Resources," for a list of books on networking.

An effective network must be broad and inclusive. Join business organizations, volunteer in a community effort, participate in your kids' school activities and get to know others in your company better. You never know where important connections will come from.

Reach out to potential networking contacts from trade associations and professional groups. Mention that you're seeking or considering a new position; actually, it's just as likely that you'll offer that contact some job leads. Your contact may introduce you to someone in the industry who provides knowledge that helps you do your job better, which leads to a promotion, which leads to interest from an outside employer.

Make sure everyone you know in the industry has a copy of your resume if you're out of work. If you're still employed, maintain confidentiality and offer your resume only to people you really trust. Give copies to your family and friends or anyone at all you think might know a company president, manager, supervisor or influential professional in your field.

In his article, "Savvy Job Hunters Learn to Network Nicely," author Doug Richardson sets out the basic rules for effective networking. If your networking efforts can use a little brushing up, keep these thoughts in mind:

1. Make sure each party feels that he is heard and respected and receives value.

2. Remember, the stakes are low, the risks nonexistent, and communication above-board and informal.

3. It's not a sales transaction. It's about building trust, gaining visibility, gathering anecdotal information and creating lasting favorable impressions.

4. Balance making your presentation with giving others the opportunity to share
their wisdom. Don't talk too much or be too quiet.

5. A networking meeting is a favor to the networker, who has little leverage. Make sure the meeting is meaningful.

In her book *Career Intelligence: Mastering the New Work and Personal Realities*, author Barbara Moses defines career intelligence as "a way of understanding yourself and the world, and a way of acting upon the world, because you can't act effectively on the world without first comprehending it properly."

In one chapter, Moses lists her 12 new rules for career success that can help you plan your career by looking ahead. Some of these are:

- Ensure your marketability.

- Be able to communicate in powerful, persuasive and unconventional ways.

- Keep on learning.

- Understand business trends.

- Prepare for areas of competence, not jobs.

- Be a ruthless time manager.

- Be kind to yourself.

Being a "career activist" in a demanding professional world with too little time in each day is a difficult challenge. But forcing yourself to stay focused on where your career is headed is the best way to keep ahead of the dynamic curve of constant change. *Career Intelligence* is one way to help keep that focus.

Job Search Facts

You can't network too much. Here are the results of a survey developed by Accountemps and conducted by an independent research firm. It includes responses from 1,400 CFOs from a stratified random sample of companies with more than 20 employees. The CFOs were asked:

"How important is networking with other professionals in your field or industry in furthering your career?"

1. A full 41 percent said very important.

2. Another 39 percent said somewhat important.

3. Only 3 percent said somewhat unimportant, while 6 percent said not at all important.

Your Current Employer

Your next great job could be with the company you're with right now. Most companies have an HR department that posts job openings, and typically, current employees are given priority consideration over outside candidates. Of course, this gives you a leg up on the competition. You have a chance to get your resume in and schedule an interview before the deluge of interviews and responses starts coming in by mail and email.

Keep an eye out for such postings, but go further in your search for internal opportunities. Talk to co-workers in other departments to learn about upcoming changes and expansions. Seek out opportunities to work on interdepartmental projects that put you in contact with *other* managers and executives. Consider gaining new experience through an outside consulting position (if it doesn't conflict with your current position). If so, you'll appear much more qualified when an opportunity presents itself.

Your Company's Competitors

There's no better place to find job openings for positions that reflect your experience and skills than other companies just like the one you're at now. Unless you've signed an agreement not to work for a competitor within a period of time after you leave your company, competing firms can be a great source of job opportunities. Remember, confidentiality regarding your job search is key, unless of course you're unemployed.

Search company websites for their most recent job openings. Of course, there's always the business section at the local library, filled with directories of all types of companies, such as the *Thomas Register of American Manufacturers*, and the bible of executive recruiters, *The Directory of Executive Recruiters* (Kennedy Publishing), which is updated annually and available on disk for sorting—and mailing to—recruiters nationwide. There's a more complete listing of these materials at the end of this book. Our company can target hundreds of top executive recruiters by industry and profession, either nationally or locally.

Trade and Industry Organizations

Trade and industry groups, as well as local Chambers of Commerce, conduct regular meetings and special events where you can meet and network with fellow executives. Most organizations have regularly published newsletters or magazines that may include job listings.

You should join at least one such organization if you haven't already and network, network, network. Consider joining your local LinkedIn chapter online. If your job search is confidential, networking just means getting to know as many people as possible. Your employer may have a policy of paying for all or part of your membership and may encourage you to be active in the group. If you're currently unemployed, that's all the more reason to join a trade organization—you can stay in touch with others in your industry and keep your knowledge and skills up to date.

Selecting Recruiters, Headhunters and Employment Agencies

Some swear by them, others swear at them. Whatever you call them, don't underestimate the power of a good agency or placement professional. In a job market with approximately 9 percent unemployment (at the time of this writing), you need to maximize every possible resource.

No matter what the company calls itself, it all boils down to individual recruiters: Are they easy to work with? Do they listen well? Will they really go to bat for you, or will they treat you like a number?

Recruiters often have positions that are not advertised. Register with the more established firms and avoid the sleazy operations that make promises they can't keep. Avoid paying clerical charges disguised as "out-of-pocket expenses." Unless you really believe the agency can help you out, let the employer pay the fees. Check *The Directory of Executive Recruiters* for annual updates of employers specializing at your income level and in your geographic or industry preference.

Try to get an idea of what types of clients an agency works with before getting too deeply involved. Do they work with Fortune 100 accounts? Fortune 500, 1000 or none of the above? Ask about their placement rate and number of years in business.

Recruiters often specialize in a particular industry, field or salary level. Some may specialize in placing CEOs, COOs or CFOs, and others place their emphasis on top VPs of sales, marketing or manufacturing. Another may focus on MIS managers or technicians, and just about all specialize in certain geographic locations.

The Growth of Internet Recruiting

Here's an excerpt that outlines the amazing growth of Internet recruiting. It's from Business Wire. Recruiter's Network (www.recruitersnetwork.com), the Association for Internet Recruiting, conducted a recent poll on the Internet recruiting practices of 1,000 organizations. The study uncovered some incredible trends:

- More than 70 percent of organizations will be spending more in the coming years on Internet recruiting.

- Almost half of the companies polled have hired 1 to 20 percent of their annual workforce as a direct result of Internet recruiting.

- Almost 35 percent of companies with more than 10,000 employees had at least one recruiter dedicated strictly to Internet recruiting.

- More than 80 percent of the organizations studied had an employment section within their company's website.

Be sure you understand what your financial commitment is with a recruiter. It's most common for the employer to pay any agency fees if a job match is made. However, you may be required to pay the agency for its services, and terms of payment vary from agency to agency. You may even be required to pay an amount equivalent to one month's salary. Personally, I wouldn't do this. My rule of thumb is that it's okay to pay for help producing custom resume materials or job leads, but never to pay anyone for a job. As in any situation, make sure you understand all terms and conditions before signing any agreement.

Trade and Newspaper Want Ads

You've probably read the statistics that up to 80 percent of all job openings are never advertised. Although this may be true, don't ignore the classified ads in your local newspaper and trade industry publications. Sunday's edition may have numerous listings, typically categorized by field.

Keep a few things in mind as you check off possibilities to contact on Monday morning. First, blind-box ads are used by companies that don't want to be identified, and they pay extra for the privilege. Respond to blind ads if the position seems right for you, but don't expect much. Often, companies will place such an ad simply to see what the pool of available talent is like. (Be aware, too, that the blind ad you're reading may have been placed by your current employer.)

Newspaper want ads tend to draw the biggest deluge of resumes. Just like you, every other job-seeker is seeing the ad and will likely respond. Your resume may be sitting in a pile with dozens or even hundreds of others (all the more reason for an excellent resume).

Advertisements in trade journals and magazines related to your field may be a little more targeted. Of course, that means the others who are responding to the ad probably have more targeted experience as well, so your competition may be stiffer.

Alumni Career Centers

Contact your school's alumni career center or placement office and see what type and level of support they can provide. Of course, some are better than others, but placement offices have some good connections with desirable employers who are looking for top-notch candidates. My own alma mater, NIU in DeKalb, Illinois, has an excellent alumni career center with job fairs, lectures and speakers on such job-search issues as networking and interview preparation.

Career and Job Fairs

Just as with the Sunday want ads, you'll be competing with a larger pool of candidates at major job fairs. Before putting in the time and effort to attend, try to find out what types of companies will be represented. Even if you don't think they're hiring executives or top managers, it's still another opportunity to drop off resumes and have them hand-delivered to top executives. This can save you time, travel and postage. You won't have to provide a cover letter, and—if your timing is right—you might even have a chance for an impromptu interview on the spot with a hiring executive.

Check the Sunday classified section for listings of upcoming job fairs. They're common in college towns as well as in cities with high demand for workers. Most job fairs are free, but occasionally you may run across one that charges admission.

Pursue the Job Lead

Once you've learned about a job opportunity, whether it's through a networking contact, an online job board or a trade publication, you aren't necessarily ready to zap off your resume—yet.

Cold Calling

Before you do anything, *research, research, research!* Whenever possible, call the company to find out exactly what they do and the name of the person who would be your supervisor. Visit your library or check company websites for the most current information and keywords about their products, services, markets and standing in their industry.

This cannot be overemphasized, because applicants who show knowledge of a company stand a much better chance of being hired—or at least interviewed—by that company. Remember, there may be hundreds of others applying for the same position. Do everything in your power to set yourself apart: Learn about the company, the position and your supervisor and then customize your resume and cover letter. The hiring executive should feel as if he is the only one getting your resume.

The Informational Interview: A Back-Door Approach

Try calling a company directly before sending a resume to request assistance in your job search. If you can reach a hiring manager, ask about industry trends, markets, and so on, but *do not* ask for a position. If that call goes well, request a personal, informational meeting (10 minutes of his time). If the person agrees to a meeting, bring a resume with you, but don't *volunteer* your resume unless requested. We train clients in this personal, verbal approach, which has led to new positions. There are books and articles devoted to this topic; call if you'd like to know more about this back-door strategy to getting hired for unadvertised positions.

All of this research, calling and networking will better prepare you for the interview, covered briefly in the next chapter.

At Last:
The Interview

The interview is your chance to elaborate on the skills and experience you've developed in your resume—and to make a personal connection with the people you hope to work with. It's your opportunity to go for the close. Therefore, it's absolutely essential that you enter the interview with the information and skills you need to make that close.

Entire books have been written on interviewing, but following are a few key tips for a job-winning interview. Check the articles in Chapter 12, "Motivation: Get Your Career in Gear," for other insights on interviewing.

Research the Company and Position

I stressed in the previous chapter the importance of learning as much as possible about job opportunities you're pursuing before developing and sending your resume and cover letter. It's even more important to walk into an interview with a clear understanding of the environment—the culture—of the firm in which you may soon be working. If you walk into the interview knowing it's a traditional business environment, you'll present yourself as more conservative, perhaps focusing on your steadfastness, reliability and long tenure at previous jobs. In that case, avoid talking about the value of radical change and how you pushed for cutting-edge management changes in a previous job.

Practice Your Answers

While it's true that you cannot predict exactly what you'll be asked in the interview, you should have some idea of the types of questions to prepare for. For example, "Tell me about yourself." "What is it you like best about the work you do?" "What are your weaknesses?"

At the very least, prepare a response to the question, "Tell me about yourself." Interviewers use this to see how well you communicate spontaneously about yourself. If you go off on a tangent about where you were born and what your hobbies are, you're not really focusing on your interviewers' interests (unless, of course, they bring this up first). Unless you feel confident that you can handle this question in the moment, you may wish to prepare a brief speech, no more than two minutes long. It should sum up the most important skills and attributes you can bring the company, as well as your work experience in relation to the company's needs

Job Search Tip

When's the best time to book an interview? Believe it or not, it can make a difference. An Accountemps survey, published in the *Chicago Tribune*, polled 200 executives. It found that job applicants who interview in the morning may be viewed more favorably than those with interviews later in the day.

A full 83 percent of those responding said they preferred to interview candidates between 9 a.m. and 11 a.m. No other time of day even came close. In general, hiring managers said they dislike interviewing near their usual break times. I think it's also because early in the morning, hiring managers are less overwhelmed with work, their busy schedules or a heavy lunch.

Present a Professional Image

This is another reason to research the company. Is it a casual corporate climate? It may be true that in some cases, dressing more casually for an interview will be entirely appropriate, but as a rule, it's always safe to wear a suit (whether you're a woman or man) to an interview.

Arrive on Time

This is basic. Your punctuality is an important measure of your reliability. Do whatever you must to arrive at the interview on time. In fact, work to get there at least 10 minutes early. This will give you time to collect yourself, review your notes and resume, use the washroom and enter into the meeting with a calm and positive attitude.

Be Positive

No matter what—you were given horrible directions, the office was hard to find, traffic was terrible—start off your interview with a positive attitude. Your interviewer wants to talk to someone who conveys enthusiasm, optimism and eagerness. No matter what sort of day you've had, keep that smile on your face; be kind to the receptionist, the doorman, everyone. If asked to complete a job application, do so—don't brush it off with, "That's all on my resume." This may be the first thing you're asked to do; by all means, do it.

Don't Be Nervous

Although it may seem that way at first, an interview is not a life-or-death situation. Relax and try to be yourself. The employer may be interviewing other candidates who come across more relaxed and confident but who don't have the skills and experience you have. *Don't let them get your job.* Remember: The person conducting the interview once sat where you are— he had to be interviewed as well.

The interview is another chance to learn more about what the employer really wants. The way I see it, you're there to interview the company to some extent. You shouldn't feel as if the burden is all on *your* shoulders to make a good impression.

Any decent interviewer understands that you may be nervous. He should know how to put you at ease right from the start with some light conversation, rather than to put you on the spot—but don't count on it.

Some interviewers actually enjoy intimidating candidates with out-of-this-world questions or impossible situations to see how you react under pressure. Just keep in mind that it's all a show to see what you're made of. Retain your composure as much as possible, thoughtfully consider your replies and maintain eye contact with the interviewer when responding.

Job Search Facts

Speak up! An Accountemps/Robert Half survey polled 150 executives from the nation's 1,000 largest companies. Fully one-third said that during interviews, applicants are often *too humble* in recounting their own achievements. The lesson: Don't take anything for granted or assume that employers already know how great you are.

When you're called in for an interview, don't overwhelm the listener and brag about yourself, but by the same token, don't downplay your ability to perform successfully for the company.

Downplay Personal Information

Interviewers are prohibited by law from asking certain questions about your personal life. Questions that attempt to ascertain your ethnic background, marital status, sexual activity, or physical or mental health are off limits.

Be careful not to offer too much personal information. Feel free to talk briefly about your favorite leisure activities (golf, and so on) if prompted, or any other personal attribute or activity you share with the interviewer. Just keep in mind that the interview is not the place to talk about how excited you are about your upcoming wedding or how you're eager to supplement your income so you can buy a new yacht.

Of course you're not perfect, and employers don't expect you to be. Sometimes they just want to hire someone who seems to have the right fit for their corporate culture—someone with the right skills, the right type of background and who they think they can get along with and train in their way of doing things.

Likability

A company can always train you in a specific task or procedure, but it can't change your personality and make you fit into its work environment. As a former corporate recruiter, I guarantee that employers are most interested in hiring someone who seems likable, reliable, trainable and a good fit with their company culture. Convey this in the first few minutes of your interview, and you're already ahead of your competition.

Stay on Message

The Profile section of your resume is your core message, your value proposition, and should remain your key reference point in face-to-face conversations, networking, telephone calls and interviews. Just like a politician running for office: Stay on message. Remain consistent and confident in all your communications. Keep a positive, upbeat tone of voice, and you'll be remembered by those who can help or hire you.

If you feel you need help in preparing for other commonly asked interview questions, check the Appendix, "Job Search Resources," at the end of this book for some great books on the topic.

Motivation:
Get Your Career in Gear

As a member of LinkedIn and a dozen other sites, organizations and professional groups, I come across articles that reflect my own ideas on the overall job search. Topics range from self-motivation and attitude adjustment to resume writing, personal networking and interview techniques.

Here are some of my favorite articles related to inspiration/motivation, networking and interviewing. I'll start with a few of my favorite quotes. As always, feel free to send your own questions, feedback and comments to my personal, direct email at Execareers@aol.com.

"People become really quite remarkable when they start thinking that they can do things. When they believe in themselves, they have the first secret of success."

—Norman Vincent Peale

"The world is more malleable than you think, and it's waiting for you to hammer it into shape."

—Bono

"What lies behind us and what lies before us are tiny matters compared to what lies within us."

—Ralph Waldo Emerson

"A happy person is not a person in a certain set of circumstances, but rather a person with a certain set of attitudes."

—Hugh Downs

"We judge a man's wisdom by his hope."

—Ralph Waldo Emerson

How to Keep from Being Your Own Worst Obstacle in the Job Search

Article originally published on hellomynameisscott.com.

- Be aware and accept the reality that we create our own obstacles.

- If we don't schedule breaks, we sometimes burn out and then take long breaks that lead to procrastination. Schedule regular short breaks to give yourself some downtime spread throughout the day.

- Organize tasks and schedules at the beginning of the week. (Saturday or Sunday, so that the week is already planned before starting the tasks first thing on Monday.)

- Schedule regular physical exercise during the week to either get in shape or stay in shape. This will help with mental health/attitude as well as the physical.

- Find a buddy or small support group (sometimes called an *accountability group*) to keep on schedule and task. Most times it's not your spouse or significant other, because they will either be too "soft" or too "hard." Outside the family seems to work best. There is a book by Orville Pearson that discusses accountability groups.

- Share with a best friend all that you are interested in doing and what you have done in your career(s). It helps to have someone close to you who really knows what you've accomplished and what your dreams are for your next career move.

- As much as possible, stay away from negative people. Concentrate on surrounding yourself with positive people, even when you are out at networking groups. If they give you energy for your journey, seek them out.

- Focus on positive inputs or results by writing down at least three per day.

- Start a "gratitude journal" with things that improved your day (blessings).

- Attend a training session on finding your strengths.

- Pray. At the best times, pray. At the worst times, pray. Keep God, however you see Him or Her, in your job search. You are not alone.

- Have music playing in the background when you're doing the job-search tasks that don't require telephone calls. Music can make the environment inviting.

- Do some volunteer work to help stimulate your sense of giving back or paying forward.

- Require structure in organizing your search so that time and effort aren't wasted.

- Have a script for networking telephone call and possibly even telephone interviews. You may not read it word for word, but at least have it there to remind you of your key points.

At the end of each day, use "The Examen of Consciousness" to remember the events and feelings of the day, pray for enlightenment, and then look forward to your plans for tomorrow. To me, it provides a deep sense of connectedness from day to day throughout the job search, with myself and with God (Higher Power).

How to Retrain Your Brain for Change

By M.J. Ryan.

M.J. Ryan is an expert on the new-millennium workplace and a former Fortune 500 HR executive. The author of many bestselling books, Ryan is a consultant with Professional Thinking Partners, where she specializes in coaching high-performance executives and leads trainings in effective teamwork in corporations, nonprofits and government agencies. Her latest book is *AdaptAbility: How to Survive Change You Didn't Ask For.* Visit her website (www.mj-ryan.com) for more change survival tips.

Big changes are happening for you. But it's (literally) easier to resist change than go with it. Your brain needs to create new pathways to perform a new behavior. Follow these tips on changing without draining your brain.

"I'm going to get better at networking."

"I'm going to increase my personal productivity."

"I'm going to learn to delegate more."

At some point we've all vowed to make some big change—or had to as a result of the huge changes around us. But all too often, our good intention soon gets pushed aside. Not because we lose motivation, but because we just don't know how to change. Especially when it comes to a career change.

Changing Your Behavior Takes Work

Our brains have enormous "plasticity," meaning they can create new cells and pathways. But our brains also create strong tendencies to do the same thing over and over.

Here's why: The brain cells that fire together wire together. Meaning, having run in a certain sequence, they are more likely to run that sequence again until it becomes a habit. It's one of the ways the brain conserves energy. By now, you've got a deeply grooved pathway to doing what you've always done. That's why change is hard; you've got to practice enough to create a new pathway that is strong enough to compete with the old one.

According to many brain scientists, it can take six to nine months to create that new automatic behavior. But it can be done. I just finished working with a micromanaging executive who no one believed could stop meddling. His goal was to have his employees rate him great at delegating in six months. He succeeded—and so can you at whatever you want to change.

Three Limiting Beliefs That Curb Executives' Ability to Change Their Behavior

1. **Bad habits can't be broken.** Executives don't understand that the change process is not about getting rid of bad habits. The pathway to your current behavior is there for life. Instead, you want to focus on the new, more positive habit and keep at it no matter how many times your brain jumps the tracks and goes back to the tried and true.

2. **I'll forget.** Executives fail to put reminders in place in the beginning. Unless you have a trigger from the outside, like a BlackBerry reminder, a note on your computer or a coach or buddy, it's virtually guaranteed you'll keep defaulting to the old behavior.

3. **I want it all.** Executives are not concrete enough about what they want and are unrealistic about what they can reasonably ask themselves to change. Here's what an executive client of mine said he wanted to change in three months: "to be more positive with co-workers, staff and colleagues, to be more creative and productive and to take better care of myself." "How about create world peace while you're at it?" I replied. "And what does 'more' mean, anyway?" As this client demonstrated, we expect too much of ourselves, and we expect to change overnight. When that doesn't happen, we resign ourselves to staying the same, convinced that we are weak or unmotivated.

These beliefs can make us even more stuck in a rut. But there are even more ways to shake these excuses and retrain your brain.

Ways to Retrain Your Brain

1. **Make it nonnegotiable.** Promise yourself that you are absolutely going to do it. When you do it, where you do it and how you do it can—and most likely will— change according to circumstances. But that you *will* do it is not open for consideration. Making it compulsory is a tool for overcoming backsliding after your initial enthusiasm fades.

2. **Make it actionable.** You have to know what actions you're going to take: 10 cold calls a day, for instance. Or asking more questions. Then be sure to track yourself so you can tell if you're succeeding.

3. **Come up with solutions for your usual excuses.** Instead of just hoping it will be different this time, write down your typical rationalizations and create coping strategies in advance. That way, you won't get stopped in your tracks and lose forward momentum when they arise. And yes, they will!

4. **Schedule it in.** Want to have blue-sky thinking time? Block it out on your calendar. Want to work out? Schedule it. Make a specific, time-bound appointment with yourself, and you'll be much more likely to do it.

5. **Do it daily.** The more you make what you want part of your everyday life, the more it will become so routine that soon you won't even have to think about it. If you want to get better at networking, for instance, do something every day: one email, call or meeting.

6. **Focus on the horizon.** Take a tip from high-performance athletes. Look at how far you've come, not how much you have left to do. Scientists call this the *horizon effect*. It creates encouragement—"I've done twice as much as a week ago!"—and builds determination—"I've made it this far; I might as well keep going." Don't forget to ask yourself how you've accomplished the task, so you can mine your success for ideas on how to keep going.

7. **Don't turn goof-ups into give-ups.** You will mess up or forget. Remember, you're learning. How many times does a baby fall before learning to walk? When you treat yourself as a learner, you don't collapse into shame or guilt, but can try again with greater wisdom. Keep at it no matter how many times you blow it.

The ability to adapt to change is one of our greatest capacities as leaders, particularly in these turbulent times. When you have this invaluable tool in your arsenal, you'll be empowered to bring anything you want into reality and be better equipped to help those around you change, too.

Networking Tips and Strategies

Remember the number-one way to get that new position: networking. How you present yourself on paper, on the phone and in-person should be clear, strong and most of all, consistent. People are drawn to consistency; it's calming, comfortable, attractive and memorable. That's what you must become throughout your job search, and for that matter, your entire career.

Adopt These 10 Traits, and You'll Have People Knocking Down Your Door, Trying to Do Business with You

By Ivan Misner, Ph.D.

Ivan Misner is co-author of *The New York Times* bestseller *Masters of Networking*. He is the founder and CEO of BNI, the world's largest referral organization, with more than 2,400 chapters in 13 countries around the world. He also teaches business courses at California State Polytechnic University, Pomona, and resides in Southern California with his wife and three children.

Networking is more than just shaking hands and passing out business cards. Based on a survey I conducted of more than 2,000 people throughout the United States, the United Kingdom, Canada and Australia, it's about building your "social capital." The highest-rated traits in the survey were the ones related to developing and maintaining good relationships. For years, I've been teaching people that this process is more about "farming" than it is about "hunting." It's about cultivating relationships with other business professionals. It's about realizing the capital that comes from building social relationships. The following traits were ranked in order of their perceived importance to networking. They're the traits that will make you a "master networker."

1. **Follow up on referrals.** This was ranked as the No. 1 trait of successful networkers. If you present an opportunity, whether it's a simple piece of information, a special contact or a qualified business referral, to someone who consistently fails to follow up successfully, it's no secret that you'll eventually stop wasting your time with this person.

2. **Positive attitude.** A consistently negative attitude makes people dislike being around you and drives away referrals; a positive attitude makes people want to associate and cooperate with you. Positive business professionals are like magnets. Others want to be around them and will send their friends, family and associates to them.

3. **Enthusiastic/motivated.** Think about the people you know. Who gets the most referrals? People who show the most motivation, right? It's been said that the best sales characteristic is enthusiasm. To be respected within our networks, we at least need to sell ourselves with enthusiasm. Once we've done an effective job of selling ourselves, we'll be able to reap the reward of seeing our contacts sell us to others! That's motivation in and of itself!

4. **Trustworthy.** When you refer one person to another, you're putting your reputation on the line. You have to be able to trust your referral partner and be trusted in return. Neither you nor anyone else will refer a contact or valuable information to someone who can't be trusted to handle it well.

5. **Good listening skills.** Our success as networkers depends on how well we can listen and learn. The faster you and your networking partner learn what you need to know about each other, the faster you'll establish a valuable relationship. Communicate well and listen well.

6. **Network always.** Master networkers are never off duty. Networking is so natural to them that they can be found networking in the grocery-store line, at the doctor's office and while picking the kids up from school, as well as at chamber mixers and networking meetings.

7. **Thank people.** Gratitude is sorely lacking in today's business world. Expressing gratitude to business associates and clients is just another building block in the cultivation of relationships that will lead to increased referrals. People like to refer others to business professionals who go above and beyond. Thanking others at every opportunity will help you stand out from the crowd.

8. **Enjoy helping.** Helping others can be done in a variety of ways, from literally showing up to help with an office move to clipping a helpful and interesting article and mailing it to an associate or client. Master networkers keep their eyes and ears open for opportunities to advance other people's interests whenever they can.

9. **Sincere.** Insincerity is like a cake without frosting! You can offer the help, the thanks, the listening ear, but if you aren't sincerely interested in the other person, he'll know it! Those who have developed successful networking skills convey their sincerity at every turn. One of the best ways to develop this trait is to give the individual with whom you're developing a referral relationship your undivided attention.

10. **Work your network.** It's not net-sit or net-eat, it's net-work, and master networkers don't let any opportunity to work their networks pass them by. They manage their contacts with contact-management software, organize their email address files and carry their referral partners' business cards as well as their own. They set up appointments to get better acquainted with new contacts so that they can learn as much about them as possible so that they can truly become part of each other's networks.

Do you see the trend with these 10 points? They all tie into long-term relationship building, not to stalking the prey for the big kill. People who take the time to build their social capital are the ones who will have new business referred to them over and over. The key is to build mutually beneficial business relationships. Only then will you succeed as a master networker.

Harness the Power of Networking©:
Easy Steps to Make Your Connections Count!

By Susan Fignar, Pur-sue, Inc.

With today's topsy-turvy economy and uncertain job market, the one thing you want to be able to count on is support from business colleagues, clients, vendors and even family and friends. It's not only who we know, but what we know about them and how we can help each other.

Remember, even the Lone Ranger couldn't do it alone. He had his trusty partners, Tonto and Silver!

Networking vs. Partnerships

Networking is only the tip of the iceberg in furthering career aspirations. If not managed properly, it can soon become a numbers game based on how many events attended, business cards collected, speaking engagements given and associations joined. While networking brings visibility, it doesn't necessarily bring credibility. However, business partnerships, which are built on a higher level, can bring credibility, trust, integrity and a positive reputation. The important thing to remember is that it's not how visible you make yourself, but how you are perceived.

So, how can you stop the numbers game and build a quality network to develop/strengthen your business partnerships?

The Partnership Factor: Build and Strengthen Your Business Partnerships

Strive to become a connector versus a giver or taker; focus your efforts to develop and deepen relationships, not contacts. Simply meeting people is not the best use of anyone's time. It's better to be known by fewer people who can speak to your unique capabilities and abilities and will work on your behalf. Building trust with key individuals is the first priority and will take time, so be patient. Listed below are four proven tips to move you closer to building and strengthening successful business partnerships:

1. **Be approachable and proactive.** Look open and initiate conversation rather than wait for others to approach or contact you via email, telephone and/or in-person.

2. **Participate only in organizations and events that are relevant to you and your business** vs. trying to be in too many places.

3. **Concentrate on leadership roles vs. membership.** You will get more out of an organization if you volunteer to be on a committee or take on a board position, rather than being a regular member. It's better to be seen and singled out as a leader in one or two organizations than to be a passive member of several groups.

4. **Follow through with your commitments.** If you take on a volunteer role, be sure to deliver what you promised. The quickest way to develop a negative reputation is to fail to follow through. Commit to those activities you have the time and ability to accomplish.

Take action: Partnerships take time. You don't build solid relationships/partnerships overnight! If your partnerships are not mutually beneficial, it's time to reevaluate them, move on, and replace the ones on your A and B lists that are not mutually beneficial. Following are a few questions to explore:

1. List three to five steps you take to build/strengthen your business partnerships (i.e., colleagues, clients, vendors, prospects).

2. What do you know about the skill set and reputation of the person you want to partner with for business purposes? Are they complementary, or do they overlap with your services?

3. What strengths / core values / personality attributes are important to you and to the individual(s) you would like to partner with?

4. How many introductions have you made on behalf of others over the past three months, and how many introductions have others made on your behalf? Remember, we judge others and they judge us on our actions, not our words.

Track your progress: Over the next 12 months, record and share your progress and any challenges you may experience along the way with an accountability partner who is known for his ability to successfully relate and connect to others. For the first 60 days, track your progress weekly; after that, bimonthly or monthly. You will be pleasantly surprised by your successes and lessons learned along the way.

You Are Not Alone

By Mike Robbins, author/speaker, www.Mike-Robbins.com

Sometimes I feel like I'm all alone. Even though my relationship with my wife Michelle is amazing, the love I feel for and from my girls is profound, and there are so many incredible people in my life (family, friends, and clients)—I still find that in my darkest moments, I feel like there's no one who really gets me, knows what I'm going through or even cares enough to truly have my back. Do you ever feel like this yourself?

I'm facing some pretty intense challenges in my life right now. Earlier this week, I was standing in the center of the circle at my men's group, and I allowed myself to really get vulnerable about what's been going on and the underlying pain and fear I've been feeling. As I fell to the floor and sobbed uncontrollably, I realized that two of my deepest fears have been "I can't handle all of this myself" and "I'm all alone."

As I allowed myself to both feel and express the intensity of these painful fears, two amazing things happened. First of all, I felt liberated (which is what almost always happens when we express ourselves vulnerably and authentically). Second of all, I felt the acceptance, support, and love of the men in my group in that moment, which reminded me (both mentally and, more important, emotionally and experientially) that I'm not, in fact, alone—there are so many incredible people in my life who do have my back.

We're never truly alone, even when we feel that way. Most of us have important, loving and caring people in our lives who are there to support us—if we're willing to open up, ask for and receive their help. And, regardless of how many people are around us; what our current relationship, family, or work situation may be; or any of the other external circumstances in our lives—each of us has access to a higher power, whether we call it God, Spirit, Source or anything else.

One of the deepest and most basic fears of being human is the fear of loneliness—no one to be with us, love us, accept us, support us and take care of us if and when we need it. Although this fear seems very real, and there's nothing wrong with us for feeling it, the paradox is that we aren't ever really alone—we're surrounded by love and support all the time, from others and, of course, from God. The idea that we're alone is simply a "story" we tell ourselves, especially when things get difficult, scary, or both.

Here are some things you can do to let go of this "story" of being alone when it shows up in your life:

1. **Open Up Vulnerably.** Acknowledging, owning and sharing your deepest truth is one of the best ways to liberate yourself and connect with other people in an authentic way (hence, reminding you that you're not alone). So often we think that if we really let others know how we feel, what we fear and what's truly going inside our head and our heart, they will judge us, reject us or not understand us. In most cases, the exact opposite is true.

2. **Ask for Help.** As the saying goes, "The answer is always 'no' if you don't ask." When we have the courage and vulnerability to ask for the help and support we need, a few important things happen. First of all, we're liberated from the pressure of trying to take care of everything ourselves. Second of all, we give other people the opportunity to contribute to us and be of service (which most people love to do). And finally, we're able to tap into the energy, brilliance and creativity of other human beings— which is almost always helpful and is also a good reminder that we have access to a great deal of love and support.

3. **Allow Yourself to Be Supported.** Being "supportable" is something many of us, myself included, struggle with. Even if we're vulnerable enough to tell the truth about how we really feel and ask for the support we truly want, it takes a certain amount of maturity, self-respect and humility to allow other people to support us. Even if it's scary and feels uncomfortable at first, practicing and expanding your capacity to receive the support of others are both generous (as it allows other people to make a difference) and wise (you don't have to work so hard and struggle so much).

4. **Have Faith.** Faith is the belief in things not seen or proven. At some level, our ability to grow, expand and evolve in life is directly related to our ability to live with a deep sense of faith—in ourselves, others and a higher power. In our lowest moments, when it feels like we truly are alone and that things will never turn around, work out or go the way we want them to in life, our faith is what can pull us through. Waiting for a "guarantee" or until we think we're "ready" or "deserving" of support sets us up to fail and creates more fear and anxiety. Having faith in ourselves, others, life and God is what can remind us, in an instant, that we're not alone—because we're not!

Interview Tips and Strategies

Ten Good Ways to "Tell Me about Yourself": "If Hollywood Made a Movie about My Life, It Would Be Called…" and Nine More Memorable Answers to This Dreaded Job-Interview Question

By Scott Ginsberg, hellomynameisscott.com

You know it's coming.

It's the most feared question during any job interview: Do you think I would look good in a cowboy hat?

Just kidding. The real question is: Can you tell me about yourself?

Blech. What a boring, vague, open-ended question. Who likes answering that?

I know. I'm with you. But unfortunately, hiring managers and executive recruiters ask the question. Even if you're not interviewing and you're out networking in the community, you need to be ready to hear it and answer it. At all times.

Now, before I share a list of 10 memorable answers, consider the two essential elements behind the answers:

The medium is the message. The interviewer cares less about your answer to this question and more about the confidence, enthusiasm and passion with which you answer it.

The speed of the response is the response. The biggest mistake you could make is pausing, stalling or fumbling at the onset of your answer, thus demonstrating a lack of self-awareness and self-esteem.

Next time you're faced with the dreaded, "Tell me about yourself…" question, try these:

1. **"I can summarize who I am in three words."** Grabs their attention immediately. Demonstrates your ability to be concise, creative and compelling.

2. **"The quotation I live my life by is…"** Proves that personal development is an essential part of your growth plan. Also shows your ability to motivate yourself.

3. **"My personal philosophy is…"** Companies hire athletes—not shortstops. This line indicates your position as a thinker, not just an employee.

4. **"People who know me best say that I'm…"** This response offers insight into your own level of self-awareness.

5. **"Well, I Googled myself this morning, and here's what I found…"** Tech-savvy, fun, cool people would say this. Unexpected and memorable.

6. **"My passion is…"** People don't care what you do—people care who you are. And what you're passionate about is who you are. Plus, passion unearths enthusiasm.

7. **"When I was seven years old, I always wanted to be…"** An answer like this shows that you've been preparing for this job your whole life, not just the night before.

8. **"If Hollywood made a move about my life, it would be called…"** Engaging, interesting and entertaining.

9. **"Can I show you, instead of tell you?"** Then, pull something out of your pocket that represents who you are. Who could resist this answer? Who could forget this answer?

10. **"The compliment people give me most frequently is…"** Almost like a testimonial, this response also indicates self-awareness and openness to feedback.

Keep in mind that these examples are just the opener. The secret is thinking how you will follow up each answer with relevant, interesting and concise explanations that make the already bored interviewer look up from his stale coffee and think, "Wow! That's the best answer I've heard all day!"

Ultimately, it's about answering quickly, it's about speaking creatively and it's about breaking people's patterns.

I understand your fear with such answers. Responses like these are risky, unexpected and unorthodox. And that's exactly why they work. Otherwise, you become (yet another) nonentity in the gray mass of blah, blah, blah.

You're hirable because of your answers. When people ask you to tell them about yourself, make them glad they asked.

Let me ask you this: How much time did you dedicate this week to becoming more interesting? Let me suggest this: For the list called "61 Stupid Things to Stop Doing Before It's Too Late," send an email to me, and you win it for free!

Make-or-Break Interview Mistakes: To Get on HR's Good Side, Avoid Certain Behaviors. A Major Faux Pas, and Your Name Gets Crossed Off That List of Potential Candidates

By Liz Ryan, Yahoo! Jobs

Some people go into human resources thinking that it's like social work. Here's a news flash for anyone who thinks in those terms: If you're the kind of person who wants to adopt every stray kitten and advise every needy person you meet, you may want to find a different profession.

The plain truth is that HR people have limits on how supportive they can be. They can help employees only to the extent that what's good for them is good for the company. They can help job candidates even less because the HR person's job is to evaluate applicants—and eliminate from consideration those the company just doesn't need.

A perfect example of the limits of HR compassion involves the job seeker who needs professional advice. Every HR person has stories about people who have come to interviews in wildly unsuitable attire, or who have said something so outrageous within the first five minutes of the interview that the rest of the conversation was a waste. As much as they may joke after the fact, most HR people—myself included—dread these situations.

Your natural instinct is to be helpful, to tell the candidate where he went wrong. But you can't—you might get sued; you might offend someone. And in any case, there's no benefit to the company in being so, well, caring. Instead, you clam up, smile that lips-together fake smile that corporate HR people are so good at, and say to the candidate: "We'll be in touch."

So, if hapless job seekers are making the same mistakes during interview after interview, who's going to tell them? Unless their friends somehow see the picture, no one. That task falls to me, right here, right now. Pay attention to these suggestions for avoiding five major "we're done" interview behaviors, and tell your friends:

Dress for the Occasion

I interviewed a gentleman for a product-manager position who was smart and friendly. He arrived in a lovely wool suit, but wearing a necktie with a large Taz on it—you know, the Tasmanian devil. Now why, I couldn't stop thinking, did this guy wear a Taz tie to an interview? He didn't mention it, so it wasn't some sort of rapport-building device.

I sure as heck didn't mention it, but the Taz tie took up more and more space in the room, until I couldn't tear my gaze from it. Why a Taz tie, in a business job interview? Does the guy own the whole Looney Tunes character collection? It was too weird—a big deal. Why didn't he wear a different tie?

You don't have to wear Brooks Brothers to a job interview, but you have to look businesslike. There are still plenty of funky startups that would welcome a job seeker in one of those 1950s bowling shirts that Kramer used to wear on *Seinfeld*. But if you're applying at a standard, buttoned-down company, dress the part. And please, gentleman: If you have any '80s vintage three-piece suits, donate them! Burn them! (If three-piece suits are back and I missed it, somebody let me know. But the '80s ones are unmistakable, and they have to go.)

Restrain the Camaraderie

It's great to be friendly. In fact, it's essential, unless you're applying for an actuarial job (just kidding). But engaging in too much camaraderie with a complete stranger is clingy and pathetic.

I interviewed a woman who had worked for a company for which I had also worked. She had arrived about six months after I'd left. At the interview, she asked about a few people we knew in common from the other company. Of course, I knew them. Sally Jones? Yep. Joe Bartlett? Roger that. Jose Quintera? You betcha. After six or seven names, I thought, "Look, lady, we know the same people." But she kept going, until she'd run down the whole employee roster. It was spooky—and it didn't help her case.

Be pleasant, be warm, but keep interview banter professional. This is not a new friend of yours; this is a person who is interviewing you for a position. Go ahead and recommend a dog groomer if the conversation turns to dogs, but don't offer to take her dog to the groomer the next time you go. You think I'm joking? I'm not.

Control Your Nerves

You get nervous on a job interview. That's normal. But if you can't sit relatively still for an hour, you'll want to work on that. I've had candidates get up and pace around the room mid-conversation. I've had them walk over to the window, look out, and begin commenting on the street scene. These are not pluses. I've had a candidate say: "I'm tired of sitting. Can we walk somewhere?"

Now, if you worked for the company for even one day, and we were chatting, and you said: "I'm tired of sitting. Want to walk somewhere?" that would be perfectly fine. Everyone gets tired of sitting. But if I'm an HR person—well, I *am* an HR person—and I walk up and down the blocks-long building many times a day escorting job candidates to and fro, then I need to sit sometimes. Once we get to a job offer, we can negotiate terms. Right now, it's sort of—sorry to say this—my terms, and I want to sit some more.

Avoid Offering Too Much Information

I want to know everything about you, professionally. I want to know your interests and what motivates you. The history of your car's mechanical problems? I couldn't care less. Too much information, or TMI, is a big problem for some job seekers. Every interviewer has a different tolerance level, but I think I'm pretty forgiving. That's why it's so astounding when people go past even my limit—and start talking about their difficult relationships or their problems with their bookies.

Somewhere, buried deep in their subconscious, I believe that such people have the idea that employers give jobs to people who seem to really, really need the job. This is not the case. Keep personal issues to yourself. Once we become workmates, we'll have time to learn all about your soap operas, and you'll learn about ours.

For now, clam up. If you're going into the third chapter of your saga about the horrible boss you left behind at your last employer, and I'm furiously taking notes, here's what I'm writing: Shoot me. Poison me. Kill me now. Kill me now. Please, please kill me now....

Cut the Puffy Stuff

You want to promote yourself, I know. But too much puff is a huge turnoff to employers. The key to presenting yourself as accomplished yet modest is to introduce all self-promoting topics with an air of humble gratitude, even mild bewilderment. "I'm not quite sure how it happened, but I won the Nobel Prize."

If, instead, you start every sentence with something like: "After I beat out two other guys for the VP spot and then blew away the goals and made the last guy look like a turkey, well, you could say I became the Golden Boy," you need not finish. The interviewer will be jotting "not in this lifetime" on his little pad of paper.

By the way, there are certain initials that can follow your name on your résumé: MD, PhD and JD are among the most common. There are certain technical and professional designations that can sit up there, too: CPA, SPHR and CFA are some of them. Also, PMP for project manager, and lots of others.

MBA is not one of them. An MBA is something you have, not something you are. Including MBA in your title is excessive self-promotion. Those three initials will help you every bit as much down in the body of your resume (under Education, duh) as they would next to your name at the top.

Now that you have these hints, you should be unstoppable. Just remember the four Ps: No puff, no pacing, no palling around, and no personal info. What did I forget? Oh, yes—no three-piece suits and no Taz. Now go get 'em!

Cover Letter Essentials and Examples

Following your research, it's essential to create a custom cover letter outlining what you know about the company's market, product lines and current condition. Even changing only the first two lines of your cover letter or simply addressing it to the hiring authority helps differentiate you from the pack of applicants who send impersonal resumes all over the place. Of course, research isn't possible with blind ads, but you can still write a letter emphasizing keywords used in the job posting.

As in your resume, avoid negatives when possible and emphasize the positive. Check the cover letter samples here, and always put the best spin on your motivations: You're seeking new challenges with more exciting product lines (mention up-and-coming technologies if applicable), or you want to better utilize your knowledge of changing industry trends or fast-paced, leading-edge products and/or marketing concepts. This tells employers you're highly motivated to learn more about—and utilize—the most recent advances in products, services or creative marketing. Employers will see obvious benefits in interviewing an executive who's in tune with the absolute latest industry trends. This is also a good place to reemphasize recent training in new technologies, personal communications or leadership.

The one thing your cover letter should *not* do is repeat too many details found in your resume. You can certainly elaborate on one or two achievements or skills applicable to the position, but you don't want to sound redundant or waste space.

The cover letter is also a good place to clarify situations that might be confusing to the reader. Let's say your resume indicates years of experience as an executive in a certain industry. Complementing the Profile section of your resume, which develops transferable skills, the letter allows you to explain why you want to work in a new industry, with a new product line and so on.

You might use your cover letter to point out that the favorite aspect of your current job is "total project management, from initial staff hiring, training and team leadership to product launch and international marketing," for example, and that you can now bring the wealth of this experience to the new company and expand its bottom line.

Length

Keep your cover letter to one page. Lead with a catchy introduction and focus on the needs of the employer—not just your needs—then identify three or four points that expand upon and complement key aspects of your resume.

Close the Sale

Finally, conclude with some plan of action, such as, "I'll follow up next week to discuss mutual interests or whether you would like to schedule an interview." If that's not possible, request that the reader call you to arrange an interview. If you're relocating, indicate when you'll be in town and available for interviews. Remind readers that they may always call or write for more information.

Your cover letter allows you to personalize your presentation, which is especially valuable if you omitted a title or objective on your resume. It also gives you the chance to write less formally about who you are, what you can accomplish in the position and what you know about the firm. Use Internet or library resources to research companies and demonstrate your knowledge of:

1. Their company mission, culture or long/short-term goals.

2. Their products and/or services—the company's unique value in the marketplace.

3. Their major markets: business, general consumer, national or international.

4. What their current hiring needs are (or could be) and how you can help fill those needs.

General Procedure

■ Send a customized, personalized letter with your resume whenever possible. If all you change is the first sentence, you're ahead of the crowd that doesn't bother with this key element. Exceptions can be made for blind-box ads, but if it looks like an exceptional position, then by all means include a letter addressed to the name of the hiring manager (see below); otherwise, send it to "Dear Hiring Executive:", "Ladies/Gentlemen:", "Dear Hiring Manager:" or "Dear Prospective Employer:". Use a colon (:) when you've never spoken to the individual and a comma when you have. When emailing directly to employers, attach your resume in MS Word or PDF format and then use the body of the email for your cover letter, in text format.

- Especially important in the executive job search: Personalize and address your letters to the actual hiring manager whenever possible. If you don't have a name, call the company and get the exact spelling of the hiring authority's name and job title. If you can't find this by calling the company, I recommend ReferenceUSA.com, available through most libraries at no charge. If the target company is listed there, you may find the name of the department head or hiring manager. If that's not available, send it to the personnel manager, human resources representative or corporate recruiter, with a name if possible.

- Make your letters brief and to the point—they stand a much better chance of getting read. Some employers skip the letter entirely and get to it only if they like what they see in your resume, so limit it to three or four short paragraphs.

- Unless you have excellent handwriting and are writing a personal note to someone you've met, cover letters should always be typed. Try to match paper colors of resumes and letters, but don't worry too much about this. White goes well with everything and doesn't look mass produced. It also looks more personal and immediate.

- Just as with your resume, proofread your letter very closely. Proofread once for content and once for grammar and typing mistakes. Then read it backwards and have someone else read it, too.

Writing the Cover Letter

Expanding on the points mentioned earlier, your cover letter should contain:

- The exact title of the position you are seeking. If that's not possible, then the general type of work for which you are applying.

- Why you want to work for the company. Remember: "What can you do for me?"

- A dazzling sample of what you know about the company: product lines, marketing strategies, their quality and quantity of clientele and where they stand among their competitors. For example, "I understand you will be introducing your new robotic CNC widget assembly system in the Australian market this fall. I have several ideas that may help you compete with Intel's established line."

- Personal attributes, or "soft" skills—just don't overdo it. One or two lines is enough, and keep it as objective as possible: "My peers would tell you I'm self-motivated and energetic, with a sharp eye for detail," or, "I feel certain my skills in personal client relations, networking and communications will expand your client base and develop strong repeat business, as demonstrated in my position with XYZ company."

- Whether you're willing to travel or relocate. Omit this if it's not requested or if you are not willing to travel or relocate.

- Other specifics about yourself or the job. If the posting says: "Include salary requirements" and not salary history, give them a desired salary range and avoid a specific number. For example: "Upper $90s/year, negotiable, depending on benefits." You may include this in a letter, but if they ask for salary requirements *and* salary

Job Search Facts

Professional writer and manager Stan Wynett conducted one of my favorite surveys of all time, and it was printed in the *National Business Employment Weekly*. Wynett conducted a poll of 200 companies and found that 94 percent said they consider every cover letter and resume they receive, *whether or not salary history is included*. He found this to be true even if the company stated in their advertising that "resumes without salary history will not be considered." Essentially, if they like you enough, they'll call, if only to learn more about your salary requirements; but then you have them on the phone and can ask about other factors: benefits such as insurance, a company car, stock options, location, advancement potential and so on.

history, include them on a separate salary history sheet and end the page with "Salary requirements are open to negotiation." However, be sure to consider the following survey:

Check annual reports at the library, newspaper and magazine articles, trade journals, CNBC or *The Nightly Business Report* on television. Any and all sources can spark new ideas or bring to mind new companies to target.

Call the firm before mailing your cover letter and resume and try to speak directly with the manager or hiring authority. If that's impossible, talk to the personnel representative. Tell him your name and that you'll be sending a resume for "X" position. Try to strike up a conversation about your qualifications and how they're just right for the job. But don't oversell yourself if the person sounds too busy to talk.

Of course, if the advertisement or posting says "NO CALLS, PLEASE," don't call—unless you can anonymously learn the hiring authority's name and/or title from the receptionist. In that case, try calling that person directly to inquire about opportunities in your field, as if you've never seen the ad and you heard about her or the company through industry contacts or a friend. As discussed earlier, you can also try to arrange an informational interview with the hiring manager and bring your resume with you. Be prepared to handle yourself well if you try this!

Track Your Progress

Keep a detailed list or card file of which resumes you sent to whom and on what date. You should call the company three to four days after sending the resume and try to speak with the actual hiring authority. Tell him you want to confirm receipt of your resume and that you would like to arrange an interview. Again, try to speak directly with the manager or supervisor, but if that's impossible, try the personnel representative. Be sure not to make a pest of yourself! Hounding anyone on the telephone is perceived as pushy and desperate.

If the manager or representative refuses to speak with you or set up an interview, wait a few days and give it one more try. Then sit tight or send a follow-up letter. Don't be discouraged by the standard "We're reviewing the applications and will be arranging interviews as soon as we've screened them all." This is the standard "don't call us, we'll call you." And it's not without justification. Sometimes employers really *do* want to sift through resumes first and then decide who to meet.

The whole idea of resume follow-up is to drop your name into the mind of the executive or HR representative and distinguish yourself from the silent stack of resumes. If you can set up an interview, fine. But remember that employers have time constraints and perhaps hundreds of resumes to screen. Don't be discouraged.

Some people approach employers with a "me against them" attitude. This can be fatal to a job search, and as hard as it may seem, you need to project yourself as an ally to all staff and managers at the target company. Rather than using an adversarial approach, act as if you're already part of their operation. Try to create a "we" scenario without being presumptuous. Remember, these are people you may soon be working with. A career coach I work with, Merri Smith, put it best; here's her personal mantra to repeat before every interview:

- I am a professional.
- I have no problems.
- I will cause no problems.
- I will solve all of your problems.

No matter what, keep on smilin'.

According to a survey by Robert Half and Accountemps recruiters, a full 60 percent of executives from the nation's largest companies said they consider their administrative assistants' opinions of applicants to be an important part of the selection process.

The survey found that "the interview begins from the moment you start speaking with the executive's assistant." Assistants are seen as being increasingly skilled at gauging whether candidates will be a good fit for the company's business environment, and executives take this into account when making hiring decisions. Some assistants actually interview candidates, either formally if they serve as office managers or informally as a means of facilitating the screening process.

With all respect to the invaluable administrative assistant, I think this shows just how subjective the hiring process can become. Hiring managers may have their opinions tainted by a subjective, personal bias even before objectively considering your skills and experience. That's why a smile, a positive attitude and eye contact may do more to win the day than you think. As management guru Tom Peters once put it, "People like to do business with people who like to do business."

The first eight cover letter examples that follow correspond to the first eight resumes in Chapter 15, "Executive Resume Examples." You should not use these verbatim, but rather modify and customize them for each resume you distribute. There are also sample follow-up letters, a salary history and a reference sheet. Again, personalization and customization are the keys to making a cover letter and resume produce the next step toward your new position: the interview.

Remember to check the three additional cover letters and resumes in Chapter 14, "Case Study: Before and After Resume Examples."

Lee A. Smith
36 Congress Road
New City, NY 10956
845/555-3620
smit@online.net

Dear Hiring Executive:

If expanding revenue is among your goals for 2012, then my experience in sales and marketing should be of interest to you. I have profitably applied skills in sales, marketing and client development to become a top producer in the wireless field. My background includes full responsibility for new business development, client relations and product introductions. My success has been the result of consistently making the needs of the customer my top priority and producing a strong referral business. Areas of expertise and transferable skills include:

Account Management	Customer Relations	New Account
Development	Negotiations	Business
Forecasting	Market Penetration	Marketing Analysis
Sales Forecasting	Sales Development	Strategic Planning
Lead Generation	Territory Development	

My peers would tell you that I thrive in an atmosphere of challenge. I'm an effective negotiator with the ability to maintain margins while building client loyalty. An in-depth knowledge of all phases of sales activity, along with specialized abilities that set my performance apart, enables me to offer a truly unique talent. I'm confident I can bring to the table a package of skills, experience and abilities that will provide you with an invaluable resource. In addition, I am a self-motivated performer who gets the job done and enjoys the challenges inherent in growing new business.

I will follow up with you in a few days to arrange a meeting to discuss mutual business interests. In the meantime, if you have any questions, you may reach me at the above phone number or via email. I look forward to our meeting and thank you for your time and consideration.

Sincerely,

Lee A. Smith

CARL STEVENS, C.P.A.
227 Alex Road
Linwood, KS 66052

C: 913-555-9434   steve@nzaro.cc   H: 785-555-1743

(Date)

(Name)
(Title)
(Company)
(Address)
(City), (State), (Zip)

Dear (Salutation) (Last Name),

I am exploring new opportunities in financial leadership, where I may leverage my skills to drive successful business development and operations. Specifically, I can bring you experience and success in improving operations, technology and the people and processes associated with them.

Recognized for polished communication, management, and problem-solving skills, I've excelled in positions where strategic planning, exceptional CRM and the ability to serve as a high-level advisor to C-level management have resulted in the profitable growth of more than five companies in various industries.

With my experience in finance, accounting, supply chain management, sales, marketing, public relations and advertising, I have been privileged to serve as CEO for two successful technology-based startups and as CFO for organizations in retail, fast-food franchising and construction. I personally developed and sold one of these businesses for a net profit of more than $4M after only six years of operation.

Accomplished in the strategic utilization of financial, marketing and process improvement initiatives driving top financial performance, I can easily translate this experience to bring out the best in your organization's business development and operations efforts as well.

I am available to interview at your convenience, and I look forward to your response.

Sincerely,

Carl Stevens, CPA

Mick Jackson

312 Main Street, #412   **Win@job.net**
Philadelphia, PA 19127   **212/555-1232**

Dear Hiring Executive:

If expanding revenue is among your goals for 2012, then my leadership experience in sales and marketing should be of interest to you. I have profitably applied skills in sales, marketing and client development to become a top producer in the financial investment field. My background includes full responsibility for new business development, client relations and sales strategies. My success has been the result of consistently making the needs of the customer my top priority and producing a strong referral business. Areas of expertise and transferable skills include:

Account Management	Customer Relations	New Account Development
Negotiations	Business Forecasting	Market Penetration
Marketing Analysis	Sales Forecasting	Sales Development
Strategic Planning	Team Leadership	Training & Development
Recruiting	Motivation	Strategic Marketing

During my career I have:

→ Demonstrated the ability to identify markets through strategic thinking, planning and problem solving.
→ Shown strong leadership of sales teams and the willingness to take bottom-line responsibility for marketing.
→ Increased accounts from 0 to 780, achieving more than $30 million in managed assets and generated revenue of $1 million.

My peers will tell you that I thrive in an atmosphere of challenge. I'm an effective negotiator with the ability to increase sales while building client loyalty. In addition, I am a self-motivated performer who gets the job done and enjoys the challenges inherent in growing new business.

I will follow up with you in a few days to arrange a meeting to discuss mutual business interests. In the meantime, if you have any questions, you may reach me at the above number or via email. I look forward to our meeting and thank you for your time and consideration.

Sincerely,

Mick Jackson

Anthony Provenzano
122 East 334th Street, Apt. 26G
New York, NY 10016

Res: 212/555-7492   E-mail: anthony@yahoo.com

[today's date]

[name]
[title]
[company name]
[address]
[city], [state] [zip]

Dear [salutation] [last name]:

I am forwarding my resume to you in response to your advertisement [search or announcement] for a [title of position]. I believe that you will find my background fits what you are seeking.

Currently, I am completing an assignment with Scream Puff, Inc., to evaluate and qualify vendor websites for hyperlink sales, banner advertising and other e-commerce marketing channels. This project is one of many that I have directed as an independent consultant to major accounts, such as Federated Marketing Services/Macy's, Ann Taylor and the Rowland Company.

During the past three years of working with these businesses, I have gained practical client-oriented experience in bringing technological solutions to the rapidly changing, complex management of information vital to a business' competitive advantage. Most important, I communicate ideas well and build strong, lasting client relationships.

[*Optional*: My technical knowledge includes _____]

I am willing to travel [and/or relocate for the right opportunity]. Please contact me soon to arrange an interview at your earliest convenience. Thank you for your time and consideration.

Sincerely,

Anthony Provenzano
Enclosure

Adam R. Nephew
221 Palm Bay Drive
Baldwin, NE 63021

Res: 314/555-0109   E-mail: nq74A@prodigy.com   Ofc: 314/555-7291

[date]

[name]
[title]
[company]
[address]
[city], [state] [zip]

Dear [salutation] [last name]:

I am forwarding my resume to you in response to your advertisement for (**position name**). I would like to explore this opportunity further. Specifically, I would like to better utilize my analytical skills and extensive background in information management systems.

As EDP supervisor at the Merchandising Corporation, I direct a staff in processing imported merchandise orders, with attention to cost analysis and pricing, for more than 200 stores nationwide. I ensure 100% accuracy of all financial and statistical data to preserve information technology across a broad spectrum of applications.

This past year, I reengineered several processes. I reduced report generation and distribution time to within 24 hours and classified merchandise items by a Uniform Product Code. The latter change smoothed inventory levels by matching items replenished to actual items sold.

Additionally, I speak and write basic Spanish. My computer knowledge covers both mainframe and PC-based systems, including UNIX, Windows 7/NT and the MS Office suite.

I am willing to relocate for the right opportunity and am available for an interview at your convenience. I look forward to your response.

Sincerely,

Adam R. Nephew
Enclosure

GOSHEN D. NANI
Coni 2280
Buenos Aires, Argentina

Cellular Phone: 541/555-3907   Business: 541/555-1001   E-mail: Goshen@hotmail.com

[date]

[name]
[title]
[company]
[address]
[city], [state] [zip]

Dear Hiring Executive:

I specialize in capital investment projects, hold an MBA, and believe you will find that my experience in senior-level management fits what you are seeking.

Currently, I'm the director of operations for Sync, Inc., a company owned by Tock-Tic Investment Group. Most notably, I recently broke through a competitive barrier worldwide and launched Sync in Argentina and Uruguay; I immediately captured an unheard-of 30 percent of total sales for the apparel division.

Prior to this position, as controller of the Latin American operations for two other ventures of Tock-Tic, the Hard Rock Cafe and Planet Hollywood, I opened and managed several theme restaurants new to Latin America. More important, I identified several successful new business development opportunities, such as the acquisition of a radio station and the backing of Disney's *Beauty and the Beast* theater production.

I am willing to travel or relocate to the United States for the right opportunity. Please contact me soon to arrange a meeting at your convenience to discuss mutual interests, and thank you for your time and consideration.

Sincerely,

Goshen D. Nani
Enclosure

Note: For use with executive search firms.

Johnathan Bishop

122 Tuna Can Road
Topanga, OH 44290

Res: 610/555-0350
E-mail: john@net.att.net

[date]

[name]
[title]
[company name]
[address]
[city], [state] [zip]

Dear [salutation] [last name]:

I am seeking senior-level positions in U.S./international corporate business development and management through your firm and have enclosed my resume for your review.

Throughout my career, my ambition and ability to motivate others have allowed me to recruit and develop high-performance teams while managing budgets and resources for bottom-line results. Most importantly, I've proven my ability to determine and meet specific client needs.

As president at Focus Research, Inc., I met the challenge of turning the company into a profitable business and penetrated major markets worldwide. This successful turnaround and market expansion enabled the parent company, Cel Technology, Inc., to sell Personal Research in November 1996. I am now providing consulting services in strategic direction and management to the newly hired president, with a focus on market development and product innovation.

Highlights of my career include:

➢ Forging and managing distributorship alliances in Korea, South Africa and Argentina and immediately increasing foreign sales by 15%.
➢ Developing and launching highly competitive, technically advanced instrumentation products and techniques, including X-ray fluorescence, spectro-photometry and bio-medical fluorometers.

Additionally, I have published and presented several scientific papers at international conferences and hold U.S. and international patents. Please contact me soon to arrange a meeting to discuss mutual interests, and thank you for your time and consideration.

Sincerely,

Johnathan Bishop
Enclosure

General cover letter template:

David Salute

5 Justice Drive		**Res: (317) 555-4898**
Mooresville, IN 46158	**godshouse@netspade.com**	**Cell: (317) 555-8127**

Receiver's name and address here.

Dear Hiring Executive:

I believe you will find my experience in supply chain logistics and operations management *{customize}* of interest. Specifically, I specialize in xxxxxxxxx, xxxxx and xxxxxx. With additional experience in xxxxxx, I feel certain I can make a valuable contribution to your goals. My areas of expertise and applicable skills include:

Skill word / phrase	Skill	Skill
Skill	Skill	Skill

During my career I have:

➤ Accomplishment
➤ Accomplishment
➤ Accomplishment

My peers would tell you that I thrive in an atmosphere of challenge. An in-depth knowledge of all phases of xxxxxxx activity, along with specialized abilities that set my performance apart, enables me to offer a truly unique talent. I'm confident I can bring you a package of skills, experience and abilities that will prove invaluable to your team.

I will follow up with you in a few days to answer any questions you may have. In the meantime, you may reach me at xxxxxx or via email at xxxxxxx. I look forward to our conversation, and thank you for your time and consideration.

Sincerely,

David Salute

Advice/referral meeting letter: Either cold call the company to speak with the hiring manager for "advice" in your job search or send this letter (customized) prior to calling. Remember, don't ask for a job here. This is used to develop advice/referral meetings and a base of networking contacts. The intent is to drop your name in the head of the hiring manager—to become noticed when job opportunities arise— often before HR hears about the position. Refine and customize this per the contact.

Denny Flapjack
39 Touraine Terrace
Northbrook, IL 60062
847/555-1554
rousse@attbi.com

Dear (Target Name):

I have spent several years in senior management roles while successfully turning around a company by analyzing and streamlining their business operations. This has been very exciting and allowed me to implement many of the latest methodologies for business management.

Much of my success in building businesses is a direct result of my previous experience, including guiding a company from $9 million to $38 million in sales. With P&L responsibility and experience in sales and marketing, I've enjoyed the challenge of playing a key role in creating and implementing changes to improve operations and increase profits, while focusing on the bottom line and making substantial contributions to sales.

My current situation has become such that I have elected to explore other career opportunities, and I thought I would drop you this note as a precursor to my call. I'd like your input on current industry trends, markets, products and how you'd like to see your company grow in the near term.

Thank you in advance for taking my call, and I will plan to call your office in the next few days.

Sincerely,

Denny Flapjack

Follow-up letter. The day after your interview, send a note like this or call your interviewer to restate your interest in the position and thank him for the interview.

David Robertson
972 Woodsy Trail #B2
Northbrook, IL 60062
707/555-1265

October 25, 2011

John B. Smith
National Sales Manager
ICB Corporation
228 Microchip Drive
Chicago, IL 60683

Dear Mr. Smith,

Thank you for your time and for an excellent [or very informative] interview on [Monday]. It was a pleasure meeting you, and I was most impressed by the high professional standards demonstrated by your staff.

I am certain my [leadership, marketing, management, etc.] skills would prove extremely valuable to your executive team. Your product line is excellent, and your company has proven its ability to penetrate both new and expanding markets.

Once again, thank you for your consideration, and I look forward to new career challenges with your excellent firm.

Sincerely,

David Robertson

Job Search Facts
An Accountemps survey of 150 executives found that 76 percent of respondents consider a post-interview thank-you note of value when evaluating candidates, while only 36 percent of job applicants actually follow through with this simple courtesy.

Reference Sheet Example

John A. Caller

References

Business:

Jim E. Shields, President
Shields Southwest Sales, Inc.
1008 Brady Avenue N.W
Atlanta, GA 30318
404/555-1133

Bruce Gin, President
Fairfield Marine, Inc.
5739 Dixie Highway
Fairfield, OH 45014
513/555-0825

Brian Krixen, Partner
Ernst & Young, L.L.P
150 South Wacker Drive
Chicago, IL 60606
312/555-1800

Personal:

Daniel Rosati, CPA
Conklin Accounting & Tax Service
5262 South Rt. 83 #308
Willowbrook, IL 60514
708/555-8800

Rick Baeson
Business Development Manager
Yamaha
PO. Box 8234
Barrington, IL 60011
708/555-4446

Bob Redson, Salesman
Central Photo Engraving
712 South Prairie Avenue
Chicago, IL 60616
708/555-9119

Salary History Example

STEVEN A. WRITER

SALARY HISTORY
(Annual Basis)

People Search, Inc.
Director of Human Resources $150,000

Anderson Publishing Service, Inc.
Chief Writer Up to $85,000: commission-based

National Van Lines
Director of Recruiting $77,000

Professional Career Consultants
Writer and Branch Manager Up to $29,000: commission-based

Notes:

In general, never include salary requirements unless requested by the employer, but also consider:

- You could add: "Current salary requirements are open to negotiation and depend on variables such as benefits, geographic location and advancement potential."

- If salary *requirements* are requested, you could add something like this in your cover letter: "Currently seeking a position in the upper $90s [$80s, etc.] per year." (Caution! This could label you as over- or underpriced for the position. That's one reason they ask for a salary history in the first place.) Remember the survey of more than 200 employers who said they would still consider you even if you didn't include requested salary information; add only if you feel it's essential, on a case-by-case basis.

Case Study: Before and After Resume Examples

Following are graphic examples of how three job applicants can be presented in a completely different light. In the first "Before" example here, I've used **bold** to highlight the most obvious errors and mistakes. Yes, the "Before" resumes were written by other firms; we're often called upon to rewrite resumes from companies such as Internet job boards attempting to write resumes as a sideline. As with all resumes in this book, applicant and company names have been changed.

Notice the new titles used on each; the first is specific: Project / Product Manager. The second targets an overall industry where Craig seeks to utilize his talents: Finance / Insurance. The third replaces a wordy, subjective Personal Summary sentence with a title focusing on level of position in a technical capacity: Management - IT Operations. All titles are followed by concise Profile/Skill sections developing their most important, most relevant skills and abilities, consisting primarily of keywords.

Before:

Pervez Success

256 Miram Drive • Wheaton, IL 60187 • Tel: 630-555-5058 • hp@sbcglobal.net

---

NEEDS TITLE HERE
CAREER SUMMARY

Broad **(Vague)** technical knowledge combined with outstanding **(Subjective)** leadership ability and creative problem **(Hyphen missing)** solving skills in both technical and strategic areas. Result **(Missing s and hyphen)** oriented, decisive leader, with **(missing a)** proven record in **(Should be of)** on-time delivery, increase **(Missing d)** profitability and enhanced customer relationship. **(Missing s)** Outstanding **(Subjective)** manager with domestic and international experience in project & product management, quality assurance and testing, release & change management, strategic positioning and software development.

Project Management (PMP) … Risk Management ... Global Product Management (PMM) ... Wireline/Wireless Technologies ... Management Information System & Technology ... Network & Data Communication (CCNA, CCDA) … Multiple technology domain ... (IBM, Amdahl, SUN) ... Quality Assurance/Test Automation … ISO9000 … Software development (SDLC) ... SAP... Customer relation **(Missing s)** *and technical support ... Strategic Business planning … Profitability, Pricing & Positioning ... Competitors* **(Extra 's' here, not needed, also awkward)** *& Marketing Intelligence ... Joint Venture & outsourcing ... Problem solving and Analysis ... Mentoring and coaching*

(Major Problem: All items below should be under the companies where occurred; this is a type of Functional resume and should not be in this format!)

PROFESSIONAL ACHIVEMENT (Note typo here: *Achievement!*)

- Provided pre-sale support **(Missing s)** in winning **(Missing a)** $20 million in annual sale **(Missing s and a)** for next **(Missing hyphen)** generation Telecommunication Messaging Product, AnyPath (supporting VoIP, WAP, wireless/wireline services, LDAP, IMAP, LAN, WAN, OSI model and associated protocols).

- Worked with technical marketing and sales teams (AWS, US Cellular, Qwest, Cinguler **(Typo)**, Verizon, Eircom etc **(Missing period)** to identify and generate requirements for new features bringing in additional $5M revenues. **(Awkward and missing in)**.

- Designed and implemented guidelines for warranty and maintenance services in the field to increase revenues (15% of total revenue) **(Missing period)**

- Managed a group of 20 engineers in Saudi Arabia in **(Delete in, replace with comma)** certifying major deliveries of Lucent Switching equipments **(Typo, s needs to be removed)** (Intelligent Network, 5ESS, ISDN features, OSPS, COM, Multimedia, Internet, LAN, WAN) using System Quality Test (SQT) and First Office Application (FOA) processes **(Missing comma)** validating 2000 generic specification requirements based on White/Blue Books. It helped building **(Typo)** solid customer relationship, **(Missing s)** gaining customer trust and winning additional $500M (Missing in and the) revenue for next few years.

- Initiated a comprehensive process enhancement of **(Missing a)** customer technical support team in Saudi Arabia 1) improved issue tracking processes 2) improved communication between cross-functional teams and senior management 3) shortened delivery intervals and 4) reduced operating expenses by 30%.

- Developed and implemented an ISO9000 registered software quality management system. Worked with development and internal QA group **(Missing s)** to define and implement procedures for the whole product life cycle. Helped to acquire both IS9000 and Malcolm Baldrige **(Typo)** awards, which resulted in reducing field problem find rate (60% of development cost) and improving customer perceptions of quality of our product.

- Managed a project of **(Change of to: to)** migrating **(Should be migrate a)** software development environment from mainframe to **(Missing a)** SUN **(Missing Hyphen)** based environment. Identified tasks, resources and set goals, implemented system in tracking **(Should be: to track)** issues and measuring **(measure)** progress. Worked with internal and external users to determine requirements and negotiated with stakeholders to resolve conflicting needs. Successfully completed project ahead of schedules **(delete s; add comma)** meeting all requirements, **(New sentence here)** improved performance by 30%, reduced maintenance cost in half and increased employee's **(should be employee productivity)** productivities by ten fold.

- Introduced Software Test Automation concept to decrease validation interval of regression and functional testing. Key contributor in developing that environment **(awkward)**. Brought funding ($100K) from SUN Microsystems in developing next generation front-end interface to existing testing environment using JAVA technology.

- Designed, developed and managed a comprehensive **(should be on-line)** On-line information/training system to facilitate development and customer technical support teams. It **(should be Helped...or This helped)** helped reduced **(should be reduce)** supporting staffing budget by 50%.

Pervez Success   **Page Three**

EXPERIENCE

Crane Technologies - Naperville, Illinois   **1986-2002**
Designs **(third person, present tense, should be Designed)** network equipment and software for communications service providers.

Product Manager, Naperville, Illinois   **2000-2002**
(Passive voice) Responsibilities were to manage a next generation messaging solution (associated with VoIP, internet, LAN, WAN, voice and data networks) **(Missing comma)** including identification of revenue **(Missing hyphen)** generating telecommunications features. Managed and supporting **(should be past tense; missing the)** whole product development cycle **(Missing comma)** from initial design to commercial product launch. Additional responsibility was to **(Passive voice)** develop the long term **(Missing hyphen)** strategic direction to increase revenue and market share. Performed marketing **(Should be market)** analysis of many **(Provide amount, rather than many)** telecom products to understand capabilities **(the capability of)** of other **(Delete other; add s after offerings)** vendors offering including cost, pricing and feature contents.

Project Manager and New Product Support Manager, Saudi Arabia   **1996-2000**
(Passive voice: *Note: I'll stop my bolding here; you get the idea!*)
Responsibility was to manage a multi-culture group of 20 engineers in certifying major deliveries and technical support of switching equipments of Saudi Telecom Company (STC). Responsible to identify and obtain needed resources and skills for the project; to set directions and document objectives. Strengths include assessing customer problems and finding creative solutions using technical knowledge and troubleshooting capabilities; building rapport over the phone, resolving issues and educating the customer on product usage.

Software Development & Quality Assurance, Naperville, Illinois   **1991- 1996**
Main responsibility was to oversee the full range of software development activities across the entire lifecycle for complex software projects. Including managing of front-end planning activities for new feature releases; documenting technical specifications; designing and developing of new features; developing customer documentation and installation procedures for a variety of platforms; ensuring on time delivery of project. Additional responsibility was to develop and implement an ISO9000 registered software quality management system.

QA Testing, Naperville, Illinois   **1986-1991**
Responsibility was to lead integration and customer acceptance testing activities for major software releases. Included estimating testing effort, preparing plans for test execution, assigning activities, and writing test scripts based on requirement documents and functional specification. Responsibilities were also to enhance processes to decrease validation interval and ensure adequate product testing prior to product release to the field.

AG Communication System, Phoenix, Arizona 1981-1986

AG Communication Systems, a subsidiary of Lucent Technologies, offers service providers advanced network-based solutions, including circuit and packet switching, voice-over-Internet protocol (VoIP) and IP Centrex.

Lead Engineer:

Responsibility was to oversee the full range of software development activities for diagnostic and maintenance features (remote office test line, 3/6-way conference circuits, and automatic number identification receivers). Included writing features specifications, designing software architecture and developing code.

Marsh & McLennan, Chicago, Illinois **1978-1981**

Marsh provides global risk management consulting, insurance broking, financial solutions, and insurance programs.

System Analyst:

Responsibilities were to maintain WANG payroll system, relation database for Marsh & McLennan employee records (bi-weekly pay-stub, W-2).

EDUCATION & PROFESSIONAL DEVELOPMENT

University of Illinois, Chicago, Illinois   University of Karachi, Pakistan
BSEE in Electrical Engineering, August 1978   B.SC Science, 1972
Majors: Computer System and Information   Majors: Physics, Chemistry, and Math

Project/Program Management (PMP, PMBOK knowledge), Business Case, Product Management, Managing Conflict, Quality Function Deployment, ISO9000, Network & Data Communication (LAN, WAN, Routers, Bridges, Repeaters etc), RF, SS7, Telecommunication (5ESS, GTD-5), VoIP, CDMA, UNIX, Shell, C, Java, Pascal, HTML, MS Project/word/excel/PowerPoint.

After, including a new cover letter, below:

Pervez Success

256 Miram Drive   (630) 555-5058
Wheaton, IL 60187   hp@sbcglobal.net

Project / Product Manager

PROFILE:
➢ Comprehensive experience in high-level strategic planning for advanced information systems and technology functions, including domestic and global product, project, risk and vendor management, as well as joint-venture outsourcing.

➢ Proven ability to execute large-scale software development and implementation projects, including quality assurance, testing, test automation, software releases and change management.

➢ Skilled in competitive and marketing analysis, product pricing and strategic product positioning, as well as client relations, needs identification and troubleshooting.

➢ Solid technical and architectural skills; consistently deliver quality software and business solutions on time and within budget; manage high-performance, multi-cultural teams; establish goals and monitor progress to meet objectives.

EXPERIENCE: Crane Technologies, Naperville, IL   1986-2002
Crane Technologies designs network equipment and software for major communications service providers.
Progressed through a series of positions, most recent first:
Product Manager   2000-2002
Directed and supported the product development cycle from initial design to commercial product launch of a next-generation messaging solution (associated with VoIP, Internet, LAN, WAN, voice and data networks), including identification of revenue-generating telecommunications features.
Developed long-term strategic direction to increase revenue and market share.
Performed market analysis of competitive telecom products, reviewing capabilities, costs, pricing and features.

→ Provided pre-sales support, winning $20 million in annual sales.
→ Designed and implemented guidelines for warranty and maintenance services in the field that increased total revenues by 15%.
→ Interacted with technical marketing and sales teams of AWS, US Cellular, Qwest, Cingular, Verizon and Eircom to identify and generate requirements for new features, bringing in an additional $5 million in revenue.

Project Manager & New Product Support Manager, Saudi Arabia 1996-2000
Oversaw a multi-cultural group of 20 engineers in certifying major switching equipment, including Intelligent Network, 5ESS, ISDN features, OSPS, COM, Multimedia, Internet, LAN and WAN deliveries, and providing technical support to the Saudi Telephone Company.

Performed project and risk management while identifying and obtaining needed resources and skills; set direction and documented objectives.

Analyzed, assessed and resolved customer problems using technical knowledge and troubleshooting capabilities.

→ Directed the validating of 2,000 generic-specification requirements based on White/Blue Books and using System Quality Test and First Office applications.

→ Played a key role in negotiating an additional $500 million in revenue for several years via a System Quality Test testing agreement with the Saudi Telephone Company; continued to provide a high level of sales support.

Software Development & Quality Assurance, Naperville, IL   1991-1996
Managed the full range of software development activities across the entire lifecycle for complex software projects, including front-end planning activities for new feature releases.

→ Successfully completed projects ahead of schedule, meeting all requirements.

→ Developed and designed new features while creating customer documentation and installation procedures for a variety of platforms.

→ Designed and implemented guidelines for warranty and maintenance services in the field that increased total revenues by 15%.

→ Managed the migrating of the software development environment from mainframe to SUN-based environment.

→ Performed as resource manager for both environments.

→ Worked with internal and external users to determine requirements and negotiated with stakeholders to resolve conflicting needs.

→ Created and implemented an ISO–9000 registered, software quality management system.

→ Interfaced with development and internal QA groups to define and implement procedures for product lifecycle.

→ Instrumental in acquiring ISO 9000 and Malcolm Baldridge awards, resulting in reducing field problem find rate (60% of development cost) and improving customer perceptions of product quality.

Lead Engineer - System Testing & Integration, Naperville, IL 1986-1991
Led integration and customer acceptance testing activities for major software releases.

Estimated testing effort and prepared plans for test execution, including assigning tasks and writing test scripts based on requirement documents and functional specifications.

→ Reduced support-staffing budget by 50% through the creation and management of a comprehensive online information/training system that facilitated development of customer technical support teams.

→ Secured funding of $100,000 from SUN Microsystems to develop a next-generation front-end interface to existing testing environments using JAVA technology.

→ Decreased validation interval through the enhancement of processes and the introduction of Software Test Automation concepts.

AG Communication System, Phoenix, AZ   1981-1986
Lead Engineer – Oversaw software development activities for telecom products.

University of Illinois Medical Center, Chicago IL   1978-1981
System Analyst – Supported, maintained and enhanced operating environment.

EDUCATION &   **University of Illinois,** Chicago, IL
DEVELOPMENT: BSEE Degree - Electrical Engineering

University of Karachi, Pakistan
B.S. Degree - Science

TRAINING: Lucent PMP and PMBOK Certified, Business Case, Product Management, Managing Conflict, Quality Function Deployment, ISO 9000, Network & Data Communication, including LAN, WAN, Routers, Bridges and Repeaters, RF, SS7, 5ESS, GTD 5, VoIP, CDMA, UNIX, Shell, C, Java, Pascal, HTML, Windows systems, MS Project, MS Word, MS Excel and MS PowerPoint.

Pervez Success
256 Miram Drive
Wheaton, IL 60187
630/555-5058
hp@sbcglobal.net

Dear Hiring Executive:

I believe you will find my experience as a project and product manager for developing software solutions and programs of interest. Specifically, I specialize in problem analysis and resolution and team leadership. With my experience in domestic and global product management and development, I feel certain I can make a positive and valuable contribution to your goals. My areas of expertise and transferable skills include:

Software Architecture	Strategic Planning	Risk Management
Staff Management	Global Product Management	Product Positioning
Multiculture Team Leadership	Joint Venture Outsourcing	Team Facilitation
Quality Assurance/Testing Automation	Competitive Analysis	Client Relations
System Analysis / Integration	Process Improvement	Technical Support
Resource / Operation Management	Release Management	Vendor Management

During my career I have:

→ Played a key role in negotiating an additional $500 million in revenue for several years.
→ Managed a multicultural, cross-functional team in delivering, installing and supporting major Lucent products.
→ Provided pre-sales support in winning $20 million in annual sales.
→ Reduced operating expenses by 30%.

My peers will tell you that I thrive in an atmosphere of challenge. An in-depth knowledge of all phases of project management, along with specialized abilities that set my performance apart, enables me to offer a truly unique talent. I'm confident I can bring to the table a package of skills, experience and abilities that will provide you with an invaluable resource.

I will follow up with you in a few days to answer any questions you may have. In the meantime, you may reach me at the above telephone number or via email. I look forward to our conversation and thank you for your time and consideration.

Sincerely,

Pervez Success

Before:

CRAIG B. POLICY, CIC
18 DAWSON DRIVE
SAN DIEGO, CA 92117-1038
CELL: (815) 555-7935
CRAIG@GAIL.COM

OBJECTIVE

To obtain a position in the insurance industry which will enable me to use my strong organizational skills, educational background, previous experience, extensive knowledge of the insurance industry and its automation systems, and ability to work well with people.

EXPERIENCE

1975 - 1977   Brook School District Brookfield, WI
Junior High School Teacher – Industrial Arts
➤ Coordinated the industrial arts departments between two schools
➤ Created new curriculum that exceeded the district's directives
➤ Made a lasting impact on students by their learning the safe use of basic shop tools and equipment

1995 – 2010   Craig Insurance Agency, Inc DeKalb, IL
President
➤ Increased retail insurance agency from a 1 man firm to 7 professionals
➤ Created and coordinated an education track for new insurance producers to allow them to excel
➤ Implemented the first computer system in an insurance agency in our local area
➤ Implemented voice over IP telephone system to expand our communication abilities while reducing operational costs
➤ Traveled to Washington, DC to meet with members of Congress to discuss legislative issues important to the insurance industry
➤ Developed long term profitable relationships with many national and regional insurance carriers
➤ Developed long term friendships with other insurance agents throughout the country
➤ Continued family tradition with my daughter and son now being the 4th generation of insurance professionals

2003 – 2006   NASPA   National
President of the SIS Semci Partner Agency ManagementUsers Group
Volunteer position
➤ Coordinated joint marketing activities with Strategic Insurance Software
➤ Suggested numerous improvements to Semci Partner which were implemented by SIS
➤ Planned and hosted national user group conferences
➤ Attended national and regional seminars such as the Acord Loma Insurance Systems Forum

2004 – 2006   AUGIE   National
Participating member of Acord User Group Information Exchange
Volunteer position

During my tenure, AUGIE made great strides in insurance automation including:

➤ Creating an online insurance industry survey that revealed technology trends and their implementation in the insurance industry
➤ Setting standards for commercial policy data download
➤ Setting standards for direct bill commission data download
➤ Setting standards for mixed case text download
➤ Settings standards for real time policy inquiry

2006   AMSUG   National
Participating member of the AMS Users' Group Research & Development Committee for AMS360 agency management system
Volunteer position

➤ My extension experience with competing agency management systems allowed further improvement to AMS360 to make it the nation's leading agency management system

2005-2007   PIIAI   Illinois
Participating member of the Professional Independent Agents of Illinois Automation Committee
Volunteer position

➤ Committee organized regional meetings on insurance agency automation systems and their implementation

EDUCATION

1975   University of Wisconsin - Stout   Menomonie, WI
➤ B.A., Industrial Arts Education
1994   National Alliance for Insurance Education & Research
➤ Certified Insurance Counselor (CIC)

INTERESTS

Assembly/maintaining of PCs & networks and their software
Reviewing latest technology for its potential usefullness & impact on the insurance industry

AFILIATIONS

Member of the National Academy for Insurance Education & Research; Member of the Independent Insurance Agents of IL; Member of Independent Insurance Agents & Brokers of America; Member of the Professional Insurance Agents

After:

CRAIG B. POLICY, CIC

18 Dawson Drive • San Diego, CA 92117-1038
Cell: 815.555.7935 • craig@gail.com

FINANCE / INSURANCE

*Sales • Broker • Marketing & Business Development • Operations Management
Financial Analysis • Technology Implementation • Strategic Planning*

Comprehensive experience driving operations and expanding profitability in the insurance industry. Skilled in new business development, client relationship management and sales. Proven ability to build and grow agencies through creative marketing and advertising plans, communication enhancements and technology implementation. Strong in recruiting and hiring top-performing talent, leveraging skills in team leadership and quality control.

Areas of Expertise Include:

- Territory Management
- Staff Management
- Goal Attainment
- Organizational Development
- Program Development

- Account Expansion/Retention
- Marketing & Sales Plans
- Agent Training
- Problem Solving
- Process Improvement

EXPERIENCE

CRAIG INSURANCE AGENCY, INC. • DeKalb, IL 1995-Present

Operations Manager

Manage P&L and oversee budget and finance, including accounting activities. Perform financial and trend analysis. Drive and develop marketing and advertising initiatives, leveraging social networking websites and media outlets to generate revenue. Lead a team of seven staff members. Ensure optimal client relations, consistent improvements in operational processes and cost containment.

Highlights

- **Grew this retail insurance agency** from one employee to seven. Identified and recruited top-performing talent to ensure operational excellence and future growth. Helped build a profitable business that now employs the family's 4th generation of insurance professionals.

- Propelled new insurance producers to higher levels of success by **developing and coordinating an education track**, providing in-house training to empower employees.

- **Expanded communication abilities and reduced operational costs** by $6K+ annually, through implementing a voice over IP telephone system that allowed staff to work remotely.

- Increased **operational efficiency** and further supported staff working remotely by transitioning agency management software to AMS 360.

- Improved accounting operations and competitive edge through implementing the first computer system in an insurance agency in the community.

- Traveled to Washington, D.C., and met with members of Congress to discuss legislative issues related to the insurance agency.

- Cultivated long-term, solid relationships with many national and regional insurance carriers.

PROFESSIONAL AFFILIATIONS

President of the SIS Semci Partner Agency Management Users Group • NASPA • 2003 to 2006

Arranged joint marketing activities utilizing strategic insurance software. Recommended numerous improvements to a Semci Partner, which were adopted and implemented by SIS. Planned and hosted national user group conferences. Attended national and regional seminars, such as the Acord Loma Insurance Systems Forum.

Member of Accord User Group Information Exchange • AUGIE • 2004 to 2006

Contributed to developing an online insurance industry survey that revealed technology trends and their implementation in the insurance industry. Established standards for commercial policy data download, direct bill commission data download, mixed case text download and real-time policy inquiries.

Member of the AMS Users' Group Research & Development Committee for AMS 360 Agency Management System • AMSUG • 2006

Contributed extension experience with competing agency management systems, which facilitated improvements to AMS 360, elevating it to become the nation's leading agency management system.

Member of the Professional Independent Agents of IL Automation Committee
PILAI • 2005 to 2007
Participated on a committee that organized regional meetings on insurance agency automation systems and their implementation.

Current Affiliations Include: *National Academy for Insurance and Education; Independent Insurance Agents of IL; Independent Insurance Agents & Brokers of America; Professional Insurance Agents*

EDUCATION & CREDENTIALS

Bachelor of Arts Degree, Industrial Arts Education
UNIVERSITY OF WISCONSIN ☐ Menomonie, IL

Certified Insurance Counselor (CIC)

Before:

DAN SANDERS
236 W 124th Pl • Palos Heights IL 60463
phone: 708.555.1123 • fax: 708.555.1996 • email: bm@comcast.net

PERSONAL SUMMARY

I am an intelligent, motivated self-starter who would like to use my IT management experience along with strong analytical, problem-solving and communication skills to help implement successful solutions for both internal and external clients.

EDUCATION
B.B.A., Management Information Systems
University of Iowa, Iowa City, IA, 1999

TECHNICAL
Microsoft SQL Server, MS Reporting Services, Analysis Services, Proclarity Analytics Server, Visual SourceSafe, Visual Studio, Query Analyzer, Visio, Astra SiteTest, HTML, VB, Java, MS Access, CCC/Harvest, Openmake, PVCS Tracker

EXPERIENCE
Iridium Resources Incorporated (IRI) – Chicago IL

Director, Quality Assurance and Delivery 08/2004 – Present
- Responsible for overall Data Quality and Data Reporting for IRI In Store Solutions Group (formerly Mosaic Infoforce) reporting to the Senior Vice President of Information Technology
- Instrumental in taking group considered 'overhead' to being widely viewed as a revenue generating opportunity
- Manage they day to day activities of 12 individuals consisting of SQL Developers (Data Analysts, QA) and OLAP Developers (Business Intelligence Analysts, Delivery)
- Serve as Six Sigma project lead utilizing Green Belt skills to effectively improve internal processes including automation and standardization
- Provide thought leadership in determining the 'right solution' to meet/exceed client expectations from a data delivery standpoint and ensure delivering against the solution
- Managed departmental budget ($1M+) and held accountable to delivering stretch commitments against budget
- Create and maintain department objectives, measure effectiveness/efficiency utilizing department dashboard, and maintain standard operating procedures
- Utilized Proclarity dashboard technology to measure ISG compliance relative to Service Level Agreements (SLAs)
- Responsible for department hiring

Mosaic Infoforce – Chicago IL

Manager, Quality Assurance and Delivery 11/2003 – 8/2004

- Implement OLAP solutions using Microsoft Analysis Services for data cube creation and Proclarity as a front end tool.
- Work with clients to understand reporting needs and act as consultant regarding the solutions we offer that address their needs
- Coordinate initiative to bring in house several previously outsourced projects thereby reducing cost without the need for additional resources
- Led implementation of internal reporting tool using Microsoft Reporting Services which allowed field force to understand quality of data on the same day data collected
- Worked on Six Sigma project to enhance the company client engagement model to identify current points of failure and solve for them.

Manager, Quality Assurance 09/2001 – 11/2003

- Lead Quality Assurance initiative of migrating Quality Procedures from Mainframe/SAS code to Microsoft SQL Data Transformation Services (DTS) Packages
- Utilized DTS to create automated jobs to process, format, update and report data to both internal and external clients
- Help coordinate and implement standards and efficiencies which led to 80% decrease in average overall delivery time
- As an administrator on a SQL server managed security, job scheduling/maintenance, script / stored procedure creation and maintenance along with various troubleshooting
- Helped establish traditional Software Testing role in company Quality Assurance department by creating standards and documented process
- Trained QA Group on Microsoft SQL Server Enterprise Manager, Query Analyzer and Data Transformation Services

ProAlliance Corporation – Rosemont IL

Consultant, 06/2001 – 09/2001

- Design and execute system test plan and system test cases for Windows NT software application migration project for a large Credit Card/Financial Services organization
- Coordinate and Manage User Acceptance Testing effort in various geographic regions
- Manage builds for development team using Build Automation tool (Openmake)
- Utilize version control software (Harvest) for maintaining different versions of software application in single environment
- Identify application defects and work with I.T. Development Team to determine root cause and solution /fix
- Manage in-house Intranet-based defect tracking system (PVCS Tracker) for migration project; system utilized by internal staff and external (UA Testers)

SALON123, Inc. – Chicago IL

Quality Analyst, 06/2000 – 5/2001
- Responsible for day-to-day quality assurance of both large-scale custom Internet-based (ASP) software application (www.salon123.com) and E-Commerce (B2B) store (www.beehivebuys.com) within a pure Microsoft client/server environment.
- Create and execute test cases, plans, and strategies for both ASP and E-Commerce brands through full software development life cycle in a fast-paced "start-up" environment.
- Develop quality assurance standards; define and track quality assurance metrics such as defect densities and open defect counts.
- Utilize stress and performance tools on both brands using various test environments
- Identify application defects and work with I.T. Development Team to determine root cause and solution / fix.
- Established and manage in-house Internet-based defect tracking system for both ASP and E-Commerce brands; system utilized by internal staff and external (outsourced) Customer Service Center.
- Declare software versions "complete" and act as gatekeeper for version release.
- Assist in live software application and version releases and ensure quality of deliverables (e.g., ensure new / current features meet documented business requirements).
- Train and support Customer Service, Marketing, and Sales staff on troubleshooting of both ASP and E-Commerce brands.
- Spearhead weekly QA corporate team meetings with Customer Service and Marketing Staff.

MORAINE VALLEY COMMUNITY COLLEGE – Palos Hills IL

Instructor, Introduction to Internet Technologies, 08/1999 – 06/2000
- Instructed college students on general Internet technologies including browsers, search engines, Internet protocols and languages (e.g., ftp, tcp/ip, html, smtp) in both classroom and lab settings.
- Created course materials and progress measurement tests based on course outline for a credited course.
- Acted as student mentor/teacher.

KELLY NISSAN – Oak Lawn IL

Internet Project Manager / Consultant, 06/1999 – 06/2000
- Created corporate web presence.
- Developed business processes and strategies for conducting business via the Internet.
- Maintained inventory and web-based promotions in accordance with business needs and direction.

REFERENCES   Available upon request.

After, including a new cover letter, below:

DAN SANDERS

236 West 124th Place   708/555-3854
Palos Heights, IL 60463   bm@comcast.net

MANAGEMENT - IT OPERATIONS

PROFILE:

➤ Comprehensive leadership experience in business intelligence, quality assurance, data warehousing, database management and the creation of data mining tools in diverse IT environments.

➤ Expert in data validation, application design & testing and requirements identification; effectively manage the entire software development lifecycle.

➤ Highly skilled in budgeting and cost controls; knowledge of conducting business and outsourcing in international marketplaces, particularly in Europe, India and North America.

➤ Demonstrated ability to meet and exceed all performance metrics, greatly improve operating processes, analyze vast amounts of data with cutting-edge technology and ensure total client satisfaction.

TECHNICAL BACKGROUND:

• Visual SourceSafe, Visual Studio, Query Analyzer, Visio, Astra SiteTest, CCC/ Harvest, Openmake, PVCS Tracker, IBM QMF, MS Reporting Services, Analysis Services and Proclarity.

• MS Office, HTML, VB, Java, SQL Server and other business applications on Windows and Macintosh platforms.

EMPLOYMENT:

Iridium Resources Inc. (IRI), Chicago, IL   2001-Present
Director - Quality Assurance & Delivery   2003-Present
In charge of building and leading a team of 12 data analysts and information analysts in overall data reporting and quality for the In-Store Solutions Group.
Collate and track business intelligence by producing and supporting extensive reporting of consumer trends and industry developments.
Continue to gain expertise in staff hiring, training, mentoring and supervision in all operating policies and procedures.

→ Consolidated and streamlined 50 reporting functions into a single dashboard in support of 1,700 field representatives, Utilizing MS Reporting Services.

→ Key participant in generating $2 million in new business through effective sales and product support.

→ Team lead for a Six Sigma project that utilized Green Belt skills to greatly improve engagement turnaround times and increase overall capacity; as subject matter expert, helped with several other successful Six Sigma projects.

→ Finished a course, "Designing and Implementing OLAP Solutions Using MS SQL Server 2000."
→ Key participant in the acquisition and transition process of Mosaic Infoforce in 2004.
→ Introduced OLAP solutions with MS Analysis Services for creating data cubes of up to 200 gigabytes; utilized Proclarity as a front-end tool.
→ Facilitator of outsourcing efforts with vendors in India.
→ Primary contact for a $300,000 contract with a US-based external vendor.
→ Promoted to this position in 2004 from **Manager - Quality Assurance & Delivery.**

Manager - Quality Assurance   2001-2003

Spearheaded the introduction of new technologies and migration of quality procedures from mainframe/SAS code to MS SQL Data Transformation (DTS) packages.

As Systems Administrator, oversaw security issues, job scheduling, maintenance and general troubleshooting.

→ Succeeded in decreasing average overall delivery time by 80% with better operating policies and procedures.
→ Instrumental in establishing a traditional software-testing function in this department.
→ Trained the QA Group in MS SQL Server Enterprise Manager, Query Analyzer and Data Transformation Services.

ProAlliance Corporation, Rosemont, IL   2001
Consultant

Contracted to produce a system test plan and cases for a Windows NT software application migration project for a large credit card/financial services leader.

Handled the in-house intranet-based defect tracking system (PVCS Tracker), which was used by internal staff and external testers.

→ Frequently traveled to different company sites to coordinate the user acceptance testing process.
→ Managed builds for the development team with Openmake.
→ Utilized Harvest to control new versions of this application in a single environment.

SALON123, Inc., Chicago, IL   2000-2001
Quality Analyst

In charge of all aspects of quality assurance for two large-scale custom applications in a pure Microsoft environment for Internet (ASP) and B2B (E-Commerce) marketplaces.

Defined and set up all quality control standards.

Generated and instituted a wide range of processes and tools to support the entire software development lifecycle.

→ Headed up weekly QA team meetings with Customer Service and Marketing groups.

→ Established in-house Internet-based systems for quickly tracking and resolving defects for both brands.

→ Personally ensured version completion and final release.

→ Trained staff in different departments on troubleshooting ASP and E-Commerce brands.

<u>Kelly Nissan,</u> Oak Lawn, IL   1999-2000
Consultant
Responsible for creating and maintaining the corporate web presence, along with instituting processes to supporting e-commerce activity.

→ Designed and implemented unique inventory and web-based promotions to generate new business and provide strategic direction.

RELATED EXPERIENCE: ○ As an **Instructor**, taught undergraduates in Internet technologies at <u>Moraine Valley Community College</u> in Palos Hills, IL for one year.

○ Personally created and updated curricula, lesson plans and testing materials, along with maintenance of accurate student records.

○ Continued to build skills as a mentor and career counselor for students.

EDUCATION: <u>University of Iowa,</u> Iowa City, IA   1999
B.B.A. Degree in Management Information Science
* Active member of the Kappa Sigma social fraternity.

DAN SANDERS
236 West 124th Place
Palos Heights, IL 60463
708/555-3854
bm@comcast.net

Dear Hiring Executive:

I am exploring leadership opportunities in IT Operations with your company. With my successful background in new business development, I can build your company and expand its market position in highly competitive marketplaces. Areas of transferable skills include:

Business Intelligence	Data Analysis	Quality Validation
Data Mining	Data Warehousing	Strategic Planning
Executive Presentations	Market Trend Analysis	

Throughout my career, I have:

→ Always met or exceeded corporate goals and performance metrics, while facilitating corporate engagements, database management and application design.
→ Been instrumental in generating millions of dollars in new business and supporting major account activity.
→ Gained a reputation for being a team leader, creative troubleshooter and hands-on problem solver of complex business growth issues.

Executives and industry peers would tell you I thrive in an atmosphere of challenge and complex problem resolution. My in-depth knowledge of all phases of business operations ensures that I will be an invaluable resource to your company's future.

I will follow up with you in a few days to answer any questions and arrange for a meeting to discuss mutual business interests. You may always reach me at **708/555-3854** or via email at **bm@comcast.net.**

Yours truly,

Dan Sanders

encl.

Executive Resume Examples

ll of the real life resume examples here resulted in calls from employers, interviews, potential interviews, job offers or new positions. I've changed company and job seekers' names to maintain confidentiality.

I called all of these applicants, asked them about the results of their resume and included their feedback at the top of each example. Many may have received even stronger results by the time you read this.

Each resume had to result in at least one employer's offering to interview the applicant, usually by phone. In the vast majority of cases, clients accepted those interview offers and actually discussed the position at hand. You and the employer can then square off and see whether the position is right for you, but without the best possible resume (preferably modified somewhat for each position), you may never get that chance.

Keep in mind that if you use too much of anyone else's resume, you run the risk of looking like—someone else! These samples are presented with the idea that you'll use them only for help in writing your own unique presentation. Any inconsistencies here are intentional: Some names are capitalized and bold, some are not; many use italics for headings, others are lowercase, bold, capitalized and so on. Again, if you have any questions, feel free to call or send us your current materials for analysis; check the last page of this book for details.

Sent 12 resumes; received two interviews and a new position as account executive. (See corresponding letter.)

Lee A. Smith

36 Congress Road
New City, NY 10956

(845) 555-3620
lsmith@online.net

Executive Leadership: New Business Development

PROFILE:

> Comprehensive experience in C-level business development and sales, including full responsibility for account acquisition, retention and market penetration in the wireless cellular industry.

> Skilled in strategic planning, territory development and sales presentations to high-level executives, including contract negotiations, competitive analysis and lead generation.

> Proven abilities in opportunity identification, proposal development and building personal client relationships with top executives at Fortune 500 firms.

> Determine and meet specific client needs; handle lead development and post-sale support, including total account servicing to meet business and financial goals.

EXPERIENCE:

Smart Money Mortgage, Inc., Spring Valley, NY   1/02-Present
Director: Mortgage Support
Coordinate sales, marketing and account management from referrals and leads for this mortgage broker, while managing a staff of three, including a loan processor, a loan closer and an administrative assistant.
Train and supervise staff in account prospecting and full processing for mortgage applications.
Plan, implement and streamline procedures related to mortgage rates, programs, qualifications, closing costs and paperwork required for applications.
Underwrite loans before final approval is issued.

→ Developed a daily report to track the number of bookings, followup calls and sales closings.

→ In charge of office during owner absence for the last two months, maintaining strong volume and productivity.

→ Obtain referrals and repeat business from a wide range of corporate accounts.

→ Recruited to work 20 hours part-time and went full time in 4/03.

Auricle Wireless, Ramsey, NJ   4/02-4/03
Executive Sales
Sold and activated new corporate cell phone accounts and performed upgrades for an authorized Verizon Wireless retailer.
Explained rate plan changes and answered questions concerning Verizon Wireless products and services.
Completed daily reports and performed cash reconciliation.

→ Personally developed and implemented an email-marketing program targeted to former customers and contacts.

→ Joined the Chamber of Commerce to conduct network marketing.

<u>AT&T Wireless,</u> Nanuet, NY   9/00-4/02
Communications Specialist
Hired on a permanent basis to sell Wireless products and services.
Spent 10–15% of the week marketing products and services to corporate clients through outside sales calls and telemarketing.

→ Consistently met and exceeded sales goals of 50 sales per month, performing 60–65 and more than 100 during holidays and sales promotions.
→ Teamed with B2B sales representatives and accompanied them on sales calls.
→ Maintained an active networking meeting schedule.
→ Followed up with all customers, utilizing thank-you cards and phone calls.
→ Processed credit checks and equipment orders, and performed activations and handled customer questions.
→ Updated and maintained seasonal point of sale marketing materials.
→ Conducted a corporate open house wireless event.
→ Developed and implemented direct email marketing programs on own initiative.
→ Created and maintained a database of prior customers.
→ Winner of two consecutive holiday contests in 2000 and 2001 for the most sales.
→ Recognized as the top sales representative of eight.

<u>Adecco,</u> Paramus, NJ   5/00-9/00
Customer Care/Technical Support
Assigned as a temporary to <u>AT&T Wireless Services, Inc.,</u> National Employee Account Services (NEAS) call center division with varied responsibilities.
Handled inbound calls to troubleshoot wireless phone problems, set up wireless web service, perform rate plan changes and check status of equipment orders.

→ Trained employees in use of the NEAS website to submit equipment orders, activate employee and dependent phone lines, submit action requests and provide other information as needed.

RELATED   Held a variety of positions in the residential mortgage loan industry. 6/91-5/00
SALES   **Financial Services Representative**
EXPERIENCE: **Loan Officer**
                    Mortgage Advisor
                    Loan Consultant
                    Loan Officer
                    Sales Associate

EDUCATION   <u>University of West Florida,</u> Pensacola, FL
& TRAINING: **B.S. Degree - Marketing, Major - Marketing Management**

                    <u>United States Air Force Community College</u>
                    A.A. Degree - Business

                    <u>AT&T Wireless,</u> Nanuet, NY
                    Completed numerous sales training courses, including Closing Techniques, Lead Generation, Prospecting Techniques, Product Knowledge, Plan Services, Features and Benefits.

CARL STEVENS, C.P.A.
227 Alex Road
Linwood, KS 66052

C: 913-555-9434   steve@nzaro.cc   H: 785-555-1743

BUSINESS DEVELOPMENT / OPERATIONS
Improving Business Performance through Systems Development and Operations Streamlining

PROFILE

Leadership talents in finance, accounting, supply chain management, sales, marketing, public relations and advertising, with success as CEO for two successful technology-based startups and CFO for organizations in retail, fast food franchising and construction.

Executive skills in P&L management, profit building, organizational development, staff management, team leadership, strategic planning, policy development and change management. Adept in leading startups, mergers, acquisitions and turnarounds.

Expert in financial management, with proven strengths in financial analysis, statement development, budget planning/forecasting, expense control, audits, business forecasting, risk management, internal controls and general accounting.

Well versed in cutting-edge IT systems; knowledge of technology architecture, business analysis, data warehousing, infrastructure design, IT security and strategy.

Skilled in network design and administration, system streamlining and integration, and full quality assurance; proven ability to advance eCommerce through Internet, Intranet and web resources.

EXPERIENCE

EMR, Inc., Lawrence, KS   2008-2011
A NeoSystems Corporation spin-off and $50M environmental construction company with 12 divisions. NeoSystems is a multi-divisional consulting and accounting service company.

Chief Financial Officer
Originally retained as a consultant and project manager by NeoSystems to provide interim leadership over its accounting and finance functions following the spinoff of EMR. Recruited by EMR senior management to provide interim financial leadership.
Trained and directed four professionals, while closely managing DCAA-compliant accounting for time & material, fixed price and cost plus government contracts.

- Established the organization's first internal controls to ensure the proper recording of company operations.
- Successfully negotiated a $3M line of credit, including a $1.5M revolving letter of credit facility, by aggressively managing the company's most strategic banking relationships.
- Increased company bonding limits by effectively negotiating with bonding companies.
- Saved the company $156,000 a year by moving its accounting back in house from an outsourced provider.
- Streamlined accounting by eliminating more than 56,000 dormant accounts from the general ledger.

CARL STEVENS, C.P.A.   PAGE TWO

Itty-Bitty Dog Store, LLC, St. Louis, MO   2000-2007
A start-up e-commerce company specializing in retail and wholesale supplies for small-breed dogs.

Vice President of Operations /Owner

Guided all business development and operations efforts of the firm, including finance, accounting, supply chain management, product development and launch, sales and marketing. Fueled development of a catalogue of more than 500 products, driving more than 60 orders a week with as many as 10 items per order.

- Personally developed and programmed the functionality and features of a B2C and B2B website, incorporating leading-edge technology to improve the customer experience and drive continuous growth in sales.
- Drove new product development by personally guiding the design and manufacturing of more than 60 products, strategically developed in alignment with the customer's requirements.
- Grew the repeat customer base to 656 customers, while nearly tripling average sale revenue.

InLink Communications Company, LLC, St. Louis, MO   1993-1999
A $4M startup company providing Internet connectivity, web hosting and web development to the public. The first St. Louis area public Internet service provider, with 34 employees and more than 10,000 satisfied customers.

President and CEO/Owner

Founded and managed the growth of this company in the early days of Internet commercialization. Developed and directed a professional force of 34 employees comprised of network engineers, web designers and essential customer support personnel.

- Successfully positioned the organization for a highly profitable $5M sale, while avoiding consequences of the dot.com crash in early 2000.
- Took the lead in technological innovation by personally administering multiple, concurrent web design and network programming projects through their lifecycle.
- Ensured consistently high levels of customer satisfaction by serving as the company's strategic advisor to clients in the areas of network management, security and disaster recovery.
- Grew the customer base to 10,000 accounts in six years, while driving a 45% increase in revenues in the company's last two years of operation.

EARLY CAREER

Chief Financial Officer of Zipps Double Drive Thru Inc., a $10M fast food franchisor with 440 employees in 15 restaurants located throughout Missouri.

Controller for Golde's Department Stores, a $7M general merchandise department store chain and a division of Interco.

Controller for Creve Coeur Camera, Inc., a multi-unit retail chain specializing in retail photo processing and camera equipment.

EDUCATION

B.S. Degree: Accounting, Southern Illinois University, Edwardsville, IL

Certified Public Accountant, University of Illinois.
Past President Delta Sigma Pi Business Fraternity.
Past President Clayton Area Jaycees.

Sent about 30; no less than one out of eight responded. Received several interviews; hired for two consecutive positions. (See corresponding letter.)

Mick Jackson

312 Main Street, #412   Win@job.net
Philadelphia, PA 19127   212/555-1232

Executive Sales / Financial Products

PROFILE:

➢ Comprehensive experience in new business development, contract negotiations and sales, including full responsibility for account acquisition, management, retention and market penetration.

➢ Proven abilities in opportunity identification, proposal development and building personal client relationships.

➢ Determine and meet specific client needs and handle post-sale support, including total account servicing to exceed business and financial goals.

➢ Skilled in strategic planning, team leadership, staff management and sales presentations, as well as competitive analysis and lead generation.

➢ Utilize Windows and Macintosh systems, as well as MS Office, including MS Excel and MS Word for documentation and spreadsheets.

EXPERIENCE: PNC Bank, Philadelphia, PA   8/11-Present
Senior Financial Consultant
Develop and execute strategic sales plans to meet brokerage sales goals of teams at three branches.
Personally train and supervise a team of three, while motivating and educating a branch staff of up to 30 in product lines, telephone and sales techniques.
Educate the sales team in the psychology of human behavior to demonstrate competence and earn trust, as well as closing techniques and account development for increased sales.
Assess client assets, liabilities and cash flow to identify financial objectives.
Plan and conduct presentations regarding recommended financial strategies for clients.
Coach branch staff in identifying and qualifying referrals.

→ Guided teams to top 10% sales ranking in the region.
→ Obtained 780 accounts with a total of $30 million in asset management.
→ Generated more than $1 million in revenue during tenure.

Morgan Stanley, Philadelphia, PA   4/97-8/11
Financial Planner
Marketed investment services and performed sales activities, including lead generation and prospecting.

➢ Exceeded goal of 50 new accounts per year by opening 150 with $12 million in asset management.
➢ Achieved top 25% ranking in asset management sales.
➢ Promoted to this position from Financial Advisor for surpassing goals.

Toltzis Communications, Philadelphia, PA   1996-1996
Copy Writer

EDUCATION: Widener University, Chester, PA
M.B.A. Degree – Business Administration   1996-1997

Muhlenberg College, Allentown, PA
B.A. Degree – Communications & Psychology   1989-1993
→ Dean's List

Used one resume; hired by a former client. (See corresponding letter.)

Anthony Provenzano
122 East 334th Street, Apt. 26G
New York, NY 10016
Res: 212/555-7492   E-mail: anthony@yahoo.com

INTERNET AND E-MULTIMEDIA TECHNOLOGIES

PROFILE: Corporate executive experience managing advanced information technologies, specializing in web configuration and systems integration, with full responsibility for startup and growth strategies in highly competitive business environments.

▶ Advise senior management on emerging issues and industry trends; write and present business plans and proposals for electronic multimedia system projects including design, installation, migration, conversion, product rollout and digital asset management.

▶ Skilled in client needs assessment, market intelligence, product specification determination, risk analysis, change order management, budgeting and client/vendor relations.

▶ Recruit and mobilize high-performance teams; effectively communicate concepts and complex technical information to non-technical personnel at all levels.

TECHNICAL

Mac OS, Windows NT, UNIX, Outlook, Adobe Photoshop, QuarkXPress, Adobe Illustrator, MS Office, DNS, TCP/IP, AppleTalk, Ethernet, WinFrame, Reflections, Cyclone, Rumba, HTML, TCL/TK, PERL, Remote Access Software; hardware includes SGI, RAID storage solutions, 10/100Base-T hubs and ISDN; expert in Internet/intranet protocols and client-server technologies.

EXPERIENCE:

A. Provenzano & Sons, New York, NY   2005-Present
Consultant / Owner
Provide consulting services and technical assistance to major corporate clients, specializing in advanced information technologies, including web design, layout and configuration, system integration, network administration, strategic planning, project direction and account management.

Major clients and projects include:
—▶ *Scream Puff, Inc.*
Current project: evaluate and qualify vendors/distributorships for website hyperlinks and banner advertising, working with client marketing and information technology staff.

—▶ *The Glamor-Face Companies*
Directed a group of 3-8 systems administrators and vendor consultants on a variety of projects.
■ Managed system migrations from Win XP/WFW to NT and from MS Mail 5.5 to Exchange/Outlook.
■ Coordinated the installation of Mac OS 8.x for the Graphics Department.
■ Evaluated software alternatives, such as WinFrame and intranets, for in-house applications.
■ Processed domain registrations of GF's trademark names and maintained MX records.
■ Monitored and documented project progress, including milestones, change orders and budgets.

—▶ *Fed Services/Stacy's*

Managed various major projects, with budgets ranging from $25,000 to $600,000, to upgrade all computer/LAN equipment and develop special multimedia services.

- Evaluated and implemented strategies to leverage emerging technologies.
- Handled all network systems administration, including design, upgrades and trouble-shooting.
- Implemented company maintenance and repair program for desktop hardware, realizing a savings of over $100,000 annually.

—▶ *The Land Company, Squish Communications, Sam Taylor*

System migration project: converted the MS Mail 5.5 e-mail system to Novell GroupWise (PC/Mac).

- Evaluated software alternatives and selected software/hardware vendors.
- Upgraded server software and hardware to Mac systems.
- Planned, organized and supervised the interoffice relocation of staff and computer equipment.

High Octane Media Enterprises, New York, NY   1995-2005

Webmaster / Partner

Formed this startup ISP venture with two other partners, offering web development, marketing and advertising services. Sold share to partners to expand consulting services.

- Invested $5,000 of personal finances in startup costs; prepared the initial business plan.
- Utilized Windows NT 3.5.1., O'Reilly's Website and Postoffice.
- Installed and maintained dedicated telecommunication lines, dial-up and fractional T-1.
- Performed network installation, troubleshooting, bandwidth monitoring and resource utilization.
- Provided website technical support for clients and fielded consumer e-mail questions.

Microcomputer Publishing Center, New York, NY   1993-1995

Systems Analyst

Responsible for servicing 125 corporate accounts for this systems integration service company.

- Developed Macintosh-based solutions for Design Studios.
- Provided one-on-one telephone support to clients, resolving network, hardware and software problems.
- Tested prototype systems prior to each software release.

EDUCATION:

School of Visual Arts, New York, NY
Coursework toward a Master of Fine Arts degree.
Concentration: Multimedia

Sent 40; received 30 interviews. (See corresponding letter.)

Adam R. Nephew
221 Palm Bay Drive
Baldwin, NE 63021

| Res: 314/555-0109 | E-mail: nq74A@prodigy.com | Ofc: 314/555-7291 |

EXECUTIVE LEADERSHIP: Information Technology / MIS
Retail, Manufacturing or Financial Services

PROFILE:

▶ Expert in retail merchandising information technology and management systems, with full responsibility for project budgets, schedules and performance for a multibillion dollar retail organization.

▶ Skilled in needs assessment, problem identification/resolution, process reengineering, cost analysis, price structuring, order expediting, inventory tracking and budget administration; coordinate and prioritize multiple tasks.

▶ Formulate and interpret financial/statistical data to facilitate critical decision making; well versed in import/export procedures and distribution logistics; knowledge of Spanish; hire, train and supervise teams to meet project goals.

▶ Efficiently develop and implement systems utilizing UNIX, zSeries, Windows 7/NT and the MS Office suite.

EMPLOYMENT: The Merchandising Corporation/Cray International, St. Louis, MO

| **EDP Supervisor, Data Center, Imports** | 6/03-Present |

Manage a three-member staff processing orders from eight subsidiary department stores and warehouses, including Gord & Talon, Famous-Bike, Hecht's and Foley's, as well as orders for imported merchandise to be distributed to stores coast-to-coast.

Administer a $745,000 departmental operating budget.

Design and generate scheduled/on-demand management decision support reports.

--> Maintain data control for merchandise ticketing including cost, duty rates, commissions, suggested selling price, classification and insurance costs.

--> Handle purchasing functions of all computer equipment, with a $1.5 million annual capital budget; negotiate contract rates and maintenance costs with such vendors as Xerox, IBM, Cadtex, CDI, Lectra and Silicon Graphics.

--> Reduced processing time and improved pricing, reporting and merchandise distribution efficiencies.

--> Ticket System Reengineering: identified and classified each item by a UPC to replenish stock by actual item sold at POS.

--> Initiated electronic reporting for international operations and generated a savings of $3,000 in DHL courier costs.

--> Increased report turnaround time to within 24 hours and reduced the number of pages from four to one per report, to achieve a cost savings of $2,000 print time/paper per report.

Coordinator, Merchandise Analysis, New York, NY   6/99-6/03
Coordinated a variety of merchandise analysis assignments and provided technical assistance to buyers and EDP on vendor/inventory management projects, with strict attention to accuracy of financial data.

--> Monitored and interpreted business/foreign vendor trends, including foreign labor costs, merchandise availability, shipping routes and political situations.

--> *Vendor Analysis Project:* Evaluated, prioritized and consolidated vendors to improve quality and gain greater purchasing leverage.

--> Designed and implemented a sales/vendor tracking system to maintain inventory levels on target.

--> *Pricepoint Project:* Audited pricepoints by classification for a decision by senior management to increase specific pricepoints.

Cost Analyst, New York, NY   8/96-6/99
Analyzed costs of merchandise imported from Asia, Subcontinent (India, Bangladesh, Sri Lanka and Dubai) and Europe for distribution to May stores throughout the U.S., including pricepoint guarantees for markup.

--> Classified items and considered routing, carriers, packing, volume, container capacity and weight ratio.

--> Developed a cost/rate manual based on average pricepoints to eliminate inaccurate and costly rate estimations.

EDUCATION: State University of New York, Buffalo, NY   Graduated 1996
B.A. Degree in mathematics and statistics
Concentration: Computer Science and Applied Mathematics

Internship: Millers Harness Company, East Rutherford, NJ 1994-1995
Research Analyst
Conducted market research project on Western Apparel.

--> Analyzed market trends and recommended targeting female client base.

--> Sales increased by 12% on implementation of recommendations.

From out of country with no green card; sent 40 resumes; received four interviews. (See corresponding letter.)

GOSHEN D. NANI

Coni 2280
Buenos Aires, Argentina
Cellular Phone: 541/555-3907   Business: 541/555-1001   E-mail: Goshen@hotmail.com

INTERNATIONAL BUSINESS DEVELOPMENT
Strategic Change Management

PROFILE:

➤ Comprehensive experience in senior-level business development in diverse, emerging and high-growth international commercial markets, with full P&L responsibility.

➤ Formulate startup, turnaround and growth strategies to take advantage of shifts in capital investment opportunities, market competitiveness and industry growth.

➤ Advise senior management on global economic and market trends; negotiate crossborder third-party client/vendor licensing/franchising and joint-venture agreements for strong market penetration and client relationships.

➤ Manage and train high-performance teams to meet strategic business goals; skilled in strategic planning, gap analysis, market positioning, capital investment/portfolio mix analysis, product launch and facility site selection/design.

➤ Well versed in intercultural communication and business practices; travel to client sites in Uruguay, Argentina, Brazil, Chile and the United States; work with suppliers in China and Korea; fluent in Spanish and English.

CAREER BACKGROUND:

Sync Investment Group, HQ, Gallup, TX

Operations Director, Sync, Inc.   1/11-Present

Direct all business development operations, including commercial, marketing, administration and distribution services, for this footwear and apparel company, acquired in 2007 for a franchiser of Sync, Hard Rock Cafe and Planet Hollywood for Latin America with $1 billion in assets.

--> Launched Vans in Argentina and Uruguay after securing $1.5 million in startup funding and generated $20 million in new revenues within the first six months of operation.

--> Ranked #1 worldwide in opening sales for apparel, at an unheard of 30% of total sales on launch.

--> Conceptualized the market expansion project, Vans Brazil investment project, expected to generate $50 million in revenues within the first six months and gain a 35% market share within the first year of implementation.

--> In charge of project control management of a $30 million tourist complex.

Controller, Hard Rock Cafe and Planet Hollywood, Latin America   6/96-1/11

Responsible for the planning, administration and policies of all financial operations for these two $65 million venture projects at 14 sites in the Caribbean, Uruguay, Argentina, Brazil and Chile.

--> Specifically developed and managed Planet Hollywood operations in Sao Paulo, Rio De Janeiro, Buenos Aires, Punta del Este and Santiago de Chile.

--> Analyzed Hard Rock Cafe operations in San Juan (Puerto Rico), St. Thomas and Buenos Aires.

--> Evaluated market opportunities in Latin America and presented investment recommendations to senior management and the Board of Directors, including a radio station and a major Disney production.

Petroken S.A., Buenos Aires, Argentina   1990-1996
Economic and Financial Planning Manager   2/92-5/96
Evaluated the financial status of company operations for this $250 million subsidiary of the Royal Dutch
Shell Group and recommended market expansion opportunities, acquisitions and new business ventures.

--> Initiated a marginal contribution review of local and export markets, which resulted in the entry into
a new $140 million niche market.

--> Introduced the first company quality improvement process and achieved earnings of 5% over sales in
cost savings and a reduction to near zero errors within the first six months of implementation.

Controller   10/90-2/92
In charge of all corporate financial administration, with a focus on planning and budget control, with a
budget of 60% over sales directly managed by a 15-person staff.
--> Produced and implemented the first corporate accounting and planning systems.

--> Developed and introduced internal control procedures; recommended corrective actions working
closely with internal and external auditors.

Prior Experience

Chief Accountant, IECSA S.A., Argentina: handled all joint venture, capital investment and construction
project audits and evaluation.

Senior Auditor, Deloitte & Touche, Argentina: audited Frigorifico Rioplatense, Consignaciones Rurales, Bull
Argentina and Argenblue S.A. (licensee of apparel manufacturers including Wrangler and Calvin Klein).

Accounting Analyst, Securities and Exchange Commission, Washington, D.C.

TRAINING: Numerous professional development seminars completed include:
                   Capital Markets, Enforcement Training Program, SEC, Washington, D.C.
                   Techniques and Analysis of External Audits, Deloitte & Touche
                   ISO 9001/14000 Normative and Quality Development in Shell Capsa
                   Certification: Internal Auditor, Bureau Veritas.

EDUCATION: University of Belgrano, Buenos Aires, Argentina
                   Master of Business Administration, 2007
                   Focus: Finance and Marketing

                   University of Belgrano, Buenos Aires, Argentina
                   Bachelor of Science Degree: Public Accounting

Sent 60 targeted resumes; received 15 interviews and three job offers. (See corresponding letter to executive search firms.)

Johnathan Bishop

122 Tuna Can Road	Res: 610/555-0350
Topanga, OH 44290	E-mail: john@net.att.net

CORPORATE BUSINESS DEVELOPMENT / MANAGEMENT

PROFILE

➢ Executive talents in senior-level planning, administration and the direction of manufacturing operations in advanced instrumentation technologies, with P&L responsibility for market penetration and expansion internationally.

➢ Skilled in strategic planning, opportunity identification, market risk analysis, venture capitalization, contract negotiation and distributor network development; recruit, train and supervise high-performance teams to meet business and financial goals.

➢ Effectively lead organizations through critical structuring and product rollouts; awarded U.S./international patents; conference author/presenter; proven ability to develop a pipeline of competitive products from concept to commercialization.

➢ Well versed in intercultural communication and negotiation; experience working with business partners in Europe, the Pacific Rim, Israel and Latin America; fluent in English and French; conversant in Dutch and familiar with Spanish.

EXPERIENCE:

<u>Focus Research, Inc.,</u> Chatsworth, IA

Consultant   11/09-Present

Provide consulting services to the president hired by the new parent company, Cel Technology, Inc. Charged with strategic planning and management, focused on market development and product innovation for this $9 million manufacturer of photometric instruments with worldwide distribution.

President   2/96-11/99

In charge of the planning, administration and direction of all company operations, with full P&L responsibility; turned an $800,000 loss in profits into a $700,000 gain.

—▶ Transformed the company culture into a consumer-driven one from an aerospace/government-driven culture, to penetrate commercial markets.

—▶ Recruited and hired a Vice President of Marketing to fill a 20-month vacancy.

—▶ Directly managed foreign distributors representing 60% of sales and increased foreign sales by 15%; contracted distributors in Korea, South Africa and Argentina.

—▶ Opened a centrally located European sales and customer service center in Germany and redesigned all products to meet EC directives to expand into European markets.

—▶ Launched two key products.

—▶ Orchestrated the sale of the company to Cel Technology, Inc., in October 2007.

General Manager and Vice President of Engineering   5/95-2/96

Recruited by the president of Kollmorgen Instruments Corporation to re-engineer the company and reverse a rapidly eroding financial position within six months.

—▶ Attended the fast-track AEA/Stanford Executive Institute.

<u>Biocircuits Corporation,</u> Sunnyvale, CA 1995
Independent Consultant
Spearheaded a nine-month redesign project to develop a first-to-market, low-cost physician
office blood analyzer into a robust, marketable product.
- ➤ FDA approval granted in October 1995.

<u>Xsirius, Inc.,</u> Marina del Rey, CA 1992-1994
XRF Instrumentation Manager
Responsible for the operation of a new products development and management function to pro-
duce portable X-ray detection instruments; drafted business plans for four product lines.
- ➤ Forged three OEM relationships representing potential revenues of $5 million.
- ➤ Designed and delivered a proof-of-concept instrument for process control to the Ford
  Motor Company within five months of operation.

Prior Experience

<u>Kevex Instruments, Inc.,</u> San Carlos, CA
Research and Development Manager
Directed all phases of research projects to develop new products in X-ray analytical instrumentation.
Provided oversight management to a staff of 26 and managed a $2.8 million budget.
- ➤ Adopted ISO 9000 guidelines and simplified documentation procedures.
- ➤ Augmented sales revenues by $10 million solely from the X-ray analytical instrument
  product line.
- ➤ Negotiated and won a multi-million-dollar contract with Intel Corporation to produce
  and deliver a semiconductor wafer process-control instrument to monitor metallic
  films on patterned wafers.

Project Group Leader
Led the team that invented and designed the first commercial XRF micro-fluorescence analyzer.
- ➤ Promoted to this position from **Electronic Engineer**.

<u>Pacific Scientific Company,</u> Menlo Park, CA
Senior Project Engineer
Designed and launched a state-of-the-art particle counter based on open cavity He-Ne lasers.

MILITARY
SERVICE: <u>Belgian Service / Developing Countries,</u> Africa
Professor of Physics, College Moderne, Ivory Coast
Professor of Mathematics, College Moulay Ismail, Morocco

EDUCATION: <u>IN.RA.CI.</u> Brussels, Belgium
Ingenieur Industrial Electronique / MSEE Degree

Military conversion to private sector. (David couldn't be located to confirm results; included to honor our veterans.

David Salute

5 Justice Drive
Mooresville, IN 46158   godshouse@netspade.com

Res: (317) 555-4898
Cell: (317) 555-8127

Operations / Management

PROFILE:
➤ Skilled in strategic planning, operations and all aspects of supply chain and project management, as well as budgeting, team leadership, Human Resources and staff training; track record of achievement as Logistical Officer.

➤ Perform cost analysis and reduction, workforce planning and quality assurance; handle worker relations and job scheduling, with a knowledge of OSHA regulations.

➤ Proficient in project management, team leadership, training and organizational development; strong knowledge of Baldridge methods and applications to establish and lead organizational and operational changes to promote efficiency and scalability.

➤ Well versed in team training, motivating and managing high-performance technicians, managers and administrative personnel in a wide variety of functional areas to meet and exceed goals and objectives.

➤ Effectively focus cross-functional teams of technical and operational personnel to meet common goals. Utilize Windows systems and MS Office, including MS Word, MS Excel, MS PowerPoint and MS Outlook; supervise programming layout to build and use national MS Access programs.

EXPERIENCE: Indiana Army National Guard, Indianapolis, IN   1992-Present
Progressed through a series of ranks and logistical responsibilities at brigade, division and headquarter levels at various locations. Requested by the Chief of Staff to stay on at the Indianapolis location after military retirement in May 2004 as a temporary civil-service employee.

Logistics Management Supervisor (Branch Chief)   2009-Present
Plan, organize, direct, monitor, control and coordinate the logistical services support operations of the Plans and Operations Branch, the Defense Movement and Coordination Branch, the Automations Branch and the Budget Branch.
Validate the usage of funding obligations, as well as inventory, while supervising a budget staff of three in tracking $10 billion in expenditures for the state of Indiana.
Provide written guidance documents on proper logistical procedures that have been utilized not only in the state, but adopted by other army organizations.
Develop and enforce rules, regulations and policies.
Ensure compliance to regulatory procedures and reinforce internal management controls; supervise the inspection of warehouses to validate inventory and control procedures.
Coordinate and plan the training activities for 169 units and 4 major headquarters; train all newly hired logistical personnel.

▶ Implemented automated programs that increased management analysis, and provided senior leadership success measures for all areas of logistical readiness.

▶ Assisted in the deployment of early activation deployed troops and was instrumental in the first Army National Guard Mobilization station to operate with full mobilization requirements and minimal staffing; tracked all expenditures to be reimbursed by higher headquarters.

▶ Implemented Baldridge Quality criteria, benchmarking and metrics methodologies, resulting in APICS certification.

Deputy Chief of Staff/Logistics   2009-Present

Planned and managed a $15 million budget and supervised more than 100 military employees supporting 12,000 soldiers for a major command that covered five states.

Developed and enforced rules, regulations and policies for this activity.

▶ Provided army standard logistics training to five Third-World countries; assisted with the development of newly activated organizations to ensure the organization met all criteria for logistical readiness.

▶ Increased readiness to 100% from 50%-65% for the command with prioritization of funds to maximize increasing equipment on hand and improve quality of organization and deployment capability.

Command Logistics Officer/Property Book Officer (Staff Officer)

1997-1999

Responsible for P&L funding to support 1 of 15 new separate infantry brigades; organized people, equipment and resources, including food service.

Supported all logistical requirements for the organization, including preparing acquisition plans valued up to $20 million annually.

Supervised 40 military employees supporting 3,000 soldiers in 26 units.

▶ Prepared logistics doctrine in standard operating procedures format that increased readiness within the organization and impacted on war fighting support skills.

▶ Implemented automated programs that increased management analysis and provided senior leadership with success measures for all areas of logistical readiness.

▶ Synchronized the growth and progress of the organization that increased the capabilities of the organization, noted nationally by the U.S. Army Connelly Award for food service.

Operations Officer for Medical Battalion   1996-1997

In charge of the medical services/support for a five-state organization, including purchasing, inventory control and facility management.

▶ Reorganized medical community to support the needs of the organization, in accordance with doctrine throughout the Army, thus greatly increasing readiness.

David Salute   **Page Three**

Command Logistics Officer (Staff Officer) Bedford, IN   1995-1996
Performed same duties as at Indianapolis, 1994-1997.

Administrative Officer (Staff Officer/Company Commander)
New Albany, IN   1994-1995
Directed, monitored, controlled and coordinated all services, training, and budget-ary requirements for 700 soldiers supported from five locations.
▶ Supervised five civilian and 20 military employees while holding Company Command of 200 soldiers.

Operations Officer (Staff Officer/Executive Officer)
New Albany, IN   1992-1995

EDUCATION: Oakland City University, Oakland City, IN   1997
                   B.S. Degree – Management of Human Resources

                   Vincennes University, Vincennes, IN   1990
                   A.A. Degree – Applied Science

AWARDS: Distinguished Quartermaster Award (2 awards), Indiana Commendation Medal, Recruiting and Retention Award, Meritorious Service, Distinguished Service Award, Army Achievement Medal (2 awards), Army Commendation Medal (3 awards), Artillery Leadership Award (OCS), Overseas Ribbons (2 awards) and Distinguished Hoosier Award (Governor).

As a consultant, sent one resume, leading to a new consulting position.

Thomas Xavier

938 Grove Avenue	**847-555-9065**
Schaumburg, IL 60193	**thom@real.com**

Director: Human Capital Management

PROFILE:

> ➢ Senior-level experience in strategic planning, human capital management and operations, including program implementation and full responsibility for start-up and established organizations.

> ➢ Establish and manage a wide range of recruiting and HR services, including account maintenance, contract negotiations, industry networking, presentations, special events planning, budgeting, recruiting and quality control.

> ➢ Skilled in lead generation, marketing programs, staffing functions and creating comprehensive recruiting structures; build partnerships with hiring managers, identify creative sourcing methods and maintain proactive, cost-effective recruitment strategies.

> ➢ Strong knowledge of Executive Order 11246 Diversity and Inclusion; prepare Affirmative Action plans and conduct EEO reporting.

> ➢ Effectively recruit, hire, train, motivate and supervise teams in company policies and procedures.

> ➢ Protect corporate investment in human capital by creating a strong atmosphere of job satisfaction and employee loyalty.

EXPERIENCE:

We Click, Schaumburg, IL   2003-Present
Consultant / Owner - **Human Capital Management Consulting Firm**
Provide Human Capital Management solutions to clients throughout the U.S. from recruitment and selection to creating recruiting operations and divisions for start-ups, expansions and established multinational companies.

Major clients and projects include:
Abbott Laboratories, Abbott Park, IL
• Talent Acquisition
  Direct an in-house recruitment and search team, addressing all issues as selection expert.
  Develop strategies to position Abbott as an employer of choice.
  Implement best practice procedures, such as an applicant tracking system, source identification, pre-employment screening and related compliance with Diversity and Inclusion Initiatives – Executive Order 11246.
  Create recruiting metrics, an employee referral program and build partnerships with hiring managers.
  Primary areas of focus include Molecular, Diagnostics, Engineering, Legal, Information Technology, Finance and Human Resources.
  Assess candidate fit and qualifications and determine competency matches.
  Prepare and maintain Affirmative Action plans and conduct EEO reporting.

• Transportation Security Administration, Washington, D.C.
  Managed and facilitated the hiring process for Federal Passenger Screeners in Philadelphia, PA and Milwaukee, WI.

Ensured compliance with EEO/Diversity policies.

- Directed the operation and setup of multiple assessment centers and led applicants through an extensive application process, including computer-based evaluations, behavioral interviews, medical and physical examinations, fingerprinting and the accurate completion of more than a dozen government forms.
- Supervised continual improvements to call center operations by creating mass candidate monitoring systems and overseeing quality assurance process prior to entry into national database (Seibel). Directed a temporary staff of employees in the development of spreadsheets and call lists; prepared scripts and weekly reports.
- Responsible for new hire orientations, Affirmative Action law, compensation, benefits and exit interviews. Project required 100% travel for a 7-day operation that averaged 70-80 work hours per week.

- Hr Value Group, Middleton, WI
  Acted as Chief Operating Officer and Director of Human Resources for a start-up Human Capital Management consulting firm, specializing in servicing credit unions. Authored the business plan, set goals, performed recruiting and presented status reports to board of directors. Additionally, developed revenue streams. Established offices in IL, PA, OH and WI.
  Focused on Personnel Policy Manuals, pre-employment, compensation and benefits, Federal Affirmative Action Requirements, Employee Performance and Development Evaluations. Project required 80% travel.

- Visual Insights, Downers Grove, IL
  Instrumental in assisting the establishment and development of an eBusiness performance company. Expanded work force in Human Resources, Information Technology, Executive levels and Sales/Marketing. Responsible for developing and enhancing human resource programs to support business.

- Totality (formerly Mimecom), San Francisco, CA
  Established recruiting functions with up to 30 professionals in New York and San Francisco. Jump-started recruiting procedures and hired staff to ensure continuation of operating policies and procedures. Project required 100% travel.

- divine, (formerly Data Return) Irving, TX
  Created entire recruiting division, *Talent divine*, with 40 professionals. Established staffing methodologies, operating policies and procedures. In eight months, brought company to IPO critical mass by hiring all executive-level and 300 technical-level employees.

Web/CKS, (formerly Modern Business Technology), Schaumburg, IL   1996-2003
Staffing Manager
Responsible for all recruiting and several personnel functions for this company, providing enterprise wide Internet solutions to Fortune 500 clients.

- Assisted with new business development and outplacement functions; served as liaison for college recruiting efforts and vendor relations.
- Played a key role in expanding revenue from $1 million to $8.5 million in two years, requiring a staff increase from 6 to 80.

- Reduced operating costs through utilization of the RTRA organization and personally recruited two principals.

<u>New Resources Corporation,</u> Rolling Meadows, IL   1996-2003
Senior Technical Recruiter
Responsible for all aspects of recruiting and new business development, including interviewing, screening and new hire orientation for this software development company with a client base of Fortune 500 firms.

- Hired, trained and supervised five recruiters in daily operations and procedures.
- Trained new support staff in company policies and procedures.

<u>Accustaff (formerly Debbie Temps),</u> Schaumburg, IL   1993-1996
Staff Coordinator
Performed recruiting and personnel functions while establishing new policies and procedures; improved advertising and telemarketing techniques resulting in increased market exposure.

TRAINING AND CERTIFICATIONS:
Certified Internet Recruiter (CIR) and Certified Diversity Recruiter (CDR)
Certified Human Capital Management professional - 1/03 (SHRM – SPHR and PHR)

Airs - Professional Internet Recruiting Training - Search Labs I and II completed:

Recruiting
Spot a phony resume
Recruiting strategies
Recruiting basics
Negotiating employment deals
Recruiting, Retention, and Development

Interviewing
Advanced interviewing skills
Interviewing and selecting high performers
Core competency-based interviewing
Behavior description interviewing
The evaluation interview

Human Resources
Staffing the contemporary organization
Managing people
Human resources writing guide
Personnel forms book
Employee relations
Managing HR
Executive benefits
Legal Issues in Human Resource Manager

Employment Law
Work place law
Labor law
Hiring and firing legal issues
Worker's compensation
Minority employment

MEMBERSHIPS:
Current president of The Regional Technical Recruiters Association
Active member of the NAACP

EDUCATION:
<u>American Intercontinental University</u>
    B.S. Degree in Business Administration

<u>William Rainey Harper College</u>
    A.S. Degree in Political Science/Criminal Justice

Received 30 interviews over one year and a new position.

GABRIEL CART

503 Salizar   152/664-6744363

San Diego, CA 92111   cartaya@yahoo.com

COO - INTERNATIONAL BUSINESS OPERATIONS

PROFILE:
- Skilled at combining **business experience, plant operations and technical expertise** to initiate growth strategies and penetrate new global markets.
- Proficient in budgeting, detailed contract negotiations, production planning, MIS and equipment maintenance; successful team leader and project manager in time-sensitive situations.
- Hands-on knowledge of essential quality initiatives such as Six Sigma, TQM, ERP and ISO; exposure to **maquiladora** operations, foreign government regulations, NAFTA and MEFTA trade agreements.
- Experience in international markets and multicultural issues, particularly in Latin America, Europe and the U.S.; fluent in Spanish and Italian.
- Recognized as an innovative **Researcher** of new technologies in the plastic, metalworking and oil industries.
- Proven track record of always meeting strict deadlines, ensuring full customer satisfaction, greatly increasing profit margins and reducing operating costs.

EMPLOYMENT: Confidential, Tijuana, Mexico/Minneapolis, MN   2008-Present

Chief Operating Officer

In charge of all start-up functions for a new manufacturing plant in Tijuana, Mexico, including effectively negotiating contracts, setting prices and performing new business development in the U.S. for the largest company ($100 million) in the plastic netting industry.

Set up and maintain automated facilities to produce unique products, control operating costs, ensure top quality and avoid machinery shutdowns.

Effectively network with sales managers in Spain, France, Mexico and the U.S., while dealing with subcontractors and off-site production activity.

Implement and support such crucial quality programs as Six Sigma, TQM, TPM, ERP, ISO 9001 and 14000; ensure full compliance with government regulations.

Established, staffed and grew departments for R&D, quality assurance, production planning, customer service, import/export, building maintenance/security, IS and human resources, with more than 100 employees.

Active member of the senior executive team in Europe.

Excellent technical knowledge of electromechanics, fluid mechanics, process automatization, polymers, metalworking and technology transfer.

→ Earned recognition from state officials as a Facilitator for foreign investments in Tijuana, Mexico.

→ Ranked among top company executives for rapid and successful start-up of this production facility and improving sales from $2 million to $6 million.

→ Succeeded in increasing productivity by 21% and reducing scrap by 4% over European standards.

→ Achieved zero delivery delays in shipping and no bad quality claims from clients; installed ERP applications.

→ Designed and launched a unique product that took 30% of business volume from a competitor.

→ Coordinated the integration of a subsidiary in Mexico City, Mexico.

→ Performed detailed studies of business conditions and production facilities in Mexico, Brazil, Argentina, Venezuela and the U.S.

→ Initially hired as an **R&D Senior** Engineer and quickly promoted to **Chief Operating Officer** for America at company headquarters in Spain.

Université Joseph Fourier, Grenoble, France   2007
Researcher
Successfully completed a technical project involving the interaction of fluid mechanics linked with emulsions.

→ Recognized for detailed investigation of emulsions through the Rheology Laboratory.

Trical, Caracas, Venezuela   1996-2007
Technical Manager
In charge of manufacturing functions involving a wide range of materials, processes (geosynthetics) and plastic net products for this $20 million operation. Oversaw teams in production forecasting, equipment maintenance, quality control, resource allocation and strategic planning.

→ Rated for "Best Productivity," increasing production by 110%, best in the company's history in 1999.

→ Succeeded in developing new technologies, including an $800,000 piece of equipment, through applied engineering.

→ Gained experience in team building strategies, conceptual engineering, staff training and new technologies.

→ Coordinated technology transfer between this firm and a joint venture with Guimatra, including new product development and process installation, for six months in Brazil.

PDVSA-Intevep, Caracas, Venezuela   1994-1996

Developer - Instruments and Automation

Hired at the highest technical level as the driving force in the design, analysis and improvement of several measurement instruments for non-conventional fluids for this $5 billion dollar petroleum company.

Directly involved in daily operations and installation activity for oil fields and refineries.

→ The most important instrument measured hydrocarbons/non-Newtonians, utilizing detailed physical and mathematical models per specific rheology of the fluids in the study, saving $300,000 in costs.

→ Achieved much more accurate results than expected by scientists.

→ Trained extensively in metalworking, CNC machines, CAD/CAM and dimensional metrology.

EDUCATION: University Simón Bolívar, Caracas, Venezuela   1994

B.S. Degree in Mechanical Engineering; specialization in Fluid Mechanics.

- Recognized for "Best Thesis in Mechanical Engineering" in Venezuela and France; honorable mention for thesis works.

TECHNICAL
BACKGROUND:
- Fully familiar with Windows NT, MS Office, CAD/CAM, MATH, UNIX, ERP and different programming languages.
- Extensive knowledge of the plastics process, including extrusion, netting, injection, blown, film, lamination and other processes.
- Hands-on skills in electrical engineering, applied physics, turbomachines, pipeline flexibility, pressure recipients, special steel treatments, geosynthetics, PLCs and power quality.
- Member of the College of Engineers of Venezuela.

Used about five with personal contacts; hired for new position.

Thomas Daily
12 Strawberry Hill Avenue, #6
Stamford, CT 06902   Res: 203/555-9548   daily@gmail.com

EXECUTIVE LEADERSHIP
C.E.O./President/C.O.O.

PROFILE:
- Comprehensive, senior-level experience in small-to-large service, manufacturing and distribution operations, specializing in business expansion and new product development, with full P&L responsibility in a variety of U.S.-based and international industries.
- Advise CEO/president and directors on emerging industry trends; proven ability to lead organizations through turnaround, critical startup and growth strategies; effectively spearhead acquisitions and joint ventures; private placement/IPO experience.
- Skilled in strategic planning, market positioning, sales and account management, product rollout, process reengineering; contract negotiation, licensing agreements, client/supplier relations, government affairs and recruiting and managing high-performance teams.
- Well versed in intercultural business communication; consistently develop solid business contacts and relationships; in-depth knowledge of multiple-site MIS and electronic commerce.

\

CAREER BACKGROUND:

Dedicated Pharm Co., Inc., Long Island, NY   2007-Present
C.E.O. / President
Hired to turn around this international manufacturer and distributor of pharmaceutical products, employing 122, with direct P&L responsibility for $10 million in annual revenues.
- Increased sales by 40% to overcome a five-year deficit.
- Eliminated 30% of overhead costs in the manufacturing functions and improved productivity by 50%.
- Repositioned the Rx and OTC product lines to target three new high-growth market segments.
- Developed and introduced seven new ANDAs (FDA-approved Rx products).
- Established licensing and distribution agreements with distributorships in the Ukraine, China, Taiwan, Hong Kong and Nigeria; other countries in process.

Nuthouse Consultants, HQ, New Canaan, CT   1997-2007
Partner and co-founder of this consulting firm, specializing in turnaround and interim management projects.

Chef. Inc., HQ, Dallas, TX   1996-1997
Vice President / General Manager
Directed startup operations to expand into the hospitality and institutional feeding markets.
- Generated sales revenue of $10 million in the first year.
- Produced a business plan for a joint venture between Cendant and a hotel franchise chain.

PRIOR EXPERIENCE

Veri Corporation, St. Petersburg, FL
Executive Vice President/C.O.O./Director
Developed and implemented a five-year strategic plan, with a focus on export trade for this startup $1.5 million manufacturer of infection control products for institutional, industrial and retail clients.
- Hired, trained and directed a 114-person sales and telemarketing group in less than two months.

Kushi Macrobiotics Corporation, Stamford, CT
President/C.E.O./Director
Founded this natural/health foods marketer and manufacturing company in partnership with the internationally acclaimed Michio Kushi.
> Raised $2 million from a Private Placement Memorandum and $7 million from an IPO Prospectus; led due diligence presentations to the financial community.
> Created and rolled out a 33-item premium product line in nine months.

Culinar Sales Corporation, Blandon, PA
President / C.O.O.
Hired to turn around operations and improve profits of this U.S. specialty and fancy food manufacturing subsidiary of Culinar, Inc., of Canada; positioned the company for divestiture.
> Increased sales by 92% and reduced sales costs by more than 50%.
> Improved ACV distribution from 15% to more than 70% in less than two years.

Rim Industries. Inc., Mt. Vernon, NY, **President/C.O.O./Partner**

Savoy Industries. Inc., New York, NY, **Executive Vice President/C.O.O.**

Hickson Advertising Agency, New York, NY, **Senior Vice President/General Manager**

EDUCATION: Long Island University, New York, NY
Coursework in the Master of Business Administration program.

Ohio State University, Columbus, OH
Bachelor of Science Degree: Chemistry and Marketing Research

Combined resume with letter and biography we wrote, sent 10 resumes and 25 bios; received 80% interviews in the first 2 months.

KEN RONALD

9608 Embarcadero Terrace
Fremont, CA 94538
ken@don.com 302/555-1234

EXECUTIVE LEADERSHIP

Operations • Finance • Product Development

Commercializing and Differentiating Technology to Meet the Customer's Needs

Consistently in the vanguard of high quality, new technology product and service launches that enable superior productivity in the organization through continuing commercialization of the Internet. Spearhead entrepreneurial management that anticipates the future direction and contribution of technology to the enterprise and its customers. Active participant in the development and growth of industry leaders including AT&T Yahoo!, eBay, GetThere, Voyence and more.

➢ Trusted advisor to startups and established companies requiring a dramatic turnaround, as well as to organizations that promote growth and viability. Graduate of and Alumni Advisor to the Sacramento Entrepreneurship Academy, and Operations Director of the VC Taskforce.

➢ Provide a guiding force in organizations noted for venture capital input and direction to early stage companies that benefit investors and their portfolio companies and real world education programs for students with entrepreneurial aspirations.

➢ Expert in corporate financing, business development and supporting operations with proven project management skills. Team player and leader, recognized and recruited to develop high-performance teams with the judgment and confidence to promote and actualize winning business concepts through strategic planning and tactical excellence.

➢ Skilled in marketing, sales and business development, investor and public relations, business planning and fundraising, budgeting, M&A, P&L analysis and contract negotiations.

EXPERIENCE

Comment Software, Inc., DBA ZeroVirtual, Palo Alto, CA   2002-2011

A company marketing embedded media applications and appliances for mobile devices, allowing Facebook and YouTube users to capture, store, view and share user-generated flash video from their profiles and view the portable content offline. The company now operates as ZeroVirtual.

VP Operations & CFO / VP Marketing
Co-founded this company, driving the development and marketing of virtualization software for Internet devices. Played a pivotal role in developing the overall strategy and company building process, while serving as a member of the Board of Directors.

Directed the execution of all business operations from product and service conception to implementation and marketing. Developed processes and worked with partners to support end-to-end business service delivery.

Achievements:

- Fueled the company's early stage growth by raising more than $2M through the effective management of both investor and public relations.
- Ensured the continued success of this startup by personally closing a contract representing $50M-$250M in revenue with the Chief Evangelist of Intel's Atom™ processor.
- Produced run rates of 150,000 visitors and 350,000 page views per month by directing the development and launch of the company's online beta release.
- Won Best of Show Award from Intel at the Consumer Electronics Show.

WowCo Productions, LLC, Fremont, CA   2000-2002
A firm producing technology startups by providing hands-on management consulting.

Managing Director
Co-founded the company; directed all business development and the subsequent execution and completion of engagements with technology startups including Voyence. Directed engagements ranging from seed stage startups to post Series A ventures backed by Atlas, Centerpoint, Interwest and Sevin Rosen.

Achievements:

- Served as a trusted advisor to the Voyence CEO in several engagements; rationalized and developed the revenue forecast that justified $18M in Series B funding prior to EMC's acquisition in 2008.

Tent Corporation, San Francisco, CA   1998-2000
Once a major force in the e-consulting industry, Scient was known as "The eBusiness Systems Innovator," and provided its clients with a full range of e-business services, from technology expertise to business strategy.

Director
Recruited by the CEO to lead pre- and post-IPO engagements for eBay. Fueled the development of a high-performance infrastructure organization, comprised of more than 100 professionals on the East and West Coasts by personally directing all related recruitment and hiring efforts.

Achievements:

- Won a much-valued and published endorsement for Scient's IPO from eBay CEO Meg Whitman, after having successfully guided the development of eBay's network strategy, as well as all related contract negotiations with companies including Sprint and UUNet.
- Personally directed a successful engagement for GetThere (formerly Internet Travel Network), focused on stabilizing and scaling Internet operations. GetThere was acquired by Sabre in 2000.

AT&T / Yippie!, San Francisco, CA   1999-2000
An early pioneer in Internet services, formerly SBC/Pacific Bell.

Director of Business Infrastructure, Senior Project and Product Development Manager
Played a key role in the company's entry into the ISP market while serving as one of its early leaders and the 20th employee in the organization. Guided the efforts of 26 professionals after having personally staffed the organization in less than two years. Placed a consistent emphasis on the quality of the organization in favor of a quantity approach. Ensured customer-centric end-to-end service delivery and infrastructure across all functions of the company's product and service offerings.

Achievements:

- Enabled the development and launch of numerous Internet products and services with highly attractive features and benefits.
  - ✓ Powered the launch of Mac Internet Access by guiding the efforts of a cross-functional team that customized and branded Netscape's 3.0 browser.
  - ✓ Rescued a troubled Personal Home Pages development project and successfully launched a product that was eventually folded into Yahoo! GeoCities.
  - ✓ Drove the rapid growth of the Windows Internet Access customer base by bullet-proofing and securing an Internet platform that was scalable to support millions of subscribers.
- Played a critical role in funding and pricing initiatives that enabled successful product development and launch.
  - ✓ Funded Pacific Bell's first commercial Internet deployments in California; invested over $50M.
  - ✓ Saved $40M over a two year period by rescuing a troubled Internet subsidiary merger. Provided financial expertise, set the organization and channeled politics to close the merger.
  - ✓ Delivered Flat Rate Pricing for the consumer product line that increased gross margin by $9M in the first year, representing a 40% year-over-year increase.

PRIOR EXPERIENCE

BT&T Information Services, San Ramon, CA
An early leader in the development and delivery of voicemail, advanced TV and digital media. Formerly Pacific Bell.

Financial Analysis & Planning Manager, Capital Investment Manager
Key contributor to the creation of four subsidiaries and the TELE-TV joint venture with Bell Atlantic and Creative Artists to develop and commercialize the Internet as an "Information Superhighway." Administered and prioritized $30M capital budget funding five companies while simultaneously ensuring a high return on investment across a $100M capital asset base. Analyzed the Enterprise Group business portfolio for Pacific Bell's Board of Directors. Emphasized P&L Analysis, EPS Impact and Cash Value Added. Facilitated the initial development and continued modification of strategic plans to ensure the attainment of financial objectives in compliance with established business milestones.

Achievements:

- Dramatically improved operational performance and productivity by consolidating multiple subsidiaries: Pacific Bell Video, Pacific Bell Electronic Publishing and the TELE-TV joint venture.
- Promoted the delivery of digital media content by playing a key role in financing and the initial financial structuring of the company's multi-million dollar purchase of HP head-end servers.

EDUCATION
Master of Business Administration, Finance & Marketing,
California Polytechnic State University, San Luis Obispo, CA
Bachelor of Science in Business Administration, Finance
California State University, Sacramento, CA
Graduate and Active Alumnus
Sacramento Entrepreneurship Academy, Sacramento, CA

AFFILIATIONS
Startup Advisor, www.kencrittendon.com
Alumni Advisor, www.sealink.org
Operations Director, www.vctaskforce.com

Sent about 50; received 10 interviews; accepted a new position; gained many more interviews from Internet distribution.

Albert H. Kinsey

77 Pecan Drive		Ofc: 201/555-0857
Oakland, NJ 07436	Kinsey@report.com	Res: 201/555-0636

Executive Management: Sales / Marketing

A leadership position utilizing entrepreneurial talents for an advanced technology company, where skills in team building, client relations, needs analysis and growth are essential to success.

PROFILE:

- Executive background in all aspects of change management, process re-engineering, new business development and strategic planning in diverse technology environments.

- Manage P&L, budgeting, territory expansion, new product introduction, data/network consolidation, outsourcing, contract negotiation, competitive analysis, market research and account maintenance.

- Extensive systems experience with WANs, LANs, client-servers, disaster recovery operations and consulting services; proficient in TQM, ISO 9002 and other quality programs.

- Hire, train, mentor and coach management and staff in company product lines, policies and procedures.

- Top-level success with Fortune 500 clients such as Citicorp, Bank of New York, Chemical Bank, MetLife, Prudential, Paine Webber, Chubb, Morgan Stanley, ADP, Bell Atlantic, Nynex and UPS.

- Recognized by corporate leadership for consistently exceeding all objectives and for skills in troubleshooting and problem resolution in high-pressure situations.

EMPLOYMENT: Total Network Techfolks, Oakland, NJ — 2003-Present

An $85 million company with consistent growth since 1984, providing mainframe connectivity through innovative application of channel networking, as well as Gateway and client-server hardware/software solutions.

Area Sales Director

Responsible for energizing sales, marketing and customer support for 11 states in the United States' Northeast corridor.

Hire, train and supervise seven new sales representatives and six SCs, resulting in exceptional performance.

--> Increased sales by 300% in only three years with 40 new accounts; personally closed the largest transaction for 2005.

--> Directed the most profitable sales area in the company.

--> Achieved extensive market exposure for this firm with all IBM Metro trading areas.

--> Created a structured marketing plan for all national and major accounts.

--> Maximized account coverage and maintenance through unique territory assignment methods.

<u>J.D. Edwards and Company,</u> Secaucus, NJ   1992-2003
A privately held $250 million company specializing in financial software for AS/400 platforms; named "Best of Breed" for G/L, payroll, financials and manufacturing/ wholesale distribution.

Large Account Executive
In charge of sales and maintenance of domestic accounts, specializing in IBM and AT&T, as well as key clients in the NY metropolitan area.
--> Personally positioned this firm as a strategic partner with IBM/ISSC.

<u>AT&T – Paradyne,</u> Oakland, NJ   1990-1992
A high-growth, WAN communications company tasked with development and implementation of innovative communications technology, including the invention of Channel Extension and high-speed modem technology.

Senior Account Executive - Large/National Accounts
Managed sales, marketing and customer relations with clients in the NY metro, PA and New England areas for the Channel Extension product line.
--> Personally responsible for the IBM account worldwide.
--> Positioned this firm as a strategic partner with IBM/ISSC; established a greater market share nationwide.
--> Assisted ISSC in winning and fulfilling the first public outsourcing contract.
--> Nurtured additional partnerships with other sales forces.

Assistant to the Executive Vice President
Coordinated highly successful efforts to completely reengineer field sales and service worldwide through strategic sales, marketing and long-term planning with a global perspective.
--> Achieved 130% of annual project objectives on time and within budget.
--> Increased field sales productivity through streamlined operating procedures and resource allocation.
--> Facilitated cross-functional partnerships between departments, along with new goals and job models.
--> Developed and implemented unique approaches to enhance management and staff performance in sales, customer service and quality.

District Manager
Assumed sales, marketing, system engineering and administration for a NYC and Long Island non-performing territory.
--> Improved sales by 300% in 18 months and staff performance to 132% of goal from 37%, resulting in five of six candidates for the 100% club.
--> Successfully sold the first jointly marketed transaction with AT&T.
--> Oversaw the reorganization into two districts, along with a doubled staff and team-based goal setting.
--> Spearheaded a joint marketing effort after acquisition by AT&T.

Senior Account Executive

Managed sales and marketing in northern NJ in a variety of sales positions with increasing responsibility.

--> Improved sales of Channel Extension products by over 30%; won 20 different awards for performance and leadership.

--> Also served as Senior Account Manager; mentored six other Account Managers.

Prior Experience

Commerce Clearing House - Computax Inc., New York, NY
A $50 million division, specializing in tax services and in-house systems for accountants; formerly RJ Software Systems.

Assistant Division Manager

In charge of sales/marketing strategies for services and systems in the NYC area. Hired, trained, motivated and supervised a professional staff in product lines and company policies.

District Sales Manager

Created an effective sales team of three field representatives in client training, field support and excellent customer service in a NY metro, PA and New England territory.

Area Sales Manager

Personally grew the assigned sales territory in the above area with four sales representatives.

EDUCATION: Fairleigh-Dickenson University, Teaneck, NJ
B.S. Degree in Accounting

• Completed corporate seminars and workshops in Process Development, Management Principles, Successful Sales Techniques, Executive Imaging, Effectiveness Training and Managing Organizational Change.

Sent 15; received six interviews.

ANGEL GUARDIAN
119 Ridge Court
Loveland, OH 45140
Res: 513/555-1731   Ofc: 513/555-9593   angel@ix.netcom.com

CORPORATE INFORMATION SYSTEMS MANAGEMENT

PROFILE:

➤ Comprehensive experience in senior-level leadership of advanced information system and technology functions, with P&L responsibility for corporate policies, standards and strategies in rapidly changing, highly competitive growth environments.

➤ Skilled in new business development, strategic planning, risk analysis, business process reengineering, product innovation, contract negotiation and budget administration.

➤ Well versed in market research processes, including potential analysis/forecasts of demographic, economic and psychographic data and sales performance interpretation.

➤ Advise fellow executives on the business implications of technologies to achieve financial goals; effectively monitor emerging technologies and alternative IS organizational structures; direct high-performance teams through critical startup and restructuring.

➤ Extensive knowledge of object-oriented design methodologies, multiple-tier client/server, WAN/LAN and virtual system technologies; design and implement efficient consumer response, category product management and commerce-based interactive systems.

TECHNICAL:

- *Client/Server and Network Systems:* TCP/IP, Internet/Website developers, Appdesigner, Enera, PowerBuilder, Visual Basic, OSF DCESNA, Ethernet, Token Ring and Novell WAN/LAN.
- *Database Languages:* DB2, IDMS, DB2-6000 and 4GL.
- *Operating Systems:* MVS, VMS, UNIX and CICS.
- *Hardware:* IBM ES/9000s, DEC VAX 3900 and RISC 6000 UNIX.

CAREER BACKGROUND:

Eckstein Consulting, Loveland, OH   2006-Present
Provide consulting services and technical assistance in information system and technologies planning, management and operations, specializing in Year 2000 impact analysis and compliance, ECR systems and commerce-based systems, targeting consumer market businesses.

Key Client

Cruncher Company, Chicago, IL: Contracted to develop an $800,000 sales and marketing system to target demographic/psychographic data for this worldwide magazine publisher, enabling them to identify new markets, forge retail partnerships and re-engineer distribution logistics.
--> Increased sales by 29% and reduced expenses by 35% on system implementation.

G-Greetings, Inc., HQ, Cincinnati, OH   2000-2006
A $650-million, 8,000-employee, international paper product manufacturer and retailer.
Vice President, Information Systems
In charge of the planning, administration and direction of corporate information systems functions, including the Order Processing Department and Telemarketing/Marketing Research Services, with full P&L responsibility for a budget of $12.8 million.

Managed a staff of 170 at headquarters and provided oversight management of 24 IS employees located at four divisions:

- *Paper Factory*, WI, $165 million sales revenue: installed an Island Pacific Retail P.O.S., AS/400 system connecting 160 stores; involved in due diligence proceedings prior to the purchase of this company in 2002.
- *Cleo Division*, TN, $225 million sales revenue: implemented AS/400 gift wrap manufacturing, inventory and distribution systems.
- *Mexico/United Kingdom Divisions*, $16 million in sales revenue: LAN networks, UNIX, PC and distribution systems; part of senior management team to start up operations from ground zero.

Key Results

--> Initiated and produced the first comprehensive company technology strategic and operational plans, including a Year 2000 impact analysis and software/application replacement recommendations.

--> Achieved labor cost savings of $1.5 million by implementing activity-based costing procedures, automated inventory selection and financial/administrative process improvements.

--> Decreased labor costs by an additional $750,000 by implementing a vendor-developed manufacturing and distribution system for carton marking, shop scheduling and pick-to-light applications.

--> Orchestrated the development and implementation of category management, efficient replenishment and computer-assisted ordering programs, including EDI and geodemographic data, to support a rapid 6%–8% growth in sales volume by $3.8 million.

--> Reduced administrative costs by $2.5 million by implementing an EDI/EFT system between suppliers and retail customers, handling 25,000 electronic invoices monthly.

--> Effected a cost avoidance of $400,000 annually in hardware costs; developed a three-tier client/server network and prepared more than 600 customized PC configurations, providing field sales staff access to individual customer sales performance data.

--> Renegotiated hardware and maintenance contracts to increase discounts by 10% on an average annual capital expenditure of $10 million.

Caressa, Inc., Fort Lauderdale, FL   1998-2000
Vice President of Information Systems / Partner LBO
One of seven partners to purchase this family-owned, women's brand-name footwear importer/wholesaler, with five divisions and 60 retail stores nationwide.
--> Directed all information systems and voice/data telecommunications functions.

Prior Experience
R.G. Barry Corporation, Columbus, OH
Vice President of Information Systems / Divisional Officer
Responsible for the planning, administration and supervision of the MIS division for this national manufacturer of shoes and slippers, with a retail division of 110 stores.
Hired, trained and directed 90 professionals in software/systems projects, maintenance of client LAN and database management systems, and post-installation technical support.
Administrated an operating budget of $8 million.
--> Acquired and managed the full Marketing Research Group.
--> Promoted to this position from **MIS Director.**

Ward Foods, Inc., New York, NY
Corporate Director, Information Systems
In charge of the restructuring and operation of MIS, seven data centers and a marketing research team, providing services to multiple divisions of this food manufacturer of candy, snack foods, cookies, pies, seafood and ice cream products.
Managed 105 employees and a $6.8 million operating budget.

--> Created this position, centralized operations and brought marketing research into the MIS function to meet the intensified demand from expanding product lines.

--> Downloaded, compiled and distributed market information from online databases such as *American Demographics Magazine*, Nielsen strategic mapping and Claritas Area Market Management.

--> Introduced television area market research into the advertising campaign for a new candy product rollout in Ohio, Virginia and the throughout the South.

Singer Sewing Machine Company, HQ, New York, NY
Director

--> Gained a solid foundation in managing corporate information systems through progressive promotions from Systems Analyst, Senior Programmer and EDP Auditor.

RELATED EXPERIENCE:

> **Lecturer/Adjunct Faculty:** Management Issues in Technology   2000-Present
> Xavier University
> Ohio State University
> Franklin University
> Various national conferences

AFFILIATIONS:

General Merchandise Apparel Industry Committee (GMAIC)

■ *Voluntary Inter-industry Communication Standards (VICS) Retail Committee, Charter Member,* developed and implemented EDI standard for industry.

■ *Efficient Consumer Response (ECR) Industry Committee/Best Practices Operating Committee Co-Chair, EDI Technology Committee,* developed pilot test and implemented Category Product Management, Continuous Replenishment Program and computer-assisted Ordering systems.

EDUCATION:

Hofstra University, New York, NY
Financial management and auditing coursework.

M.I.T., Boston, MA
Cambridge Technologies

IBM Executive Institute, Poughkeepsie, NY
Kings Park High School, Long Island, NY

Posted on various Internet databases; received at least 50 interviews.

ANN KLEPACZ

P.O. Box 3047 714/555-5772

Newport Beach, CA 92659   Ann@msn.com

SAP CONSULTING

Comprehensive skills in SAP consulting and data warehousing, including complete business analysis and custom solution development for SAP users. Proven ability to build alliances with systems integrators and SAP partners to solve problems on time and under budget.

- Accurately translate theory and training into practice; re-engineer business processes and develop software implementation plans that clients can effectively realize and apply.

- Interface with IT executives, management, and staff, including MIS Directors, CEOs, CFOs and comptrollers, in the analysis of business operations and IT requirements.

- Experience in personal networking and intelligence gathering. Establish strategic alliances and personally manage relationships with accounts, resulting in additional sales.

- Specialize in IT Marketing and Business Development, with diversified experience in marketing, information management and accounting for competitive, high-growth and start-up companies.

ENTERPRISE SOFTWARE EXPERIENCE

Consulting Project Manager - Great Getter, Inc.   2007-Present

Design and implement data warehouses, including data requirements analysis and tools selection. Determine migration/extraction requirements for SAP R/3 and Oracle applications software.

- Trained in Data Modeling, Methodology, Prism Warehouse Executive, Prism Quality Manager, Prism Warehouse Directory, Prism Schedule Manager and Prism Web Access.

SAP Director of Marketing, Systematic Systems Integration   2006-2007

Created marketing collateral for SAP data extraction interface and provided pre-sales technical support.

Defined data access/extraction requirements for SAP projects; specialized in extraction requirements for bar-coding and RF terminals at manufacturing plants, particularly during upgrades of SAP versions.

- Developed an extensive lead tracking system from involvement with SAP user groups, referrals, and contacts met at numerous conferences. Cultivated customer-focused vendor/client relationships.

- Built alliances with vendors marketing complementary products to enable collaboration and increased market intelligence; extensive contact with Big Five, DEC/COMPAQ, HP and Intermec representatives.

SAP Consultant - KPMG   1995-2006

Analyzed business process re-engineering, workflow and SAP data requirements.

Configured FI/CO/SD/MM. Demonstrated SAP functionality and provided technical answers.

- Explained SAP options regarding accounts payable and credit limit choices to clients.

- SAP Partner Academy Training included: Introduction to Sales and Distribution, Shipping, Billing, Conditions and Pricing, Configuration and Organization, Introduction to Materials Management, Purchasing, Inventory Management, Aris Toolset, SAP Fundamental Hierarchy, SAP Navigation, SAP EDI and SAP Security Authorizations.

CONSULTING EXPERIENCE 1991-1995

Marketing, Sales and Seminar Consultant - Apple, Microsoft and Oracle
Consultant to Oracle during the planning of Financial Applications seminars; advised them on target audience, speakers, presentation materials and prospect and lead tracking systems.
Contracted by Microsoft, Apple, Times Mirror, RIA and 30 other companies to produce conferences on CD-ROM for tax research and technology for accounting firms. Contracted nationally known speakers and maintained attendee profiles for use by clients' sales representatives.

- Contracted by Apple to create reports on accountants' influence in the selection of Macintosh for their practices and clients. Focused on accountants' buying behavior, business software for Macintosh vs. PC and suggestions on increasing the use of Macintosh.
- Conceived, outlined and implemented a tax software seminar series at hotels and CPA firms.

Software Implementation and Training

- Created websites and provided consultations, maintenance and promotion to increase traffic.
- Revised accounting/medical billing software procedures and dramatically increased cash flow.
- Provided cost/benefit analysis of various software/hardware options, training and related business costs and changes needed during software implementation; responded to numerous RFPs.
- Instructor for Microsoft NT, Novell Netware and numerous desktop applications courses.
- Implemented accounting software modules, documented customization and trained users.
- Converted data from competitive tax software for numerous CPA firms.

Accounting and Business Reporting Analysis

- Licensed to practice before the IRS for audits since 1994; specialized in high-income clients.
- Successfully convinced the IRS of client's net operating loss, exceeding $400,000, due to fire, without normal documentation; reconstructed loss from secondary sources.
- Tax preparation for partnership and corporations, including consolidated corporations, with related sales tax, property tax and business tax reporting.
- Contracted by an economist for a complex litigation procedure involving 21 groups of real estate partnerships to provide analysis of conflicting financial data dating back 20 years. Reconstructed financial records and prepared spreadsheets and presentations for litigation.

EDUCATION

MBA, University of San Clemente: Concentration in Marketing and International Business.
BA, University of East Florida: Extensive Business and International Studies courses.

Professional conferences attended. SAP TechEd, SAP ASUG User Conference, Microsoft SAP Customer Workshop, SAP Year 2000 Seminar, SAP/Microsoft/DEC Seminar, Microsoft Tech-Ed, Microsoft Professional Developer Conferences and Microsoft Sitebuilder Conference.

Sent 50; received eight interviews.

RANDALL B. SEMANTIC
220 Summer Lane
Toronto, Canada, M4TlB4
Randy@interlog.com   416/555-0874

TELEVISION PRODUCTION / BROADCASTING

PROFILE:

➤ Extensive experience with the Canadian Broadcasting Corporation (CBC), the Olympic Games, the NHL, Major League Baseball, Imperial Life, White Rose and special how-to programs.

➤ Comprehensive experience in television broadcasting and production, including full responsibility for national broadcasting of live and taped sports and special events, entertainment and news programs.

➤ Perform research, writing and development of corporate training and sales videos.

➤ Coordinate all aspects of video and broadcast production, from talent coordination and set design to lighting, camera placement, editing and special effects.

➤ Proficient in all standard and state-of-the-art production techniques, including non-linear computer editing and digital technologies.

EMPLOYMENT: Ambrose College of Technology, North York, Ontario, Canada
Instructor   9/08-Present
Responsible for training 18 students in all aspects of TV production and studio operations, including related theory and lab work.
Plan and implement all lab activities and tests; work closely with students and track individual performance.
Lab subjects include scripting, floor plans, crew positions, studio camera use, ENG/EFP cameras, angle of axis, lighting, video editing, graphic layout, video switchers and systems, character generators, audio boards, set design and direction.
--> Create and supervise a wide range of practical exercises; all students must write, block and shoot a 30-second commercial.
--> Provide experience in camera operations, switching, lighting, computer graphics and all editing functions, including inserting text and graphics.

Rob Francis Productions, Toronto, Ontario   1996-Present
Independent Producer
Effectively manage corporate video productions and broadcast and freelance work, including marketing and training videos, as well as other instructional programs.
Hire and coordinate writers and assist in script writing; manage creative personnel at all levels.
Locate and hire all talent, including actors, commentators, announcers and researchers.

Key accounts include:
McDonald's, KFC, AMC, CBC Enterprises, Imperial Life, the NHL, Proctor & Gamble, Schenley and the Roy Thomson Hall.

Sports broadcast productions include:
The XV Commonwealth Games, Victoria, 2004; Isolation Director at athletics venue for host broadcaster; originated international video and audio production feed to world broadcasters.

The XW Olympic Winter Games, Calgary, 1998; Associate Director at the ski jumping venue for host broadcaster.

CBC TV News: Producer in charge of satellite news gathering and dissemination, as well as on-air coordination.

<u>Red Rose Crafts and Nursery Sales, Ltd.,</u> Unionville, Ontario   1999-2006
Executive Producer / Communications Specialist - Red Rose Productions
Responsible for all aspects of production and management for *The Hobby Garden*, a 65-episode, national TV series with broadcast sales to Global, Life and TVO Networks.

Oversee a $450,000 budget and supervise all staff and crew.

--> Managed budgets and media promotions, while personally selling commercial time to underwrite production costs.

--> Coordinated marketing departments of program sponsors; prepared and produced a wide range of commercials.

Producer and Manager for Red Rose Productions, producing training videos for staff and how-to demos for in-store customer use.

Created and produced craft video titles for retail sale, from concept to package design. In charge of producing all French versions of Red Rose projects.

--> As Co-Chair for the Canada Blooms flower show, produced a profit of $150,000.

<u>Canadian Broadcasting Corporation,</u> Toronto, Montreal, Halifax   1998-1999
Television Producer / Director
Performed full management of sports productions, including the XI Commonwealth Games in Edmonton; directed boxing venue coverage and originated international AV production feed to world satellite feed.

For the XXI Olympic Summer Games in Montreal, directed basketball coverage for ORTO and earned the **1998 TV Award.**

Other projects included (full details on request):
Sports of the XXI Olympiad, Montreal; Montreal Expos Baseball, Hockey Night in Canada, Montreal; World Cycling Championships; the Canada Summer Games and Universiade in Turin, Italy.

Entertainment productions such as: From Our Family to Yours; New Years Eve Live!; Front Page Challenge and the Bob McLean Show.

News and special events: The Journal and The Papal Visit.

RANDALL B. SEMANTIC   **Page Three**

EDUCATION: <u>Ryerson PolyTechnic University,</u> Toronto, Ontario
Radio and Television Arts Diploma
Graduate: Landscape Architecture Certificate Program

<u>McGill University</u> and <u>Concordia University,</u> Montreal
French as a Second Language

COMPUTERS: Skilled in various computer systems: Adobe Premiere for Digital Audio and
Video Editing, Microsoft Word, Excel for spreadsheets, Access for database
management and PowerPoint and Netscape for presentations and Internet access.

MEMBERSHIPS: GWAA: Garden Writers Association of America.
Civic Garden Center and the YMCA.

Sent to five internal postings; chosen as one of three among 56 applicants for interview.

MARK CHECKER
2306 Dover Drive
Hanover Park, IL 60103

630/555-8916   Checkman@yelp.com

EXECUTIVE LEADERSHIP: QUALITY / INVENTORY / COST REDUCTION

PROFILE:

➤ Comprehensive experience in a wide range of business operations, including staff management, quality control, inventory management and management reporting.

➤ Proven ability to build teams and motivate associates to achieve peak performance; skilled in problem analysis and resolution; identify the root causes, develop answers and implement solutions.

➤ Leverage professional communication skills to coordinate various activities between departments; handle multiple priorities and projects simultaneously.

➤ Proficient in Windows 7 systems including Excel, PowerPoint and Word for spreadsheets, seminar presentations, graphs/charts and professional correspondence.

EXPERIENCE: Clarity, Inc., Itasca, IL   2003-Present

Manufacturing Quality Coordinator / Analyst   2010-Present

Responsible for all aspects of quality control, including inspections, documentation, staff supervision and quality reporting for the packing division.
Coordinate the activities of quality auditors and monitor results; train and motivate personnel in procedures, operations and company policies.
Document all inspection data; utilize various spreadsheets to format reports, as well as graphs of inspection results.
Establish and implement action plans to eliminate quality defects.
Conduct regular meetings with the packing group, auditors, supervisors and managers to discuss quality issues.

--> Worked with the corporate Quality Department to develop the proper links for data retrieval from the field.
--> Wrote the quality auditing MPS for the packing group.
--> Championed a TCS / Problem Solving team to attack and resolve issues such as cycle time, cost reductions and quality.
--> Showed a 20% decrease in defects (2010).

Quality Auditor   2007-2010

Performed random inspections of packed crates to determine the quality level of the department.
Documented inspection results on hard copy and entered into UNIX Wingz spreadsheets.
Investigated and identified the root causes for defects created in packing.
Worked with the management team to develop action plans to correct quality mistakes.

Participated in weekly meetings with the Quality Department to discuss quality concerns.

--> Represented Motorola on multiple client visits to China and India.

--> Championed a quality TCS team that was responsible for a 50% decrease in defects within five months.

--> Worked with clients to identify and correct quality problems.

Field Team Leader / Refurb Inventory Control   2007

Traveled to client warehouses to lead the inventory, packing and quality evaluation of refurbishing equipment.

Led Motorola associates in preparing shipments for return back to consolidation warehouses.

Consolidated all refurbishing equipment in appropriate warehouses.

Created a showroom atmosphere for customers to view and evaluate merchandise for possible purchase.

--> Recognized and rewarded for exceptional performance and commitment to job while running an outside packing firm to handle critical customer orders.

Team Leader   2005-2007

Directed a group of 12 to 15 associates in the sorting, verifying and packaging of ancillary and warranty equipment.

Coordinated with planners and schedulers on workload capacities.

Worked with crate vendors and Motorola engineers to develop more reliable crates for our clients.

--> Installed a Productivity Metric that resulted in increased productivity through greater visibility and ownership.

--> Implemented the first Attendance Metric that focused on improving cycle time and workload capacity.

--> Installed a department Reward and Recognition program that resulted in strong morale and increased productivity.

--> Represented the department on a TCS team that streamlined processes to improve cycle time.

Packer
                                                             2003-2005

TRAINING: Completed a wide range of Motorola university courses, including:
Macintosh Excel Introduction, Intermediate and Advanced

Macintosh PowerPoint	*MPC Wingz*
The Six Steps to Six Sigma	*Alternative Thinking*
Continuous Improvement Tools	*QR Training*
Advanced Manufacturing Processes	*Emergency Evacuation*

EDUCATION: College of DuPage / Northwood University, Glen Ellyn, IL
--> Currently pursuing a Bachelor's Degree in Business Administration with a minor in International Business.

Sent 10; received one interview.

DALE EVANS

1135 Fairview Terrace   781/555-4759

Maiden, MA 02148   Dsdy@state.ma.us

EXECUTIVE CONSULTING

PROFILE:

➤ Comprehensive experience in a wide range of business operations, including contract administration, regulatory compliance, staff training and procedure planning/implementation.

➤ Proven ability to troubleshoot and develop creative, innovative solutions to business challenges; successfully manage change for improved performance and efficiency.

➤ Demonstrated success at identifying processes and complex systems; work with clients to streamline operations, establish goals and implement strategies to achieve those goals.

➤ Skilled in team development and project management; communicate objectives, plan and organize work flow and conduct personal, individualized training.

➤ Proficient in Lotus; working knowledge of Excel and Word for report preparation; experience in Internet research.

EXPERIENCE: Department of Public Health, San Francisco, CA

Fiscal Administrator   8/04-Present

Responsible for all aspects of fiscal management and contract administration, including budgeting, project management, expense authorization and training for Justice Resource Institute programs.

Motivate and supervise a staff of seven consultants; handle all personnel administration for the site, including processing of applicants and arranging benefits.

Approve and code all invoices, authorize employee expenses, reconcile bank statements and direct petty cash disbursements.

--> Perform research and data collection for development of special reports.

--> Prepare General Ledger Summary reports.

Grands Management Specialist / Consultant   12/93-8/04

Provided detailed guidance and administrative support to contract managers and agency staff with 300 contracts throughout the state.

Provided proper documentation and regulatory compliance of contracts and grants. Participated in the development of policies and procedures.

Assembled and processed contracts, subcontracts and grants administered by the AIDS bureau to ensure compliance with state policies.

--> Documented and recommended system improvements to the Director of Administration. Implemented and directed approved policy changes.

--> Trained Contract Managers on management systems, general contract requirements, procedures and protocols.

--> Acted as a primary liaison, providing technical assistance to MIS and Purchase of Service units for the development of contract policies.

Camp McKee, Cambridge, MA   1/90-9/93
Contracts Administrator
Responsible for various aspects of contract management, including project
management, client relations, and budgeting.
Worked with clients to develop and administer special billing requirements;
established billing dates according to client payment cycles.
Prepared, issued and processed client invoices.
Assisted project managers in scheduling, budgeting and controlling projects.
--> Filed contracts and related documentation with contract accounting.
--> Prepared and issued a monthly billing report to senior management.

Senior Accounts Payable Specialist
Trained new associates in accounts payable as well as organizational policies.
Coordinated the input of and payment of vendor invoices and check requests.
Disbursed, maintained and reconciled petty cash funds.

EDUCATION: Cambridge College, Cambridge, MA
                    Master of Management
                    Concentration on Organizational Theory and Behavior.
                    Received registered copyright for a thesis on Managing Workplace Diversity.
                    --> GPA 3.8/4.0

                    American International College, Springfield, MA
                    Bachelor of Science Degree
                    Major: Human Relations, minor: Psychology
                    --> Named to the Scholastic All-American Honor Society.
                    --> Received President's Recognition Award for Scholastic Achievement and
                        Leadership.

                    University of Massachusetts at Boston
                    Certificate in Government Auditing

MEMBERSHIPS: Association of Government Accountants
                    --> Recognized in *Government Financial Management Topics* (Dec. 1997)
                        "The Face of Public Service."

                    National Association of Female Executives

Sent 40; received seven interviews.

George A. Stoker

1121 E. Balmoral
Chicago, IL 60656   773/555-6600

ATTORNEY / MANAGER / CONSULTANT

PROFILE:

➤ Comprehensive experience as business manager and attorney, including full responsibility for contract negotiations, staff supervision and new business startups.

➤ Legal background includes litigation and successful resolution of complex matters related to the buying and selling of businesses, contract disputes, family law, arbitration and various real estate transactions, including development of subdivisions.

➤ Business management experience includes procedure planning and budgeting, insurance coordination, purchasing, vendor relations and inventory control.

➤ Familiar with Windows 7 and MS Office systems for data entry and retrieval, correspondence and status reporting.

CAREER BACKGROUND:

Law Offices of G. Stoker, Chicago, IL   2004-Present
Attorney & General Manager
In charge of the setup and operation of this law firm, including the hiring, training and supervision of one associate and two support personnel.
Represent individuals in a wide range of legal matters, including family law and divorce, probate, incorporations, real property transactions, title searches and examinations.
Perform contract writing and corporate asset purchases; counsel clients and oversee corporate buyouts and sales; prior experience with personal injury and worker's compensation cases.

> Supervise all matters of the practice and establish good working relationships with co-counsel and opposing counsel.
> Chosen as legal representative of United Insurance Company on various home and mortgage insurance and licensing issues.
> Advisory Board Member: Attorney's Title Guaranty Fund; County Approved Arbitrator.

All Star Foods, Schaumburg, IL   2000-2004
Manager / Owner
Responsible for profit/loss and virtually all operations of food distributor and bakery, including budgets and cost-effective purchasing and distribution in Illinois.
Developed and managed all functions, including staff hiring, training, supervision and performance review.

> Directed facility maintenance and repairs for an 8,000-square-foot building.

EDUCATION:

John Marshall Law School, Chicago, IL
Juris Doctor Degree
> Licensed to practice in the State of Illinois.

Loyola University, Chicago, IL
Bachelor of Arts Degree
Major: Political Science; Minor: English

Sent eight resumes; received five interviews.

Markus Riser
468 Prairie Avenue
Glendale Heights, IL 60139

630/555-4251   Riser@mark.com

BANKING / MARKETING

PROFILE:

➤ Profit-building skills in sales, marketing and new business development in the banking industry, including competitive analysis, market/demographic research and strategic planning.

➤ Skilled in advertising and creative promotions; plan and conduct sales presentations and communications in a professional manner; fluent in English and French; semi-fluent in Greek and Arabic.

➤ Effectively train and supervise staff in all banking procedures, with a sharp eye on personal customer service; strong background in loan origination, processing and closing.

➤ Familiar with Windows 7 and Premier II for the setup and maintenance of client accounts.

EXPERIENCE: South Urban Bank, Robbins, IL

Branch Manager   2007-Present

In charge of all branch operations, including the hiring, training, scheduling and supervision of up to nine employees in sales, customer service and new accounts.

Responsible for all outside sales, bank promotions, advertising and daily operations.

Handle creative development for print advertisements.

Designed and implemented a customer profile sheet to track client mortgages, deposits and financial status for cross selling and financial planning.

--> Assets have grown from $1 million to $30 million over the last two years.

--> Promoted to this position from:

Assistant Manager   2006

Involved in the setup and operation of the Wheaton location, including all purchase requisitions, staff recruitment, training and quality control.

Worked closely with the Federal Reserve.

--> Selected as one of four in the company to assist in the opening of this bank.

Personal Banker   2001-2006

Established new accounts and determined/met specific customer needs with a strong knowledge of all bank services.

Trainer   **1994-2001**

Conducted extensive staff training for six banks in all operations, including teller procedures and troubleshooting.

Teller   **1993-1994**

<u>Petrie Stores Corporation,</u> Bloomingdale, IL   **1990-1993**

Store Manager

Effectively hired, trained and supervised a team of 16 in all sales and customer service activities.

Coordinated the sales floor, including planning and implementing creative promotions and display setup.

Handled customer returns, quality control and problem situations with tact and a personal, yet professional approach.

--> Gained excellent experience in communications, sales and customer service.

--> Promoted to this position from:

Cashier

EDUCATION: <u>Sorbonne University,</u> Paris, France

                      B.A. Degree in French   **1999**

                      <u>Lewis University,</u> Joliet, IL

                      Trained in Interior Design   **1997**

LICENSE: Licensed Interior Designer

Sent about 70; received eight interviews.

CARL F. WALKER
221 South Windham Lane
Bloomingdale, IL 60108

Res: 630/555-9067   Ofc: 630/555-4103   E-mail: 4657@kwom.com

CORPORATE SALES: E-COMMERCE MARKETING
Willing to Travel or Relocate

PROFILE:

▶ Perform creative, executive leadership of e-commerce marketing and sales functions for consumer and industrial products, with P&L responsibility for business development in domestic and international markets.

▶ Skilled in account acquisition and management, including market research, competitor analysis, lead generation, product introduction, demand forecasting and contract negotiation.

▶ Personally recruit, train and supervise direct and independent sales representatives to meet business and financial goals; orchestrate new business relationships in Europe, Australia, Japan, Central/South America, Mexico and Canada.

▶ Leverage social media networks to identify and penetrate new markets and formulate penetration strategies.

▶ Well-versed in direct/sell-through sales organizations, manufacturing processes and EDI/JIT distribution systems; monitor industry trends and market conditions.

▶ Utilize Macintosh Excel, Windows 7, MS Word, MapLinks, PowerPoint and social media resources.

CAREER BACKGROUND:

Flawless, Inc., (formerly Vera, Inc.), Chicago, IL   2000-Present

An international subsidiary of the publicly traded, $950 million Gee Enterprises firm, manufacturing glass and mat board product for the picture framing and fine arts industries.

Director of International Sales and Marketing   7/97-Present

Promoted to this position to direct the global business expansion objectives of the company.
Handle all aspects of strategic planning for international market development, including creation of marketing plans.
Identify, contact, recruit and contract new distributors.
Arrange for the translation of all marketing materials.

     --> Opened six new distributors on three continents in the first 90 days.

Director of Sales   6/95-7/97

Responsible for a direct and sell-through sales organization nationally and internationally, working closely with a manufacturing/distribution center in Chicago and distribution centers located on the East Coast and in Paris, France.

     --> Reduced the cost of sales by 9% incrementally over three years in a mature market and doubled revenues to $28.5 million in five years.

     --> Provided oversight management of a 300-dealer distribution network; refocused field staff on distributor account maintenance and process improvement to resolve channel problems.

     --> Consolidated customer service and the direct/independent sales operations into three regional territories, and proposed implementation of an operations manufacturing computer system.

     --> Launched five new products, three in 1996, including an anti-reflective glass and mirrors packaged for a custom picture framer.

Director of Sales and Marketing   12/90-6/95

In charge of the planning, administration and direction of worldwide sales and marketing functions, including marketing and customer service, with responsibility for an operating budget of $2.8 million. Supervised three regional sales managers, eight direct sales staff and 21 independent representatives. Directed advertising agency jobs through the creative process and directed prototype testing; contracted key agencies such as Murphy Sutton, RPM Graphics and Spindler Claps Associates.

> --> Increased sales revenues from $14 million to $24 million.
> --> Key player in acquisition due diligence activities of Miller Cardboard Company in 1994, including merger plan and pro forma development.
> --> Conducted annual status report presentations to the Board of Directors and at company national sales meetings attended by the Chairman, Group VP and Division Manager.
> --> Proposed and implemented the first national industry information exchange forums, *Conservation Framing Forum* and *TruVue Forum on Framing Technology*.
> --> Negotiated and secured distributor contracts with firms in Europe, Central/South Americas, Asia/Pacific Rim and North America.

Castle Rock Manufacturing Company, Minneapolis, MN   4/89-12/89
Vice President, Sales and Marketing

Developed the initial marketing plan to pre-sell major capital equipment to the photo processing industry; pre-sold 10 units at $1 million at startup.

Clark Moulding Company, Garland, TX   1987-1989
National Sales Manager   9/88-4/89

Managed 32 independent sales and direct representatives in product development, marketing and promotion activities.

Oversaw a budget of $1.9 million for this manufacturer of extruded aluminum picture framing moldings, sold to the picture frame industry through a national distributor wholesale system.

> --> Member, Corporate Review and Planning Committee.
> --> Devised the first comprehensive sales/marketing strategic plan, generating $10 million in sales.
> --> Promoted from Eastern Sales Manager, 3/87-9/88; restructured 14 territories.

PRIOR EXPERIENCE:

Viracon, Inc., Chicago, IL
Director of Consumer and Industrial Products Division

Responsible for all national sales, marketing and customer service activities, including new product development coordination, product design and marketing strategies for this division manufacturing flat glass products for the appliance, automotive, display and picture framing industries.

> --> Increased sales to $12 million in a highly competitive market.
> --> Developed a customer profile system to improve sales forecasting, inventory control and distributor sales response to product inquiries.

Sales Manager, O.E.M. Products Division

Directed the product/marketing support for 15 company sales representatives and supervised customer service; personally handled all national account contracts.

> --> Revised quoting/pricing procedures and devised cost factors.
> --> Increased sales by 20% over 1992 sales, to $4 million.

Territory Sales Representative

EDUCATION: St. Cloud State University, St. Cloud, MN
                Bachelor of Science Degree in Recreation Business Minor: Marketing

Randy was seeking to relocate; sent about 60 overseas; received two interview offers.

RANDY PROFICIENT

234 Juncal

345 Ciudad de Buenos Aires, Argentina

E-mail: ano@perel.org

Residence: 54.11.4825.5477

EXECUTIVE MANAGEMENT: *CORPORATE OPERATIONS*
CEO, President or Senior Vice President

PROFILE:

➤ Entrepreneurial and Fortune 500 corporate leadership experience in international business development, specializing in breakthrough joint ventures and global partnerships with P&L responsibility, in rapidly changing, highly competitive environments.

➤ Advise CEO, Directors and senior managers on policy issues and emerging industry trends; formulate growth-oriented capital investment strategies to maximize ROI and market share; lead organizations through turnarounds, startups and mergers/acquisitions.

➤ Recruit and mobilize multi-functional, high-performance teams; skilled in client needs assessment, opportunity identification, market positioning and country risk analysis.

➤ Perform product/service introduction and communications logistics with advanced technologies; skilled in capital market financing and investor relations; CPA; MBA.

➤ Well versed in intercultural business practices and communication; interact with government agencies, investment/merchant banks and corporations to forge cross-border, public/private trade alliances and networks; fluent in English and Spanish.

CAREER BACKGROUND:

<u>Huron Consulting,</u> Buenos Aires, Argentina 2008-Present

Independent Contractor

Provide management consulting services in organizational leadership, strategic planning, venture financing, mergers and acquisition and marketing/communications for private and public sector organizations.

→ Fortune 500 clients include Visa, COMSAT, Bell Atlantic, Fiat and Alcatel.

Major Projects

- *TEL (SWW)*: produced and implemented a business plan to develop this company's call center operations throughout Latin America; assessed country risks and market entry strategies for Mexico and Central/South American countries.
- *COMSAT*: chief architect in the creation of a financial and telecommunication consortium for a strategic partner to launch COMSATArgentina; Consortium won the bid to privatize the basic telephone system.
- *Applied Energy Systems*: participated in the privatization of government utilities in Argentina and Brazil.
- *Alcatel*: sold the Argentine subsidiary of this telecommunications firm for a profit of $35 million.
- *Centro de Computos*: pioneered the introduction of state-of-the-art computer systems in Argentina.

<u>Goodrich Capital International,</u> New York, NY 2007-Present

President, Argentina

In charge of this investment bank's South American cross-border M & A operations, located in 12 countries.

→ Completed the Wharton School of Business program *Strategic Thinking and Management for Competitive Advantage*, at the University of Pennsylvania, PA.

Banco Mercurio, Buenos Aires, Argentina   2003-2006
C.E.O. / Board Member
Recruited by the owner of a privately held venture group to start this cross-border retail bank with full-service, technology-based operations.

→ Set up and implemented a Private Banking Division.

→ Achieved a profit of $25 million for this division, despite the continuing economic downturn due to the 2004 Mexican financial markets crisis.

→ Restructured banking and brokerage affiliate operations in Argentina, Uruguay and the Bahamas.

→ Drove up profits to a $60 million profit base from startup, despite the faltering economy.

Banco Del Buen Avre, Buenos Aires, Argentina   1993-2003
Member, Board of Directors / Executive Committee
Elected to the Board of Directors to stem a loss of $63 million in profits and transform operations into an advanced technology-based, customer-oriented financial services business.

→ Introduced the first customer self-service 24-hour banking units into the Argentina retail banking market, including home banking and ATM networks.

→ Generated a net worth of $225 million and profits of more than $50 million annually, which facilitated the sale of this bank to Banco Itau of Brazil.

Spicer and Oppenheim, HQ, New York, NY   1990-2003
Partner in Charge, Latin America
Directed all aspects of business operations in Latin America for this accounting firm, ranked first among Wall Street firms and 12th worldwide.
Other Positions
- *Associate Professor: MIS,* University of Buenos Aires, Argentina
- *Editor/Columnist,* Ambito Financiero: a daily financial journal similar to *The Wall Street Journal*
- *Chairman of the Board/Founder,* Centro de Computos, S.A.: a service bureau offering computer services
- *Board Chairman/Founder,* CAESCO: the first trade organization for the computer industry in Argentina
- *Associate Producer/Correspondent,* CBS TV News, Special Events Unit, New York, NY

DIRECTORSHIPS: Served on numerous boards of directors, including:

Motorola	Bell Atlantic
Telefunken	Visa
Comsat	Fedders
Alcatel	Fiat Group Companies
Cia. Financiera DO-AI	Cia. Financiera Del Plata

EDUCATION: University of Buenos Aires, Argentina
                      Master of Business Administration
                      Certified Public Accountant

Sent about 50; received numerous calls and five interviews.

VINCENT HAMIL

561 Thornton Way
Huntley, IL 60142

630-555-1464
Vhamil@aol.com

SENIOR MANAGEMENT - FINANCIAL OPERATIONS

PROFILE:

- Comprehensive leadership experience in all aspects of corporate finance, general accounting, strategic planning and start-up operations in diverse international markets.
- Solid expertise in budgeting, strategic forecasting, regulatory compliance and the preparation of accurate financial reports; successfully develop and supervise management and staff in all operating policies and procedures.
- Highly skilled in acquiring, implementing and supporting cutting-edge IT infrastructures; fully familiar with all key HR programs, including OSHA, EEOC, AA, ADA and others.
- Proven abilities as a Change Agent, Troubleshooter and Turnaround Specialist in greatly improving productivity, reducing operating costs, meeting strategic objectives and ensuring high morale levels.

EMPLOYMENT: E Link USA, Elk Grove Village, IL   2009-Present
US Controller

In charge of all accounting, finance, collections, HR and IT functions for U.S. operations with this British graphic branding and pre-press services company, with $12 million in revenue.

Ensure total compliance with U.S. laws and regulations relating to compensation, EEOC, AA, ADA and FMLA.

→ Improved the DSO cycle from 220 days to 55 in only three months.

→ Rolled out SAP for this business unit during the same period.

→ Converted the company payroll system to ADP, resulting in better control at three remote sites.

→ Fully supported the start-up of a new branch in Neenah, WI.

→ Saved $80,000 in healthcare costs by streamlining the benefits structure.

LSG / Sky Chefs, Inc., Chicago, IL   1987-2009
City Manager   2009

Specially chosen to oversee all daily operations for a start-up company, SCIS Air Security Corporation, to meet FAA requirements following 9/11.

Hired, staffed, deployed and supervised three supervisors and 60 employees in all new operating policies and procedures.

→ Recognized as leader of the "Department of the Month" three times.

→ Instituted a process to facilitate 10-year background checks on all employees, while raising overall security awareness.

→ Acquired full authorization for corporate operations at O'Hare Airport.

Manager: Finance & Administration   1999-2001

Directed a group of two managers, one financial analyst and 25 clerical staff in all accounting and financial functions for the $80 million Chicago, IL, office.

Continued to coordinate key IS and HR duties; active member of the IT Performance Management Team.

→ Improved department productivity by up to 35% across the board through major process improvements, resulting in higher customer satisfaction levels.

Manager of Administration   1996-1999

Responsible for all accounting functions, such as payroll, general ledger, accounts payable/receivable and collections for the $40 million San Francisco, CA, operation. Effectively handled budget planning, financial statement preparation, cost analysis and market trend studies.

Recruited, trained and supervised one HR manager and six clerical staff in all operating policies and procedures.

→ Chosen to oversee daily operations for a $5 million start-up facility servicing small retail clients in San Jose, CA.

→ Performed many of the duties of a Senior Controller and all-purpose troubleshooter, as well as for IS and HR requirements.

→ Co-leader of a team tasked with identifying and championing better standards and policies companywide.

Controller   1989-1996

Led a group of nine clerks in handling key financial duties for the Chicago, IL, office, worth $80 million in annual revenue.

Produced weekly forecasts, monthly financial statements and annual budgets.

Greatly assisted in the hiring, training and deployment of exempt and hourly employees.

→ Fully reorganized and implemented the benefits and compensation package for clerical staff.

→ Automated the preparation of billing and payroll statements.

→ Instituted new union/non-union health and 401(k) benefits, which helped integrate a new acquisition, Caterair, in Washington, D.C.

→ Promoted to this position from Accounting Supervisor in Los Angeles, CA, as well as Chicago, IL.

Supply Room Supervisor   1987-1989

In charge of leading a team of 15 employees providing adequate catering service for all flights out of Detroit, MI.

Gained hands-on experience in a wide range of operational functions, including inventory control, strategic forecasting and project management.

→ Recognized by a key client, Northwest Airlines, for excellent job performance in time-sensitive situations.

→ Worked full-time while attending university; promoted to this position through levels of increasing responsibility.

EDUCATION: Northern Illinois University, DeKalb, IL   2002

Executive M.B.A. degree; emphasis on International and Global Management.

* Selected to attend a two-week seminar on International Business in Shanghai, China, 2001.

* Participated on a quality improvement project to improve cash flow and sales tax reporting processes for Interlake, Inc.

University of Michigan, Dearborn, MI   1984

B.S. degree in Financial Management; minor in HR Management.

**PROFESSIONAL
TRAINING:**   Fully familiar with Windows XP/NT, MS Office and various financial packages, such as Peachtree, Hyperion Budgeting System (SAP), KRONOS and CODA.

Sent 18; received six interviews, three solid offers, two strong potential offers and a $10,000 increase by following our interview and salary-negotiating tips. William was unemployed for almost a year. We use this as a reference in our offices.

William J. Barrett

57 N. Dare Avenue		**Res: (773) 555-9571**
Chicago, IL 60641	**Barrett1@worldnet.net**	**Cell: (773) 555-4716**

Sales Engineer / Account Manager

PROFILE:

➢ High-impact, executive talents in new business development, strategic planning, marketing, staff management and team leadership, with P&L responsibility for market penetration, development and territory management.

➢ Skilled in business-to-business account acquisition, management and retention, as well as project management, product research and development; plan and conduct presentations to senior-level executives.

➢ Proficient in opportunity identification, lead generation and the capitalization of market opportunities to increase revenues, grow market share and maximize profitability. Author and present technical literature to scientific and trade associations; evaluate technical and project requirements.

➢ Provide effective sales leadership and training to distributors and representatives while building relationships with prestigious OEM accounts; train, motivate and manage high-performance sales teams to meet business goals and objectives.

EXPERIENCE: Uptown Motors, Torrance, CA   12/99 – 11/10
Sales Engineer

Sold industrial motors and controls to OEM engineers, as well as provided technical sales support to independent representatives and distributors.

Provided technical support and training to clients related to the use and operation of products.

Identified sales opportunities, generated leads, prepared quotes and sales reports.

Serviced the following markets: Material Handling, Industrial Automation, Automotive, Machine Tool, Medical, Laboratory, Food and Packaging.

→ Increased base accounts from 40 to 80.

→ Produced consistent increases in sales during tenure; 1999: $437,000; 2000: $953,000; 2001; $1,245,000; personal sales in 2002 were $1,168,000, down only 10% while overall company sales dropped 40%.

→ Developed marketing and pricing strategies for OEM and distribution sales channels.

→ Introduced two new products, becoming the national sales leader for one, and placing second in sales for the other.

→ Created high-level relationships with key accounts.

→ Proposed changes in products based on client requirements as necessary to meet their needs.

→ Planned and conducted technical training to client employees, independent representatives and distributors in a formal class setting, training 50 staff.

→ Diagnosed and resolved problem issues with installed equipment.

→ Sales averaged three times higher than other Sales Engineers.

→ National winner of the 2000 USA Goldrush Sales Campaign out of 23 Sales Engineers.

Itoh Denki USA, Wilkes-Barre, PA   7/98 – 10/99

Sales Executive

Performed all marketing activities for electric motors, including lead generation, account acquisition, retention and management.

→ Served as Team Leader of four that created a supplier agreement.

→ Personally negotiated and closed a supplier agreement with the #1 material handling company in the U.S.

Strandex Corporation, Madison, WI   1996 – 1998

Marketing and Product Development Consultant

Researched and developed a unique process and production system for thermoplastic composite technology used as a substitute for wood.

→ Developed strategic alliances with Washington State University and international equipment suppliers.

→ Initiated and supported commercial presentations with potential licensees, including Armstrong Flooring and Louisiana-Pacific, among others.

→ Wrote and presented technical information for scientific and trade association publications.

→ Developed and co-authored Small Business Innovation & Research Grant proposals to obtain federal funding.

Chicago Fabrication and Supply, Chicago, IL   1990 – 1998

Sales Manager

Directed all marketing strategies for this designer of custom components for industrial clients.

→ Directed and monitored a sales representative.

→ Increased sales from $800,000 to $1.3 million in the first year and $1.8 million the second year.

Matsushita Electric Corporation, AKA Panasonic, Secaucus, NJ   1987 – 1990

Sales Executive

Increased sales from $240,000 to $1.2 million in three years.

→ Developed special market sales accounts throughout 11 states with corporate and industrial clients.

→ Designed national marketing and sales promotion programs.

→ Provided sales forecasts and analyzed market conditions.

EDUCATION: University of Utah, Salt Lake City, UT

                      Architecture

                      Member of the Graduate School of Architecture Student Advisory Board

Sent about 50; received four interviews.

Janice T. Stamper

3456 Ava Road   eck@mediaone.net
Reading, MA 01867   781/555-6913

SENIOR VICE PRESIDENT / CEO

A position utilizing the ability to adapt, capitalize and thrive in rapidly changing business environments.

PROFILE:
➤ Comprehensive, executive experience in new business development, including full P&L responsibility for strategic planning and high-tech product lines.

➤ Effectively set up and manage highly profitable business units, from budgeting to effective team training, management and motivation.

➤ Proven ability to expand profits through creative planning and coordination of all essential functions, from initial concept to coalition building, PR and market establishment, to vendor sourcing and quality control.

➤ Oversee market research, creative promotions and top-level contract negotiation; analyze competitors and design/meet financial models; experience with Internet-based software and systems.

➤ Holder of several successful patents; skilled in the commercialization of new technology, including direct interface with customers, market analysis and high-level strategic planning; oversee product pricing, costing and market segmentation.

EXPERIENCE:
JCN Corporation, Rochester, NY, and Burlington, MA
Document Service Group   2005-Present
Vice President, Business Development
Oversee all P&L functions related to the commercialization of JCN technologies and integrated systems solutions.

Handle extensive primary and secondary market research and the writing of business plans, as well as industry segmentation, competitive analysis and benchmarking.

Directly involved in developing and marketing incubator systems to sell to the publishing industry, with the potential to expand JCN into billion-dollar markets.

Manage designers, architects and coders in the development of such products as high-speed, turnkey book production systems for copying, cover printing, cutting and binding.

Establish goals and controls; monitor results to consistently increase profit margins, enhance market position, reduce operating costs and meet strategic objectives.

→ Create and implement accurate financial models to maximize market penetration at the lowest possible cost.

→ Recognized by the publishing industry for the "Book In Time" program, generating more than 500 senior management leads in the publishing industry in nine months; this is now the subject of a Harvard Business School case.

→ Developed and managed the highly regarded "Pony Express" program, an Internet printing method tied to major overnight delivery carriers.

→ Primary Architect for Xerox's professional service organization (XPDS), providing systems integration focused on document management.

→ Performed competitive benchmarking work on Hewlett-Packard, resulting in total restructuring of the Channels organization (SOHO products).

<u>Electronic Data Systems (EDS),</u> Cambridge, MA   1994-2005
Partner

As partner with the management consulting group, hired and directed a strategic planning team to work with SBUs and sell additional, non-outsourcing services.

This group was eventually combined with another EDS acquisition, A.T. Kearney.

<u>Braxton Associates,</u> Strategy group of Deloitte and Touche, Boston, MA
Director / Partner   1990-1994

Full P&L responsibility for marketing and personal sales of more than $1 million annually.

Developed successful corporate and business unit strategies for a wide range of domestic and international companies.

Created new and revised strategic plans.

A sampling of companies and projects includes:

Central Regional Bell Operating Company: Researched and assessed the market for delivery of interactive and passive broadband services to homes and small businesses.

Eastern Regional Bell Operating Company: Directed a competitive benchmarking and financial analysis of regional Bell operating company ownership of cable services.

Pennsylvania Telecom Commission: Directed 20 focus groups across the state to gauge public receptivity to video-on-demand services.

A fiber optic manufacturer: Performed acquisition screening for potential candidates in the fiber optic industry. Spun-off a multilayer capacitor manufacturing operation to a major competitor.

A major cable TV electronics supplier: Determined customer needs for this major manufacturer of TV cable boxes. Assessed manufacturing options for a new diode manufacturing facility in Europe.

The largest electrical products supplier: Responsible for channel strategies, including pricing, competitive analysis, distribution streamlining, direct sales and working with manufacturers' representatives for industrial products.

An office products supplier: Developed strategic plans to transition from old to new technologies.

A major publisher: Determined manufacturing equipment needs, plant locations and consolidation efforts.

The largest photographic supplier: Determined market acceptance criteria for a CD-ROM–based product.

The government of Taiwan: Assessed social and economic effects of acquiring the multi-billion dollar McDonnell Douglas commercial airplane manufacturing operation.

A major home builder. Developed strategies for penetration of new housing segments.

* A wide range of projects—not listed—were related to printed circuit boards, photographic plates, automotive/scientific instrumentation and A/E design services.

Chomerics Corporation, Woburn, MA   1989-1990
Director of Marketing
Successfully marketed and sold computer peripherals to OEM accounts.
Note: This company was acquired by AMP, which relocated to Ohio.

Prior Experience:

Polaroid Corporation, Cambridge, MA
Engineering Manager
Directed engineering teams in the design of integrated circuits and advanced imaging technologies.
* Holder of seven patents used in millions of consumer and industrial camera systems, including analog, digital and microprocessor designs.

EDUCATION:

Massachusetts Institute of Technology, Cambridge, MA
Bachelor of Science in Electrical Engineering
GPA: 4.2/5.0

Boston University, Graduate School of Business, Boston, MA
Master of Business Administration with Honors

Harvard Business School Executive Marketing Course

Sent 35; received nine interviews: four from headhunters and five from companies.

RALPH S. OLOG

237 Heather Lane
Bartlett, IL 60103   Whynot@yep.com   630/555-9676

CFO / CONTROLLER

PROFILE:

➤ Comprehensive experience in the direction and setup of accounting, finance and information systems, with full responsibility for procedures, mergers, acquisitions and special projects.

➤ Skilled in risk management and capital equipment selection and justification, including cost-effective contract negotiations with vendors and suppliers.

➤ Utilize Platinum, Ross Renaissance systems, WAN setups, Windows 7/XP/NT, Lotus and Excel for spreadsheets and status reporting; familiar with WinView and WinFrame, Novell and UNIX, as well as MRP, ADP, Ceridian and Simplex systems.

➤ Analyze and streamline all key systems for multiple locations, including accounts payable/receivable, payroll, credit, collections and benefit plans, including 401(k) and profit sharing.

EMPLOYMENT:

<u>Millenium Pizza Products LP,</u> Version, IL
Formerly part of <u>Century Management, Inc.</u> (below)
CFO / Controller   2005-Present
In charge of all finance, accounting and MIS operations for this multi-site manufacturing company, with sales of $80 million.
Handle extensive budgeting and project reviews.
Effectively manage all treasury functions, including extensive contact with banks, insurance brokers and the evaluation of alternative financing.
Train and supervise a team of 12 in all accounting and computer services.
Oversee financial statement preparation, AP/AR, billing and payroll functions.

- Acted as lead person for the installation of a Ross MRP system, using a Novell network and a UNIX base; currently switching to NT.
- Consolidated two manufacturing companies and added a third company; merged them into one entity.
- Selected and installed a Simplex time card system.
- Secured financing for a $24 million expansion of the Schaumburg location, as well as the previous $16 million buildout, utilizing operating leases and other standard types of financing.

<u>Century Management, Inc.,</u> Chicago, IL
CFO / Controller   1990-2005
Responsible for all accounting and finance operations for this $30 million general partner, managing multiple partnerships, including two manufacturing facilities, three separate restaurants, three holding companies and a real estate partnership.
In charge of training and supervising up to six in all financial statement preparation, AP/AR, billing/payroll functions, and MIS procedures.

- Established all financial reporting systems.
- Treasury functions included the evaluation of alternative financing and working with banks and insurance brokers.

The Havi Group, L.P., Westmont, IL   1988-1990
Manager: Financial Analysis
Developed and supervised all essential corporate accounting, risk management and financial analysis functions for this $1.5 billion food service distribution and purchasing services company.
*   Projects included the analysis of acquisition candidates, strategic planning and annual budgeting.
*   Directly involved in developing and implementing all corporate finance policies and procedures.

Stalev Continental, Inc., Rolling Meadows, IL   1987-1988
Senior Internal Auditor
Conducted detailed financial, operational, capital expense, and special project audits of food and manufacturing facilities.
Supervised two staff auditors in the execution of all audit processes, including planning, fieldwork and the preparation of audit reports.
*   Directed the setup of standard accounting systems and procedures for a newly acquired company.

Anchor Hocking Corporation, Lancaster, OH   1985-1987
Staff Auditor
Performed operational and financial audits for this $750 million manufacturer of table-ware, hardware and packaging products.
Conducted plant and divisional audits of inventory, standard costs, accounts payable/receivable, insurance and payroll functions.
Reviewed and evaluated the adequacy of internal controls surrounding these functions.
*   Worked closely with senior management and produced formal reports and presentations for audit findings and recommendations for system improvements.

Prior Experience
Wasson and Company, CPAs, Newport, KY
Staff Accountant
Provided all major accounting services to businesses in Cincinnati and Kentucky, including the preparation of tax returns, audits, reviews and statements.

EDUCATION: University of Cincinnati, Cincinnati, OH
B.B.A. Degree: Accounting
Accounting GPA: 3.69/4.0

*   **Cooperative Education Program:** Gained practical accounting experience with two companies: Alexander Grant and Hydra Systems.

Certified Public Accountant: State of Ohio

Mailed 90; received 10 interviews.

STEVEN B. TIRED

3451 Gain Street
Westborough, MA 01581
Res: 508/555-5125   joinin@aol.com   Fax: 508/555-1853

MANAGEMENT / CONSULTING

PROFILE:

➤ Successful executive experience in new business development and business system analysis, including full P&L responsibility for creative sales, marketing and project management.

➤ Skilled in long- and short-term strategic planning and organizing, coordinate startup operations and quickly capitalize on rapidly changing market trends.

➤ Effectively hire, train, supervise and motivate staff and management teams in all operations, from initial product development to promotions, distribution and networking.

➤ Conduct in-depth analyses of entire business systems and communicate with technical staff and managers to improve operations, ranging from sales to accounting and internal functions.

➤ Handle multi-million-dollar contract negotiations, as well as written and oral presentations in a personal, yet professional manner.

EXPERIENCE: Stephanie's, Inc., Westborough, MA   1/07-Present
Executive Consultant
Established - and currently manage - this executive management consulting business, including extensive business analysis, system development and project execution.

Key accounts include:

June 2008-Present: **VP: Marketing/Business Development** for Interactive Stuff, Inc. Developed, produced and marketed high-quality Internet, online and PC CD-ROM games. This company owns iMagic Online, a pay-for-play online service with customers from more than 70 countries; titles are sold through 15,000 outlets worldwide.

Sept. 2007-Sept. 2008: **Interim Chief Executive** for Itchu, Int'l.
Established a new entertainment division, "The Print Club" (a $2 billion business in Japan), to produce and place photo sticker kiosks; coordinated partners in Japan.
In charge of all procedures, staffing and the development of detailed business plans.

Initial shipments began in December, 2007, with initial orders exceeding $1 million; projected 2008 sales are $20 million.

* Itochu is one of the largest trading companies in the world, with gross sales exceeding $160 billion.

Jan.-Sept., 2007: Vice President of **Sales and Marketing** for Virtual Music Entertainment, Inc.

Responsible for creative planning and new business development, including sales and marketing, the writing of business plans, coordinating corporate partners, finding new partners such as Creative Labs, and managing international relationships.

- VMS develops software with proprietary technology to add interactivity to any CD-ROM; artists include Aerosmith, The Who and the estates of Janis Joplin, Jimi Hendrix, The Grateful Dead and Stevie Ray Vaughn.

Virtual Entertainment, Inc., Needham, MA   2/99-12/06

Senior Vice President: Sales and Marketing

Directed sales and marketing for this emerging publisher of entertainment software products.

Creatively managed direct mail, retail and direct consumer response to home users. Additional responsibility for OEM bundling and the professional market.

A full range of business development efforts included creative packaging, advertising, radio & TV promotions, and various public relations events.

- Successfully doubled sales volume from under $600,000 to more than $1.2 million in nine months.
- Personally managed the largest sales rep. firm for SMP software.
- Worked closely with graphic designers to develop a "look" for product lines.
- Established corporate direct mail programs that improved cash flow, expanded the market and allowed this company to improve gross margins.

LG Electronics, Inc., formerly GoldStar, Englewood Cliffs, NJ   10/94-2/99

Vice President / General Manager

Established a new division, including all fiscal matters, team hiring, procedures and operations for this subsidiary of LG Group, a $60 billion conglomerate manufacturing products for GoldStar and Zenith based in Seoul, Korea.

Acted as corporate spokesperson for the 3DO hardware business.

Directed a complete packaging design makeover.

Developed and negotiated all contracts with software developers.

Member of the executive committee, involved in all U.S. operations.

- Created a comprehensive marketing campaign and successfully coordinated efforts of 3DO partners, including Panasonic, Electronic Arts and the 3DO company.
- Successfully launched an innovative marketing campaign and three software titles; improved market share in the 3DO category from less than 15% during the first few months to more than 65%.
- Established a new division and expanded sales volume by more than $20 million in the first year.

Sega of America, Inc., Redwood City, CA   1992-1994

Group Director: Sales / Marketing

Most recently in charge of sales and marketing for the eastern U.S.; responsible for a team of six and sales exceeding $500 million.

Responsible for customer negotiations and developing partnership programs.

Oversaw budgeting, planning and allocation for all product categories in the region.

- Directed the launch of a new toy division as National Director of Sales and Marketing for the entire country. This highly successful project expanded distribution and built first-year revenues to almost $100 million; helped establish Sega as one of the top 10 toy companies in its first year.
- Personally developed very strong relations with major corporations, while greatly improving customer relations.
- Gained computer experience in the development of sales and inventory models.

Child World, Inc., Boston, MA   1990-1992

Vice President, Merchandising

Directed a team of 12 buyers and all corporate negotiations, product selections, overseas product development and all financial planning.

- Responsible for more than $500 million in annual sales volume in such categories as electronics, video games, juvenile products, bicycles, seasonal products and preschool items.

EDUCATION: Ohio State University, Columbus, OH

                         B.A. Degree: Economics

Sent three; received two interviews and a new job.

JOHN R. CROCKER

446 Spring Drive, #315
Roselle, IL 60172   Dunno@yep.com   630/555-1363

SYSTEM ANALYSIS / DESIGN / PROGRAMMING
A position where skills in project management would be of value.

PROFILE:
- Extensive background in business application design, coding, testing, documentation, staff training, post-installation evaluation and technical assistance.
- Proven ability to communicate complex information in understandable terms to non-technical personnel.
- Plan and conduct executive presentations; research and write proposals, system documentation and client reference materials.

TECHNICAL:
- Proficient in Tandem languages, software and operating systems including Tandem TAL, COBOL, Pathway/SCOBOL, Enable, Enscribe, DDL and Tandem Guardian.
- Knowledge of IBM PL/l, Basic Assembler Language, COBOL, IMS DB-DC and MVS.

CAREER BACKGROUND:

No Problem Data, Inc., Itasca, IL   8/06-Present
Lead Programmer / Analyst
Perform detailed system analysis, design, programming, testing, documentation and installation of this company's wireless dispatching system for utility customers.
Develop and customize systems to meet specific customer needs; modify TAL and COBOL pathway servers for multiple customers and write server programs for new customers.

Quickie Computing Corporation, Elk Grove Village, IL   1987-8/06
Senior Programmer / Analyst
Responsible for all aspects of analysis, design, programming, testing, documentation and installation of online check authorization systems for retail food service businesses.
Determined customer specifications/requirements, working closely with client/company personnel, including engineers and systems trainers.
Estimated project schedules and costs; prepared job quotes for sales proposals and bids.
Trained and supervised junior programmers/analysts.
Interfaced with the Project Coordinator to produce reference and training manuals.
→ Received a letter of commendation and bonus for consistently high performance.
→ Innovated the "driver's license on-the-fly" access method for check authorization systems and provided the undergirding documentation for multimerchant systems design.

Major Projects
- *Eagle Foods, Appletree Foods, F&M*—lead analyst assigned to check authorization programs and the CRT system.
- *Safeway Foods*—shared lead analyst assignment and backup analyst for the CRT system.
- *Walgreen's, Sunrise, Schnucks and National Stores*—backup systems analyst.

<u>Control Data Corporation (CDC),</u> Park Ridge, IL   1983-1987
3M purchased the health care system and closed this facility.

Senior Programmer / Analyst, CDC   2/85-3/87
Retained to integrate the CDC and Sentry Data software.

→ Selected to write the interface between the CDC registration system and Sentry Tandem-based patient accounting system for full integration.

→ Upgraded and maintained the Sentry Data registration system under pre-existing contracts.

Senior Programmer / Analyst, Sentry Data, Inc.   5/83-2/85
Managed the Tandem-based health care system for hospitals, including module customization in accordance with client specifications.

→ Specialized in the patient registration subsystem.

→ CDC purchased the rights to Sentry Data's software.

Prior Experience:

<u>First National Bank of Chicago,</u> Chicago, IL

Senior Program / Analyst, International Systems Group
Provided technical assistance to the bank's New York Edge Act office, including business application design, development, implementation, module enhancement and modification.

→ *Applications:* accounts payable/receivable, cash management, international cash letter, profit allocation and financial statement preparation.

→ Primary resource for worldwide support of the International Banking pay-receive system.

→ Developed main customer account statement programs to provide clients with reports from the SWIFT 950 and the International Balance Reporter cash management systems.

› Created the ability for the New York office to make international clearing house payments in New York; increased payment transaction capability to a peak volume of 2,000 payments per day from 600 daily payments.

<u>Northern Trust Company,</u> Chicago, IL

Senior Programmer, Information Systems and Services
Performed a wide range of programming activities, including business system analysis pre-planning, feasibility reporting, functional specification and DDA system interface design.

→ Supervised year-end testing of the Savings system.

→ Chaired the DDA ad hoc committee to develop system maintenance procedures.

→ Served as Training Coordinator for the Retail Banking Division of the IS Department.

TRAINING: <u>Numerous seminars and courses completed include:</u>
■ Tandem seminars in Concepts and Facilities, TAL, GUARDIAN, Data Communications and System Management.

EDUCATION: <u>Roosevelt University,</u> Chicago, IL
B.G.S. degree candidate in Computer Science; Focus: Business Information Systems

<u>University of Wisconsin,</u> Madison, WI
B.A. degree candidate in Journalism

Sent 50; received seven interviews and a new job.

SUSAN BRIGHTER
2242 Hampton Street
Naperville, IL 60565

Res.: 630/555-1547   Brighter@xnet.com   Fax: 630/555-2569

TELECOMMUNICATIONS / IT PROJECTS

PROFILE:

➤ Cutting-edge skills in corporate telecommunications, including networking routing, administration, account updating and system debugging/maintenance.

➤ Effectively troubleshoot IRQ and 1/O conflicts; map Novell networks; familiar with NT application servers, including backups, monitoring, anti-virus and documentation.

➤ Skilled in MS Office and Macintosh systems, as well as Lotus, Office Works and cross-platform functions; familiar with staff hiring, training and supervision.

➤ Utilize and/or install modems, network interface cards, memory, power supplies, scanners, fax servers, local/network printers and programmable telephone equipment.

➤ Knowledge of general accounting, including accounts payable/receivable, general ledgers, budgeting, forecasting, tax preparation and status reporting.

EXPERIENCE: Barley Technical Corp., Wheaton, IL   2006-Present
Ranked #123 among the Inc. 500, with employees in 20 states.
Office Manager / System Administrator
Reporting directly to the president, administer and maintain Novell 3.12/NT 4.0 servers, a 24-node Ethernet network and all related hardware and software.
Personally maintain and administer network and local printers, scanners and a fax server.
Supervise two employees in accounts receivable, payroll and general reception, including employee relocations.
Effectively train employees on new software installations.
→ Assisted in construction buildouts, including contractor relations and loan negotiations.
→ Acted as Project Accountant for the build-out of three offices.
→ Administer 40l(k), profit sharing and medical plans.
→ Responsible for all human resources and accounting functions; procure international visas for consultants; coordinate job fairs and special occasions.

Midwest Fertility Center, Ltd., Downers Grove, IL   2006
Eight locations in two states with 50–60 Employees.
Controller: Reported to the President
Saved more than $70,000 in commissions created by software design problems.
Performed extensive research and troubleshooting to correct problems using analytical skills.
Responsible for financial accounting, reporting and analysis, as well as A/R, A/P, payroll, job costing and inventory control.
Located and negotiated with vendors and suppliers; handled cost-effective purchasing and contract supervision.
→ Acted as project coordinator for a Surgi-Center build-out and construction.
→ Consulted with owners regarding business endeavors in real estate and joint ventures.

St. Petronille Church, Glen Ellyn, IL   1992-2005
Bookkeeper
Performed all essential bookkeeping functions and reported to the chairman of finance.
This church consisted of 2,300 families, a school of 400 students K-8, and a religious ed
program with more than 600 students.
Responsible for all accounting functions, including contributions, A/P, A/R, general
ledger, payroll, budgeting, bank reconciliations and financial statements.

→ Setup a peer-to-peer system for six computers.
→ Proposed, researched, purchased and installed an 11-module, integrated accounting and
   management system by Omega C.G. Ltd.; wrote the program to convert member data.
→ Uncovered an embezzlement scheme involving over $70,000 annually of a total
   budgeted income of $2.1 million.
→ Prepared and consolidated financial statements for reporting to the Diocesan controller.
→ Implemented policies for 50 to 65 full-time and part-time employees, in compliance
   with state and federal labor laws, and maintained all personnel files.
→ Analyzed, monitored and consolidated budgets for 15 departments; prepared the
   salary budget for 13 staff managers according to Diocesan guidelines.

CJ's Accounting and Taxes, Naperville, IL   1990-1991
Self-employed: Public Accountant and Consultant
Compiled monthly financial statements for corporations and year-end financials for six
corporations, two partnerships, two sole proprietorships and approximately 35 individuals.
Utilized a Macintosh computer with Peachtree Insight G/L software and after-the-fact
payroll, processed on an Excel spreadsheet.

→ Filed all necessary tax forms, including 941, 940, 1120, 1065, 1040, STL, IL.501,
   Worker's Compensation and union reports.

Carpetland USA, Munster, IN (Headquarters)   1988-1989
Office Manager - Reported to the Regional accounting manager.
Responsible for the accounting department, including general ledger maintenance and
analysis, account reconciliations, labor and material variances and overseeing A/P and A/R.

→ Uncovered a scheme by the sales manager to alter figures on the computer.
→ Recovered $20,000 of charge invoices never processed because of a fire.

Malibu Interiors, Downers Grove, IL   1987-1988
Home furnishings retailer with annual gross sales of over $4 million.
Accounting Office Manager - Reported to the president.

Prior Experience:
* Accounting instructor for Omega Software Corporation (temporary assignment).
* Air Traffic Controller.
* Internal Revenue Collector.

EDUCATION: College of DuPage, Glen Ellyn, IL
                 Associate's Degree: Computer Information Systems
                 Associate's Degree: Accounting
                 CURRENTLY STUDYING for CNE Certification.

Sent only one to a headhunter; received three interviews and a new job.

Noel Church, CPIM, CIRM

1123 Water Park #19
Van Nuys, CA 91401
Days: 310/555-8433   lac@ey.com   Eves: 818/555-8062

SENIOR IT CONSULTANT / PARTNER

PROFILE:

➤ Comprehensive experience in complete project management, including the setup and streamlining of ERP and Oracle applications for highly profitable manufacturing and distribution.

➤ Perform detailed analysis of legacy systems, as well as cross-functional IT and logistics management; familiar with ISO 9002, FDA and GMP requirements.

➤ Experience in complete supply chain management with certification in CPIM and CIRM through APICS; analyze and streamline supply chain requirements regardless of software.

➤ Skilled in writing training materials, documentation and conducting training programs on real-time system use by staff and management.

➤ Technical background in a wide range of computer systems and networks, including state-of-the-art databases, RF terminals, bar codes and data access tools for in-depth analysis and prompt data entry/retrieval.

EXPERIENCE: Superb Controls, Chat, CA   7/03-Present

This company manufactures and distributes disposable supplies for hospitals and operating rooms.

ERP Implementation Manager

Responsible for the setup and implementation of supply chain, inventory and operations planning functions using Oracle ERP applications software for six manufacturing and seven distribution centers in the U.S. and Canada for this $270 million company.

Directly supervise a team of five in MRP, including writing - and teaching from - training materials.

Perform ERP (enterprise resource planning) with a two-year project budget exceeding $17 million.

Handle all budget planning for financial, order entry and technical systems.

Active member of the SAM (software for agile manufacturing) team; identified and purchased enterprise-wide software for running the company.

Coordinate full system implementation, including operational analysis, solution design and identification of business needs to build pilot environments, test software and meet changing business requirements.

• Perform detailed incorporation of: domestic and international forecasting, DRP, safety stock levels (specific to product volume demand history), sourcing rules, MDS and MPS options and loads, as well as MRP and min/max planning.

• Utilized an Oracle memory-based planning engine for planning runs of minutes rather than hours.

• Designed a supply-chain process to allow production and distribution to function in a demand flow environment.

- The first plant went live on time and under budget, using Oracle NCA version 10.7 for full manufacturing, encompassing inventory, BOM, costing, WIP, supply chain and full implementation of HR.
- Involved in preparing RFI and RFQ documents.

MRP II Manager

Managed systems to coordinate manufacturing resources and planning, especially related to order processing, purchasing, inventory control and shipping of $80 million in annual sales volume in the division.

Coordinated the entire operations budget while standardizing units of measure.

Redesigned production assembly areas.

- Designed, implemented and installed an RF (radio frequency) terminal network for real-time transaction processing.
- Implemented a bar code marking program.
- Substantially contributed to improving inventory accuracy to 99%.
- Established procedures for change processes that complied with FDA, BMP and ISO 9001 requirements, yet reduced lead times for quick change implementation.
- Assembled an Executive Information System (EIS) to summarize mainframe data in graphical format for daily management review of business status.
- Computerized shop finite scheduling on the shop floor for optimal allocation of machines and tooling.

Materials Management Solutions, Van Nuys, CA   3/91-6/03
Consultant

Developed and implemented materials management projects related to cost-effective purchasing, receiving, shipping, warehousing, bar coding, MRP II and computer systems.

Retained primarily by clients in both manufacturing and service industries.

Baxter Healthcare Corporation, Glendale, CA   3/81-2/91
Most recent positions first:
Project Manager

Directed special projects as well as purchasing, vendor relations, contract negotiations and inventory control for 15 Baxter plasma collection centers.

Supervised one purchasing coordinator and an inventory control coordinator.

Gained experience with EDI specifications and field layouts.

Directed the fast track, final validation of the Baxter Screening Lab computer system.

- Oversaw $1.2 million in capital projects for lab redesign and equipment.
- Negotiated a successful agreement with a major supplier, resulting in a 15% savings on production supply parts.
- Designed and implemented a bar code system for electronic ordering, receiving and inventory control for plasma centers.
- Tripled sales volume of plasma preparations to Baxter and Puerto Rico.

Senior Project Engineer

Directed various projects at all levels of manufacturing with numerous production departments.

Played an integral role in the future planning and direction of production areas, with an emphasis on materials management.

Gained experience on multiple computer platforms.

- Completed a $400,000 redesign of the Packaging Department.
- Projects resulted in cost savings and productivity improvements.

Package Engineer

Installed numerous beneficial updates and revisions in product packaging configurations and design.

Directed the installation of process equipment.

- Projects included the design of bulk-shipping configuration to Japan, resulting in annual savings of $500,000.
- Invented and patented a plastic bottle hanger.

EDUCATION: APICS Certified in Integrated Resource Management (CIRM), including logistics, customers and products, manufacturing processes, support functions and integrated enterprise management   6/92-11/93

APICS Certified in Production and Inventory Management (CPIM), including Material Requirements Planning, Just-In-Time, Capacity Requirements Planning, Master Planning, Production Activity and Control   7/90-3/91

Hebrew University, Jerusalem, Israel
Completed two-thirds of requirements toward MBA degree specializing in Marketing. Successful completion of courses, including accounting, finance, operations research, pricing and customer behavior   10/88-7/90

Bar Ilan University, Ramat Gan, Israel
B.A. Degree: Psychology; 1987

PERSONAL: Member: American Society of Healthcare Material Management, American Production and Inventory Control Society.
Member: Advisory Board Member for the School of Management Science at California State University, Northridge.

- U.S. Patent #4,413,741 for plastic IV bottle hanger.
- Honorable Mention, Pharmaceutical category, SPHE Packaging competition, 1998.

This aspiring executive sent 40 and received 18 interviews.

SAMUEL SELLER
87 Catskill Lane
Bartlett, IL 60103

laffa@msn.com   630/555-1658

EXECUTIVE SALES REPRESENTATIVE

PROFILE:

➤ Comprehensive experience in sales, account management and new business development, including full responsibility for upselling and personal client relations.

➤ Familiar with market research, strategic planning and target marketing; handle competitive analysis, forecasting and status reporting.

➤ Skilled in pricing and creative promotions and programs; determine specific customer needs and product pricing; conduct top-level presentations and negotiate contracts; write/implement bids and provide ongoing sales support.

➤ Assist in hiring, training and supervising staff in sales procedures, product lines and contract administration.

➤ Knowledge of ISO 9002 and computer systems, including Windows 7 and MS Office: Word, Publisher and Excel; basic knowledge of PowerPoint.

EXPERIENCE: Stacey & Co., Inc., Hoffman Estates, IL (sold to Ringo Corp. in 2006)

Senior Contract Administrator   1996-2012

Responsible for lead development and the sale/administration of corporate service contracts for medical equipment.

Developed leads from warranty information; quoted prices and negotiated prices via phone and in-person presentations.

Analyzed and submitted government bids for contractual agreements.

Reviewed/resolved credit disputes; conducted sales forecasts and coordinated ISO 9002 services.

Provided personal client communications and follow-up while tracking and analyzing medical business trends related to service contracts and customer needs.

Trained four contract administrators in all procedures.

--> Personally closed and processed more than $10.5 million in service contracts.

--> Initiated a telemarketing program - adopted nationwide - that improved the contract renewal rate by 25%.

--> Achieved a warranty-to-contract conversion rate of 92%.

--> Acted as liaison between the contract department and senior management for initializing two new computer systems.

--> Worked closely with the contract department and senior management to create a policies and procedures manual for ISO 9002.

--> Earned numerous awards for commitment to excellence.

--> Promoted to this position from:

Senior Service Assistant 1992-1996

Handled extensive sales forecasting and personnel issues.

Communicated with customers to ensure quality of installations and service calls and develop new policies as required.

--> Established a critical account list for prompt follow-up.

--> Created a database to track parts usage.

--> Earned numerous Outstanding Service Awards.

Senior Marketing Assistant 1990-1992

Supported the Regional Sales Manager in all aspects of sales forecasting and personnel.

Coordinated shipments of instruments to new customers through manufacturers, installers and service representatives.

--> Created a national account contact schedule for sales representatives.

--> Researched competitors' products and developed competitive profiles.

EDUCATION: Trained extensively in Partnership Selling, 1996

Hallmark Service Sales Professional Development and Contract Selling, 1995

The Glomark Institute, Columbus, OH: Sales and Marketing Program for High-Tech Service Sales, 1994

Strategic Selling, 1993

Negotiation Dynamics, Far Hills, NJ, 1992

WR. Harper College, Palatine, IL

Completed various business and marketing courses, 1989

PERSONAL:

Board Member of Single Parents, Inc.

Sunday School teacher, Fox Valley Unity Church

Sent about 90; received 18 interviews.

Albert Robinson, CPA

2348 Saple Street   515/555-5401
Fairfield, IA 52556   allioop@aol.com

EXECUTIVE LEADERSHIP

PROFILE:

➤ Detailed experience as Director, COO and CFO, including full P&L responsibility for new business development, business analysis, financial matters and system streamlining.

➤ Proven ability to build business through equity expansion, procedure planning, cost reduction, expense control and accounting oversight for nationwide operations.

➤ Research and write detailed, concise business plans and prepare financial forecasts; plan and conduct presentations to potential investors.

➤ Proficient in hiring, training and supervising technical and support staff at all levels; encourage new ideas and cultivate a creative team atmosphere to attract and retain quality people.

EXPERIENCE: New Frontiers, Fairfield, IA   3/03-Present

Director, Executive Vice President and CFO

In charge of four department managers and virtually all operations for this company, with 3,200 shipping locations nationwide.

Responsible for all financial matters, including building equity through investor relations, budgeting, forecasting, treasury administration and financial reporting.

Perform market research and strategic planning.

Full oversight of operational audits, data services, MIS, administrative departments and accounting.

Analyze call loads vs. total customer service satisfaction and overhead.

Effectively coordinate MIS in determining information requirements, prioritizing requests and managing the development process.

Handle extensive staff and management hiring, training, supervision and motivation in a strong, creative team environment.

→ Constantly develop and communicate new marketing and program strategies to middle managers, resulting in a doubling of revenue and shipping locations.

→ Developed accurate internal systems to track customer shipments, activity, cash transactions and overall customer demographics.

→ Saved more than $100,000 by renegotiating equipment warranty agreements.

→ Reduced costs by 20% by negotiating the company's communications contract.

→ Constantly recognize opportunities in functional areas to exceed customer expectations, benefit the total company culture and improve financial results.

→ In charge of selecting an investment banking organization and raising $5 million of permanent equity; prepared investment memorandums, monitored investment contacts and coordinated/participated in investor presentations and negotiations.

→ Negotiated/procured an $800,000 revolving credit facility for this early-stage enterprise.

→ Developed and negotiated a corporate lease agreement that doubled the company's office space for less than $3 per square foot and enabled the consolidation of two warehouse locations.

Chicago Holdings, Inc., Pittsburgh, PA   4/90-3/03
Vice President
As a private equity investor, identified and evaluated investment opportunities in consumer finance companies for this venture organization.
Worked with other investors and negotiated investment valuations and amounts, while providing post-investment management services.
→ This company was a major investor in The Finance Company, below.

Prior Experience
The Finance Company, Manassas, VA
Chief Financial Officer
Developed and directed investor relationships and all operational accounting, financial reporting and treasury functions for the corporate holding company and two remote regional operation sites.
→ This company underwrote consumer finance loans.

Marine Midland Capital Markets Corporation, New York, NY
Director, Chief Financial and Operations Officer
Managed the securities operations, regulatory reporting and compliance function for Marine Midland Bank's Public Security Division.

Emanuel and Company, New York, NY
Controller
In charge of broker dealer security operations and regulatory/financial reporting for the investment subsidiaries of this investment banking operation.

EDUCATION: West Virginia University, Morgantown, WV
Bachelor of Science, Business Administration

* Graduated Cum Laude

Sent about 50; received eight interviews and two job offers.

JEFFREY BURNS

500 Edison Court
Bartlett, IL 60103

E-mail: far@ibm.net   630/555-2380

ELECTRICAL ENGINEERING / MANAGEMENT

PROFILE:

➤ Extensive background in all aspects of technical support and the service/repair of high-tech equipment, including client relations, project management, staffing, financial analysis, programming and technology management.

➤ Work directly with the client base to provide high-level support, obtain feedback, build business relationships and understand the needs of the customer; effectively research and identify market needs.

➤ Proven ability to manage multisite operations; provide technical training, organizational skills and motivation; handle budgeting, P&L and financial analysis/reporting.

➤ Skilled in network installation, including layout design, groupings, set-ups, application installation and upgrades.

➤ Project management talents include team development, organization, scheduling and budgeting. Design and develop software applications; skilled in C, C++, Pascal, Visual Basic, Access, Novell 4.x, NT, Windows 7 and Novell Workstations.

EXPERIENCE: Totally Keen Surveys, Itasca, IL   1995-Present
Regional Service / IT Manager   2005-Present
Direct all aspects of service and information management for this innovative, high-tech company, manufacturing various surveying equipment using global positioning satellites.
Supervise all operations for nine workshops throughout the Americas, providing for the repair of equipment.
Manage all aspects of technical support and provide high-level support for clients.
Prepare and administer an aftermarket operating budget of $1.5 million.
Perform financial analysis, with responsibility for profits.
Work extensively with clients to gain feedback on new products and learn the particular needs of each client.
Maintain regular contact with regional offices and manage the workflow.
Prepare and submit reports on service statistics.
Analyze trends and provide feedback to headquarters.
Perform quality audits to ensure compliance with ISO 9000 requirements.
Develop various applications in C and C++.

→ Handled all aspects of installing a network for 50 users; contracted services for wiring, set up user profiles and installed software.

→ Developed and maintain database for service offices. Implemented various technology to make information more accessible to satellite offices.

→ Boosted division profitability by 28% over two years.

→ Traveled to the various shops to provide training in the technical aspects of service and new product development and to exchange information.

Service Manager   1999-2005

Responsible for managing two service offices.

Trained and directed a team of six associates.

→ Handled all client relations and technical support.

→ Determined pricing for spare parts.

Service Engineer   1998-1999

Performed equipment service and maintenance as well as technical support.

→ Reassigned to the U.S. from Sweden.

Service Engineer, Stockholm, Sweden   1997-1998

Serviced equipment brought in from sites around the world and provided technical support to satellite offices.

Set up special tools for service.

Test Engineer, Stockholm, Sweden   1995-1997

Utilized test equipment to run functional analyses of circuit boards and sub units for spare parts inventory.

EDUCATION: Kingston University, London, England
Bachelor of Science Degree in Electrical Engineering:
Concentration in Communications and Control with CAD / Computing.

LANGUAGES: Written and oral fluency in English and Swedish.

Used only one resume; received one interview and was offered the job.

Wallace Rodgers
236 North Court
Des Plaines, IL 60016

W998@aol.com   847/555-7893

OPERATIONS LEADERSHIP: Heavy Equipment

PROFILE:
➤ Comprehensive experience in the heavy equipment industry, including forecasting, competitive analysis and the negotiation of sales and leasing agreements.

➤ Familiar with market research, strategic planning and new business development, including distributor networking and contract negotiations.

➤ Skilled in finance and budget administration, forecasting and long- and short-term planning.

➤ Handle cash requirement forecasting and statement analysis, as well as loan agreements, P&L statements and balance sheets.

➤ Plan and conduct seminars and various written and oral presentations in a professional manner.

EXPERIENCE: The Construction Solutions Company, Addison, IL   2/02-Present
Vice President: Risk Management and Corporate Secretary
Responsible for developing and presenting a strong corporate image in the heavy equipment industry, with direct involvement in marketing, sales and profit expansion.
Negotiate sales and lease agreements while keeping a sharp eye on competitors' rates and product lines.
Network closely with distributors and promote product lines; constantly analyze risks associated with contracts, purchase agreements, vendors and suppliers.
Directly involved in staff training and development in company procedures and product lines.

→ Constantly analyze and reduce risks associated with sales contracts, purchase orders, litigation proceedings and employee personnel matters.

→ Maintain the quality of vendor and purchasing relationships and act as company representative in sensitive matters.

Directed a wide range of functional areas, including:
Credit Management: Worked closely with sales representatives to expand sales through credit procedures. Designed and implemented all credit department functions, including establishing and managing new accounts. Negotiated settlements and disputes, while supervising two support staff.

Manager of Human Resources, Manager of Casualty Insurance and Employee Benefits Manager: Researched and purchased/designed all employee benefit packages, including savings and profit-sharing plans. Administered all business insurance, including sourcing, cost-effective purchasing and implementation; maintained aggressive, positive programs.

Forms Manager: Establish and maintain inventory levels of forms; oversee design, purchasing, and updating of business cards and all printed matter. Analyze/control costs and reduce waste.

Safety Director: Responsible for the design, implementation and review of safety procedures and policies for adherence to OSHA and government guidelines.
Train workers on safety issues and maintain vendors' material safety data sheets.

Member: Corporate Board of Directors: (2009-Present) Directly involved in long- and short-term planning and all major business decisions of this company.

Harris Group, Arlington Heights, IL   11/95-2/02
General Manager / Part Owner
In charge of sales development through marketing, promotions and advertising for two successful restaurants.
Effectively hired, trained and supervised up to 80 in all operations, including direct customer service and upselling.
Purchased and managed all food, beverages, capital equipment and supplies.
→ Performed cost analysis, payroll processing and overall business management.

PRIOR EXPERIENCE: American Bakeries Company, HQ, Chicago, IL
General Credit Manager
Oversaw sales and credit activities for this $500 million operation, including sales expansion through more effective customer service.
Hired, trained and supervised a staff of nine and a national staff of 75.
Negotiated directly with customers, banks and attorneys regarding credit and sales contracts.
→ Established provisions for bad debts, departmental budgeting and
   expenses; forecasted credit losses.

Swift and Company, subsidiary of Esmark, Chicago, IL
Regional Credit Manager

EDUCATION: College of Great Falls, Great Falls, MT
B.S.B.A., Accounting

Attended Northwestern University in Evanston, IL, two years.

DePaul University, Chicago, IL
Law Program; enrolled 1994-1995

MEMBERSHIPS: U.S.A. National Credit Union, Homewood, IL
Member: Board of Directors

MILITARY: U.S. Air Force, **Sergeant**
Four Years

Some would say Merril is overqualified. He was very selective and was seeking a very unique position. He sent about 200; received six interviews and a job offer.

Merril Chase
99961 Snake Road
Luken, CA 92630

Res: 949/555-6465   Chase@anet.net   Cell: 949/555-4700

EXECUTIVE LEADERSHIP: International Business Development
A position utilizing the ability to adapt, capitalize and thrive in rapidly changing business environments.

- Executive talents in domestic and international business development, including full P&L responsibility for entire companies and complex, high-tech projects with top executives and government agencies.
- Proven ability to expand profits through creative strategic planning and coordination of all essential functions, from initial concept to coalition building, PR and market establishment to lease and financing packages, vendor sourcing, computer systems and quality control.
- Establish and manage entire leasing programs and related financing, including the design and implementation of operations for banks, independent lessors and major corporations; skilled in capital development and the sourcing of venture funds for multimillion dollar projects.
- Spearhead global distribution networking and international sales, including market research, creative promotions and top-level contract negotiation; analyze foreign competition and improve relations with overseas governments and partners; bilingual in Greek.
- Effectively hire, train and motivate technical staff and management teams; establish goals and controls; monitor results to consistently increase profit margins, enhance market position, reduce operating costs and meet strategic objectives.

EXPERIENCE:

Ross Funding Corporation, Luken, CA   1991-2008
President
Concurrent management and consulting roles with:
D.A.T. Holdings Ltd., UK **(Chairman);** D.A.T., AB Sweden, (a D.A.T. subsidiary); Clean Air North America, Inc., Luken **(Chairman & CEO)** and Syntec, Ltd. UK **(Chairman).**
Commercial Consultant to the City of Luken (Dept. of Water and Power) and Southern California Edison.

OVERVIEW:

Director: Electric Vehicle Initiative
Under an EPA mandate and a resolution by the City of Luken for cleaner air and commercial development, directed a highly successful, multibillion dollar international R&D program to establish the primary electric vehicle (EV) initiative, from initial strategic planning and infrastructure to financing, production and coalition building on a worldwide basis.
Performed or directed all strategic planning, contract management, lease financing and government and regulatory affairs, as well as all sales and marketing initiatives.

Diplomacy

Developed strong diplomatic and business relationships with auto industry leaders worldwide and government agencies throughout Europe and Asia, especially China, for a complete EVehicle program. Founded the Luken EV Commercial Advisory Board, composed of high ranking, Fortune 500–level executives.

Co-founder of a Washington, D.C., lobbying agency, The Electric Transportation Coalition, which acquired national visibility through key state and federal legislators and regulators.

Established acceptance by key governments and automakers through effective lobbying.

Worked closely with a top U.S. general and foreign officials on a multibillion-dollar electric transportation program for the People's Republic of China.

Communications and Coalition-Building

Worked closely with Fortune 500 firms and top officials at U.S. and foreign governments.

Promoted electric transportation to national fleet and leasing associations.

Conducted numerous speeches and presented the program worldwide to foreign governments and all major car manufacturers, with excellent response.

⇨ Wrote and distributed a highly successful request for proposal for 10,000 vehicles.

⇨ Major automakers produced at least prototype EVs as a result of this initiative.

Finance

Created financial and regulatory plans to assist automakers in market penetration.

Conducted external audits of leasing and financial portfolios for several California banks.

Infrastructure and Logistics

Addressed the entire infrastructure issue, including insurance and finance matters, with fleet companies and auto manufacturers.

Technology

Acquired and managed the latest commercial technology and manufacturing techniques with a sharp eye on diplomacy and cultural matters.

Facilitated technology transfer and defined all parts, products, systems and procedures.

Provided a catalyst for R&D efforts of the Big Three automakers, overseas automakers and various utility services.

⇨ Oversaw production of two prototype vehicles, demonstrated at auto shows in Frankfurt, Tokyo, Sweden, Hong Kong and Luken.

⇨ Earned "Best of What's New in Technology" from *Popular Science* magazine, 1992.

⇨ As Member of the Board of Directors of Syntech, Ltd., UK, directed R&D and infrastructure for the developing utility load leveling storage systems and fuel cells for electric transportation.

Marketing

Established profit potential and the ability to preserve and expand market share in the U.S. and abroad (including Asia and Europe), to spur major economies and companies to substantially invest, adapt the program and integrate their auto manufacturers' efforts.

Created commercial incentives for manufacturers and promoted a worldwide effort to manufacture and market electric vehicles.

Specific achievements include:

➪ Designed and implemented a plan for Denning Mobile Robotics to commercialize the only truly autonomous robot at the time, leading to an increase in bottom line profits of 2% on $200 million in new business.

➪ Established a $225 million line of credit for a national car rental corporation. Created a used car leasing program for vehicles removed from the rental fleet; projected annual income from leased vehicles is estimated at $750 million.

➪ Working extensively with top GM executives, announced the introduction of the Impact Vehicle in Luken.

➪ GM's vehicle launch triggered announcements of EV programs from all major auto manufacturers around the world.

Details of Hands-On Management

Personally managed companies selected by the city of LA: C.A.T. Holdings, Ltd., UK, and C.A.T. AB, Sweden, Clean Air North America, and a majority interest in Syntec, Ltd., a fuel cell development company.

As part of the EV initiative, developed and implemented a detailed plan to manufacture and market electric vehicles through C.A.T.'s Swedish subsidiary, C.A.T. AB and Clean Air North America

➪ Through strategic alliances, acquired $20 million in contingency capital.

➪ Directed development of a $55 million hybrid electric vehicle program and raised $20 million in capital from a strategic partner.

➪ Reduced overhead by $500,000 annually.

Compulease, Inc., Downey, CA   1985-1991
Founder and President
Directed systems development and integration operations, including the design and implementation of lease financing packages for newly released IBM equipment.
Performed detailed consulting for leasing companies and banks.
Directed marketing and business development.

PRIOR
EXPERIENCE: Medical Data Systems, Inc.
                    Director: Data Processing

                    Applied Data Systems
                    Manager: Computer Operations

                    Borg-Warner Corporation
                    General Data Processing Supervisor

AFFILIATIONS: Founder: Luken Electric Vehicle Commercial Advisory Board.
                    Co-Founder: Electric Transportation Coalition, Washington, D.C.
                    Member: SAF Executive Committee, Scripps College, Claremont, CA.
                    Member: Executive Committee, Hellenic Heritage Foundation, Luken, CA.

PERSONAL: Married; enjoy travel and antique car restoration.

Distributed via Internet; received six phone calls and four emails in the first four days and two interviews.

Edward Jones
233 Cat Drive
Williams, AL 75707

Home: 903/555-0133   personage@gte.net   Cell: 903/555-7731

PRESIDENT: SOFTWARE DEVELOPMENT / MARKETING

PROFILE:

- In-depth experience in multimillion-dollar turnarounds, including P&L responsibility for national and international business development, successful product rollouts and distribution, with experience in North America, Europe and the Middle East.

- Executive management experience in application software, distribution, databases, operating systems, logistics, computer hardware, client/server networks and consulting; familiar with major manufacturers, including Microsoft, Oracle and Novell; manage the design and development of Internet applications and Web-based products.

- Effectively hire, train and supervise staff and managers in all aspects of marketing, financials, account acquisition and management, as well as technical products.

- Skilled in creative project management, strategic planning, and "out-of-box" thinking, resulting in dramatic improvements in bottom-line profits.

- Effectively managed both large and small organizations, regional, national and international; coordinate financials, inventory management, customer service, help desk, warehouse management, logistics, municipal government relations and utilities.

CAREER BACKGROUND:

<u>Gray Matter, Inc.</u>, Buehler, TX   1999-2011
This is the software division of a $14 billion international corporation focused on software applications for governments, municipalities and privately held utilities.
President
Directly involved in all aspects of business turnaround, with full P&L responsibility for corporate identity, product evolution, marketing and sales.
Responsible for the hiring, training and supervision of 46 employees; directly supervised a team of five.
Effectively managed all phases of market research, product design, multimedia, Internet promotions, print, public relations and lifecycle management.

- Instrumental in expanding this company from $2 million to $7 million.
- Increased recurring revenues by over 300%.
- Increased average transaction from $6,000 to over $200,000.
- Led the company from a loss of 43% of revenue to profitability in six quarters.
- Anticipated and recognized technology and market shifts and responded quickly to these changes. Successfully aligned distribution channels with current and future product strategies, while identifying and targeting optimum vertical markets for the company's products.

- ◆ Responsible for product development and projects related to software applications for financial applications, customer service, distribution, utility, municipal government and logistics.
- ◆ Determined product priorities based upon customer needs versus development resource requirements.
- ◆ Gained experience in Web-based, mission-critical projects, client/server knowledge, databases and operating systems.
- ◆ Developed strategic plans, including the vision for a new client/server Windows 7 product to replace legacy products; obtained funding, completed projects under budget and in less than 12 months when industry estimates called for 30 months.
- ◆ Converted a staff with no Windows experience to one capable of outperforming the consultants we hired and retained 100% of staff at completion of projects.

The Thomas Group, Inc., Dallas, TX   1995-1999
Senior Consultant

Managed consulting engagements and determined and met specific client needs for this $75 million, publicly held consulting firm.

Performed task definition, options evaluation and full project management.

Specialized in process improvement for product development, customer support and sales management. (Recruited to join Sensus SofTech as President.)

- ◆ Worked with Fortune 500 companies in industries such as software development and distribution.
- ◆ Accomplished reductions in sales cycle times of up to 60%, while increasing successful close ratio from 24% of opportunities to over 60%.
- ◆ Assisted a $110 million software company in developing strategic plans for a new, Internet-based product to replace legacy product in the real estate industry.
- ◆ Performed process improvement for software development, customer service and help desk, while evaluating acquisition opportunities and sales cycle management.

UDS, Inc., Dallas, TX   1990-1995
President and CEO

Promoted due to results achieved for this distribution software application company.

Spearheaded a successful turnaround and ignited a stagnant, declining operation.

Directed the company from previous five-year record of losses to profits of 16% on revenues in five quarters.

Oversaw 92 employees and six direct reports.

- ◆ Expanded sales from $5 million to $25 million.
- ◆ Recognized for quality service and developing loyal customers, resulting in impressive sales. (Left due to hostile takeover by a major competitor.)

Executive Vice President Product Development & Marketing

Rapidly promoted and immediately successful in streamlining operations, finding more productive methods to achieve top performance, eliminate waste and reduce unnecessary expenses.

Vice-President, Sales and Marketing

Doubled revenues in two years and increased margins 40% for this leading provider of hardgoods distribution software applications and computer hardware and services. Established market share dominance domestically and in Canada.

♦ Earned Chairman's Award from parent company for performance in top 1% of over 750 employees worldwide.

♦ Generated positive cash flows of 18% of revenues, the first positive cash flow performance in company history.

♦ Reduced operating expenses by 55% in 12 months while revenues increased substantially.

♦ Improved Customer Satisfaction Survey ratings from base of 1.6 (on a scale of 1 to 5) to 4.27; achieved similar results on Employee Satisfaction surveys.

♦ Decreased Bad Debt expense from almost 10% of revenue to under 1/2 of 1% of revenue.

♦ Redesigned support and services fee structures, doubling monthly recurring revenues.

♦ Restructured the consulting services department; increased revenues six-fold while reducing staff size and operating expenses.

♦ As VP of Sales and Marketing, doubled sales in two years.

♦ Rewrote contracts, resulting in dramatically reduced sales cycles.

♦ Implemented new pricing and commission structures, which increased gross margins by 35%.

♦ As Western Regional Manager, expanded a territory with six salespeople from $1.2 million to over $6 million in 10 months.

♦ Closed the largest transaction in company history within six weeks of beginning employment.

EDUCATION: University of Tulsa, Tulsa, OK
B.S. Degree: Accounting

♦ MBA Graduate Studies; Minor: Marketing
Active in a fraternity, holding offices of President, Treasurer, Rush Chairman and Social Chairman, as well as Chapter Advisor during graduate school.

Sent about 60 through mail and email; received five interviews.

Cary Evans
213 Mar Heights Court #129
San Diego, CA 92130

Cgas@aol.com   619/555-9760

EXECUTIVE LEADERSHIP: New Business Development

PROFILE:

➤ Proven ability to acquire and manage new accounts, with P&L responsibility for marketing, intellectual property, R&D and operations management in technology industries from start-up through acquisition.

➤ Skilled in entrepreneurial-driven functions ranging from product development, staffing and procedures to long- and short-term strategic planning, media relations and the establishment of synergistic alliances.

➤ Effectively manage budgets and financial matters; negotiate contracts and coordinate vendors, suppliers and distribution channels for effective product pull-through.

➤ Proficient in applied technologies, software and systems integration.

EXPERIENCE: Super-Link Systems, Inc., Waterslide, CA   2000-Present

Founder and CEO
Responsible for the design and development of embedded firmware control systems (central server with an online service) and data communications used to optimize water use for residences, businesses and government accounts.
Plan and implement all marketing strategies, including media relations, market research, creative promotions and advertising.
Effectively hire, train and supervise staff and management teams in product lines and all marketing and sales techniques.
Develop long- and short-term plans, as well as financial projections and private placement to raise capital.
This business integrates weather data, communications over cable systems and utility cost savings to the customer.

→ Oversee circuit design, high-level software programming and all engineering functions with programmers and technical staff.

→ Successfully negotiated cable trials and beta testing with Time Warner Cable, Cox Communications and Jones Intercable and alliances with water utilities.

→ Negotiated license agreements with strategic business partners.

→ Personally secured patents with broad claims and obtained registered trademarks.

SAFE-Time Emergency Systems, Inc., Westlake Village, CA   1990-2000

Co-Founder and President

Eventually negotiated the sale of this business to DuPont (at 16 times initial investment).

This company developed and sold scientific software, bundled with advanced systems, interactive graphics, and instrumentation to the chemical and petrochemical industry for monitoring and tracking hazardous chemical leaks.

Developed business with numerous multi-national Fortune 100 companies. Personally established distribution and sales to Europe, Asia, the Middle East, Canada and Mexico and on the East Coast and Gulf Coast of the U.S. Directed 30 to 40 staff and managers with an annual, multimillion-dollar run rate.

→ Established this company as the # 1 supplier through high-visibility media, such as *The Wall Street Journal, The New York Times, Business Week, Chemical Week, CNN and other TV stations*.

→ This company grew 50% annually with high profit margins during my tenure.

→ Negotiated for up-front customer deposits, which greatly improved cash flow and reduced working capital.

→ Hired, trained and motivated a high quality, efficient team of technical and support staff and managers in engineering, sales, production and quick-response customer service.

EDUCATION: Pepperdine University, Malibu, CA
M.B.A. (Partial fulfillment, Presidential Key Executive Program) 1990

Colorado State University, Fort Collins, CO
M.S. Degree: Environmental Resources

University of Colorado, Boulder, CO
B.S. Degree: Aerospace Engineering

COMPUTER SKILLS: Proficient in spreadsheet development, graphics, word processing, e-mail, Internet, and all major Windows applications.

PERSONAL: Married with one child; enjoy skiing, hiking, boating and travel.

Sent about 22; received two interviews.

David Barnicle

239 Mercury Drive   847/555-3932
Schaumburg, IL 60193   barn@gateway.net

HEALTHCARE ADMINISTRATION

PROFILE:

➤ Proficient in healthcare and operations management, including responsibility for new startups, special projects, procedures and communications.

➤ Research and write policies, procedures and training materials; design and implement budgets and forecasts; strong knowledge of insurance codes and medical terminologies.

➤ Skilled in team training, supervision and motivation; coordinate systems and procedures in fast-paced situations.

➤ Experience in cost-effective purchasing and vendor relations, as well as overhead reduction and computerized status reporting; utilize Windows 7 and XP, MS Word and Excel for correspondence and spreadsheets.

➤ Plan and conduct written/oral presentations and meetings for staff, management and the public in a professional manner.

EXPERIENCE: Marion Medical Clinic, Ellyn, IL   2005-Present
Practice Manager
In charge of an entire OB/Gyn department and the training and supervision of 15 employees supporting seven physicians.

Reimbursement Specialist
Constantly analyze, update and implement clinic fee schedules, including all insurance procedure codes, supporting 160 physicians in 20 departments.
Create and implement office policies, procedures, business forms and monthly financial reports to meet constantly changing demands.

→ Act as liaison between clinical staff, including doctors and RNs and the billing office to maximize insurance reimbursements.
→ Effectively train and develop clerical and clinical staff.
→ Control the department budget and work directly with physicians.

Vesicare, Inc., Torrance, CA
Office Administrator   1994-2005
Created a more effective reporting system and trained numerous employees in its use.
In charge of daily profitability and operations of a regional office.

Handled extensive telephone and in-person communications with all types of patients.

Verified insurance benefits, oriented beneficiaries on coverage and produced medical reports for locations in Illinois and Colorado.

<u>Vein Clinics of America,</u> Schaumburg, IL   1991-1993
Quality Assurance & Training Manager
Computer Systems Coordinator, promoted from:
Patient Relations Coordinator / Sales Representative
Personally directed the setup, implementation and support of 17 healthcare facilities nationwide.

Utilized Gant charts to open locations within strict timelines.
→ Worked closely with computer programmers to create new menu items and perform beta testing on a proprietary system; effectively trained endusers in all system operations.
→ Trained and developed Regional Managers, Office Managers and PRCs in front-office operations.
→ Created and implemented front-office policies and procedures, as well as monthly financial reports.
→ Supervised up to six employees, including scheduling performance reviews and terminations.

Prior Experience:

<u>Obstetricians - Gvn., PC,</u> Omaha, NE
Clinical Supervisor - LPN
Effectively hired, trained, scheduled and evaluated up to seven nurses supporting 10 physicians.
Updated the policy and procedure manual and maintained optimal patient flow.
Oversaw OB-Gyn diagnostic procedures and interfaced with physicians, an administrator and other medical staff at all levels.

→ Conducted/facilitated Continuing Education Units (CEUs) for clinical staff.

EDUCATION: <u>College of DuPage,</u> Glen Ellyn, IL   2008-Present
Communications

<u>Metro Tech Community College,</u> Omaha, NE
Completed courses in Management / Supervision

<u>Southeast Community College,</u> Fairbury, NE
Licensed Practical Nurse (LPN)

Sent 10; received 10 interviews.

Lana Norris
22567 Welland Court
Roselle, IL 60172

630/555-1330   Msnorri@aol.com

OPERATIONS / MANAGEMENT

PROFILE:

> Skilled in the management of multiple locations, including the setup and improvement of departments, systems and procedures.
> Proven abilities in new business development, staffing and total project management, including cost analysis and reduction for successful operations.
> Effectively hire, train and supervise staff and managers in personal customer service, sales presentations, product lines and company policies.
> Plan and implement budgets and forecasts to increase profits, reduce payroll and improve customer satisfaction.
> Utilize in-house databases and computer systems including Windows, Amisys, Access, Accel, MS Word and Internet resources for spreadsheets, status reports and correspondence.

EMPLOYMENT: Health Plans of Illinois, Chicago, IL   2/06-Present

Director: Claims and Enrollment

Effectively manage claims and enrollment departments, including organizing and delegating jobs and hiring, training and monitoring a front-line and processing staff of 11.

Determine and meet specific department goals; conduct regular staff evaluations and motivate all team members for high-quality work and prompt turnaround.

Instrumental in planning and implementing virtually all department and company policies and procedures with the company president, CEO and CFO.

Perform detailed analysis of statistics and trends for improved quality and excellent cost control.

Coordinate third-party liability and re-insurance reimbursements.

→ Increased membership from zero to 30,000 through effective staff training, precise documentation and attention to detail.
→ As Operational Interface: Worked closely with IS department staff to evaluate and maintain the mainframe computer and update configurations as needed.
→ Assisted in configuring the Amisys database and computer system; worked closely with programmers and trained staff in effective use.
→ Earned regular bonuses for reaching financial goals.

New City Life, currently owned by Aetna, Oak Brook, IL   9/94-9/06

Account Service Representative

Provided total support to 10 service staff in customer enrollment and claim submissions for multi-product and multi-site clients.

Handled extensive communications with providers.

Worked closely with clients to resolve service issues, including claims utilization and the reporting of medical care activity.

Gained an excellent knowledge of claims, insurance codes and procedures.

Performed proofreading and correcting of certificates of coverage.

→ Effective in servicing more than 3,500 lives.

Euclid Managers, Inc., Elmhurst, IL   9/92-9/94
Marketing Representative

Responsible for the marketing and sale of group health products, primarily to brokers.

Developed sales leads and conducted presentations for lines including United Healthcare, Blue Cross/Blue Shield and Delta Dental.

Negotiated rates with brokers; conducted enrollment meetings and provided creative ideas for marketing and advertising.

→ Chairperson: Continuing Education for the DuPage Chapter of the National Association of Health Underwriters.

Share Health Plan of Illinois, Itasca, IL   7/87-9/92
and United Health Care of Illinois

PPO Coordinator   1/92-9/92

Established the PPO Customer Service Department, including the training and supervision of all customer service staff.

Created and implemented all department policies and procedures.

Provided extensive training and support of groups and individuals.

→ Member of a breakout group that streamlined ER claim processing procedures; greatly improved accuracy and processing efficiency.
→ Analyzed and improved claim processing procedures as member of the Continuous Quality Improvement Committee.

Claims Liaison   12/91-1/92

Acted as liaison between claims and customer service departments.

Provided research and resolution of claim issues.

Developed and streamlined procedures to implement claim tracking and processing efficiency.

EDUCATION: Total Polytechnic Institute, Evans, NY
                   B.S. Degree: Management

Mailed 100 over two months; received 12 interviews and accepted a new job. He checked/used Yahoo! Real Estate to find cost of living differences in various states.

MARCUS SELLER
21167 Barry #108
Bloomingdale, IL 60108

630/555-7524   bigsell@yippie.com

INTERNATIONAL SALES/MARKETING

PROFILE:
- Proven abilities in sales and product development, including profitable domestic and international experience, market penetration and total account management.
- Skilled in complete sales program planning, as well as account acquisition and competitive analysis, especially for industrial and technical product lines.
- Plan and conduct sales presentations for senior-level clients; design sales proposals and price quotes; perform new product introduction and personal client development.
- Extensive contacts worldwide with vendors, suppliers, major manufacturers and distributor networks; lived in several European and Asian countries; familiar with French and Japanese.
- Skilled in Netscape Navigator, Microsoft Outlook, Word and Excel for account tracking and updating, spreadsheet analysis and sales forecasting.

EXPERIENCE: The Hester Group, Chicago, IL   2006-Present
Account Executive - International Sales
Responsible for the promotion and sale of exhibit space around the world, primarily to major U.S. and Canadian industrial firms.
Handle relationship sales and business development with a focus on more than 400 manufacturers.
Utilize a solid background in construction and other industrial equipment, markets and business trends.
Exhibitions are held in Europe, Singapore, China, Mexico and Argentina.

- Set sales records for the World of Concrete in Asia, 1997.
- Constantly update and maintain account information for timely, accurate account follow-up.

Illini Products, Chicago, IL   1994-2006
Sales Representative
Effectively marketed and sold a variety of construction equipment and power plants, including gas and diesel engines and generator sets.
Implemented promotions and performed all aspects of lead development and account management, including needs analysis for numerous accounts throughout Illinois and Indiana.
Created and implemented custom sales proposals, pricing and contracts to expand client profitability.

Key accounts included: United Airlines, American Airlines and numerous OEMs.
Sold product lines from: Kohler, Deutz, Ford, Lister Petter and Gillette.

Travel Agents International, St. Louis, MO   1986-1994
President / Owner
Directed the setup and operation of this full-service company, including all
staffing, procedures and operations.
Oversaw sales and customer service functions on a daily basis.
Hired, trained and supervised a team of 25 in sales, order processing and
troubleshooting with tact and a personal approach.
Gained experience with a wide range of cruises, tours, hotels, rental cars and
corporate travel.

→ Ranked in the top 15% of 350 agencies every year.
→ Established the first of six agencies in the St. Louis area.
→ Introduced a unique cost-savings program to St. Louis.

Prior Experience:
Caterpillar, Inc., Peoria, IL
Management: Sales, Marketing and Advertising
Responsible for a wide range of duties in various positions, including business
expansion through effective promotions, advertising, and media relations.
Sold all major products, including construction equipment, diesel engines,
transmissions and generator sets.
Markets included construction, mining, industrial, logging, power generation
and marine.
Trained and motivated sales staff in field sales, forecasting, account tracking
and product introduction.
Lived and worked in Switzerland, Singapore, the Philippines and Japan.
Gained an excellent knowledge of Caterpillar distributors.

→ Introduced several new products, including one that captured more than
  50% of the U.S. market.
→ Lowered costs by $1 million by eliminating unnecessary attachments.
→ Managed a highly successful national sales motivation program, resulting
  in sales exceeding budget by 30% and $30 million.

EDUCATION: Rensselaer Polytechnic Institute, Troy, NY
                   B.S. Degree: Management Engineering
                   Minor: Civil Engineering

                   St. Lawrence University, Canton, NY
                   B.S. Degree: Liberal Arts

Emailed to approximately 200 companies; received 12 interviews. I mentioned he should also do regular research and mailings.

MELVIN BOWERS
777 West Lake Street
Plainfield, IL 60544

Res: 815/555-7021	chai.com@world.att.net	Cell: 312/555-6148

INTERNATIONAL BUSINESS / OPERATIONS

PROFILE:
- ➢ Comprehensive experience in new business development, startup operations and project management, including full P&L responsibility for marketing, staffing and procedures.
- ➢ Skilled in hiring training, and motivating sales teams in technical product lines; perform market research, strategic planning, creative product development and key account management.
- ➢ International experience in joint venture administration, market development, contract negotiations and financial analysis; fluent in English, Arabic and French.
- ➢ Well versed in import/export procedures and foreign business practices and customs.
- ➢ Proficient in cost reduction and business analysis to reduce fraud and theft; oversee security procedures with a knowledge of government and product regulations.

EXPERIENCE: Fraizer Board of Investigators, New York, NY   5/03-Present
Specialist
Conducted corporate investigations and analyzed/reduced theft and fraud; reported findings, and made recommendations to top management to quickly solve security problems.
Performed risk management and conducted investigations of a wide range of business transactions.
Supervised a team of five and answered internal inquiries, managed risk and protected valuable assets.
Organized investigations with various law enforcement agencies and reviewed/improved workflow and procedures.

- → Analyzed and evaluated technical intelligence for the FBI, including threats and hostile acts affecting national security.
- → Reduced a backlog of various cases to zero.
- → Granted Top Secret security clearance and utilized state-of-the-art, sensitive equipment and information.
- → Certified by the Department of Justice in Arabic (fluent in all Arabic dialects).

International Management Information Services, Paris, France   3/97-4/03
International Marketing Manager
Personally established the entire sales function, including staff hiring, training and supervision for software sales.
Conducted market research and top-level sales presentations.

Performed extensive research and test-marketed, packaged and sold OCTIMIS, an eight-module software package.

→ Successfully negotiated joint ventures with corporate America and greatly expanded markets in the Middle East.
→ Personally acquired key accounts such as Timex and IBM.
→ Successfully increased revenues by 45%.
→ Assigned as the exclusive representative for the U.S. headquarters in Langley, VA.

<u>Banque de Participation et de Placement (BPP),</u> Paris, France   5/96-3/97
International Business Consultant
Conducted extensive research and determined potential for overseas expansion for this international bank.
Performed research and compiled/wrote detailed analyses of 15 countries, with an emphasis on real estate, tourism and import/export potential.

→ Personally identified markets and potential office sites.
→ Directed the opening of a BPP branch in Libreville, Gabon.
→ Determined profitable investment alternatives in Europe and the U.S.

<u>International Business Consultant,</u> Langley, VA   6/94-4/96
On an independent basis, researched and wrote credit reports on four African and Middle Eastern nations using World Bank and International Monetary Fund (IMF) criteria, resulting in the grant or denial of aid or loans.
Coordinated and directed major international media events with local media and public relations firms.

→ Planned and supervised international conferences in the U.S., including the INTERPOL conference in Washington, D.C. in 1995.
→ Conducted international teleconferences in Arabic, French and English on key business issues involving European, African and Middle Eastern nations.
→ Conference work was supervised by the CACI and local PR firms.

PRIOR EXPERIENCE: <u>Radio-Television Morocco / RTM,</u> Morocco
Associate TV Director / Editor-in-Chief
Interviewed numerous government officials and VIPs for nationwide broadcast.
Covered local, national, and UN events.

EDUCATION: <u>University of Hartford,</u> CT
MBA Degree
Granted a USAID scholarship to the U.S.
Computer systems: familiar with Windows 7 and XP, as well as MS Word 97; knowledge of web page design and various word processing software.
Completed various software consulting courses covering SAP and Lawson.

Did not use regular mail; emailed about 250; received 20 interviews.

STEVEN ANTHONY

776 White Court

San Ramon, IL 64583

Stevie@bell.net   925/555-4250

DOMESTIC / INTERNATIONAL FACILITIES MANAGEMENT

PROFILE:
 ➤ Skilled in total project management, including plant design, facilities specifications, new construction and vendor/contractor relations; negotiate contracts and manage multimillion-dollar budgets for complex projects.

 ➤ Creatively manage the implementation of energy conservation systems for central energy centers; reduce online hours and cost of operations to improve cooling efficiency of all A/C systems.

 ➤ Manage large campus facilities, as well as multi-country sites and real estate leases for sales offices; proven ability to direct millions of s.f. of T.I. changes, upgrades and conversions.

 ➤ Detailed experience in manufacturing operations, including full responsibility for new startups of products and facilities, staffing and cost control for high-tech product lines.

FACILITIES MANAGEMENT EXPERIENCE:

O'Dell International, Poedunk, IL   2000-2011

Project Manager: Facilities Design and Construction

Reported to the president of this $1 billion international computer manufacturing company.
Effectively controlled costs for two construction sites through close scrutiny of contractors, architects and design engineers, as well as vendor relations and quality oversight.

* Reduced construction costs by 40% at a site in Germany by conducting a total redesign of factory floor layouts and functional areas of a 150,000 sq. ft. plan.
* Full responsibility for a $26 million design and construction budget.
* Analyzed facilities and managed all construction for a 100,000 sq. ft. project in the Philippines.
* Defined requirements for electrical, mechanical and architectural layouts.
* Selected and managed installation of diesel generators for back-up power.

Memorex / Svs Corp., Santa Clara, CA   1995-2000

Director of Facilities

In charge of all facilities for this $5 billion manufacturer of mainframe computer disk drives.
Responsible for 2.5 million sq. ft. of facilities (18 buildings).
Managed a $6.5 million capital budget and an annual operating budget of $22.4 million.
Directed daily plant maintenance, including grounds, janitorial, electrical, HVAC, clean rooms, DI water, solid waste, fire sprinkler, central energy plant and emergency power/UPS systems.
Researched/performed all space planning, layouts and the remodeling of buildings.

* Coordinated all facility engineering for factories in Mexico, Canada and Singapore.
* Selected sites for regional sales offices, including design and lease-hold improvements.
* Directed site selection and the setup of a 150,000 sq. ft. facility in Singapore.

<u>Corus System, Inc.,</u> San Jose, CA
1992-1995

Director of Corporate Facilities and Security

Initially designed and managed the construction of a 30,000 sq. ft. factory for disk-drive assembly in Oregon.

Executed total project responsibility for contractor selection and procurement of capital equipment. Managed daily plant safety and security, plus facility engineering and maintenance.

* Managed the installation and qualified all manufacturing process equipment.
* Promoted in one year and relocated to San Jose.
* Directed the layout of a new 225,000 sq. ft. facility in San Jose.
* Provided floor plans to architects, defined HVAC and electrical loads to contractors for a "build-to-suit" complex. As Construction Project Manager, maintained daily on-site inspections to monitor all "build-to-suit" tenant requirements.
* Assisted in relocating more than 500 people from six buildings.

MANUFACTURING MANAGEMENT EXPERIENCE:

<u>Infant Advantage, Inc.,</u> San Ramon, CA
1990-1992

Director of Operations

Directed a new start-up product into volume manufacturing, from product redesign to prototyping and high-volume production.

Personally hired, trained, developed and managed a technical and support team.

Directed the installation and configuration/establishment of a full MPR-order fulfillment system.

Managed all functions in various departments, including Design Engineering, Materials, Contract Manufacturing, Document Control and Quality Control.

* Directed the total redesign of the product, greatly improving robustness and quality; reduced RMAs by 75%.
* Researched and selected an offshore manufacturing vendor and directed the prototyping and preparations of documentation and tooling for the transfer of manufacturing to China.

<u>Read-Rite Corporation,</u> Milpitas, CA
1986-1990

Director of Manufacturing

Specifically chosen to create a new group for the manufacturing of Thin Film MR tape recording heads at this $800 million disk drive recording head company.

Recruited and hired a team of designers and engineers to move a product from R&D labs into production.

Successfully transferred all processes to a China contract manufacturer for high volume.

* Conducted all planning and execution for rapid-process development and tool designs.
* Managed staff and procedures in various departments, including Engineering Tool Design and Drafting, Manufacturing, Manufacturing Engineers, Quality Control, Material Control and Document Control.
* Performed fast-track tooling and directed prototype acceptance.
* Provided full process documentation for tools and all assembly processes.

Prior Experience

Applied Magnetics Corporation, Goleta, CA
Director of Operations
Recruited to join this $600 million magnetic recording head manufacturer.
In charge of manufacturing configuration, scheduling and quality for ferrite recording heads.
  * Developed cost-effective processes for manufacturing operations in Korean factories.
  * Completed extensive training and performed detailed documentation and process transfers.
  * Developed and improved yields through cost-effective process changes.

Seagate Technology, Campbell, CA
Director of Operations
Created a new division to develop and prototype mini-composite recording heads; successfully transferred all operations to Thailand.
Personally recruited and hired all technical/support staff and management.
Designed and built a laboratory facility, including equipment selection, tooling, jig setup and the development of manufacturing processes.
Effectively managed the daily operations of Engineering, Administration, Facilities, Materials and Manufacturing departments.
  * Conducted competitive analysis and handled extensive vendor research and selection/ negotiations.
  * Gained full product qualification and acceptance for profitable production.
  * Provided full documentation and tool design, while controlling the start-up budget.

PRIOR EXPERIENCE: Project Engineer: 3M: Minnesota Mining and Manufacturing
Manufacturing Manager: National Semiconductor

EDUCATION: California Polytechnic University, San Luis Obispo, CA
Bachelor of Science, Industrial Engineering
Minor in Electrical and Electronics

TRAINING & CERTIFICATION: University of California at Santa Barbara
Hazardous Materials Management Certificate, currently half complete.

SPC Certificate and Gage Capability; TQM; JIT training;
LTP: Licensed Tax Preparer (H&R Block)
Federal and California State Personal Tax Preparation
Memberships: ASTME; AIIE; SPIE; SQE
Skilled in computer systems including MS Windows 7, Excel, Word, PowerPoint and Project.

DISTINCTIONS: Highest achievement of "Programs for Profit" (two years) Commendation for "Outstanding Performance."

Sent 10; received two interviews in the first two weeks.

SAMUEL REDHEAD

925 Fox Court

Gaithersburg, MD 20882

Residence: 301/555-8621   Business: 202/555-8197   E-mail: samhed@nas.com

---

INVESTOR RELATIONS: Director or Vice President

Comprehensive senior-level experience in investor and media relations management, specializing in global capital markets, stock market structures and trade policies in fast-paced, rapidly changing environments.

▶ Advise CEOs, CFOs, directors, senior management and clients on industry issues and emerging trends; formulate strategies for best ROI on institutional and individual client investments in the NASDAQ-AMEX stock markets.

▶ Partner with top management on consulting services to European, Eastern European, African and Asian government agencies for solid investments in U.S. markets; skilled in client needs assessment, risk management, media/public relations and financial services.

▶ Recruit and mobilize cross-functional high performance teams; effectively explain technical, complex matters in understandable terms at all levels; company spokesperson featured in the national press, global trade journals and newspapers.

▶ Utilize Bloomberg, NASDAQ NWII, FactSet, dBase/Foxpro, MS Access, Lotus, MS Excel, MS Word, ISQL and various graphics packages; well versed in Internet technologies and implications.

CAREER BACKGROUND:

<u>The Investment Group,</u> HQ, Washington, D.C.   2002-Present

Manager and Spokesperson, Media Relations   4/07-Present

In charge of all aspects of media relations, including investment relations programs for the largest stock market worldwide.

Specialize in policy and technical issues, with P&L responsibility for public information.

⇨ Media spokesperson on policy and market issues.

⇨ Formulate responses to inquiries on such matters as the market making system, trading rules and systems and the economics of markets.

⇨ Compile and provide financial, statistical and trend analyses to internal and external constituents.

⇨ Prepare press releases on market, firm and technology issues; conduct media and company briefings.

⇨ Meet regularly with international dignitaries to discuss salient features of an efficient capital market, capital formation and trading systems during the process of restructuring domestic capital market infrastructures.

⇨ Current Special Assignment: Interim Director, The AMEX Stock Exchange New York office.

Market Analyst, NASDAQ International, London, United Kingdom   7/05-10/07
Recruited to restructure and develop the infrastructure and personnel of this international headquarters.

➪   Trained marketing staff on stock market functions, theories and practices.

➪   Consulted prospective new issuers on requirements and options for raising capital on U.S. markets.

➪   Liaison to investment banks and consultants; coordinated "road shows" and director visits.

➪   Prepared and edited marketing material for non-U.S. marketing initiatives.

➪   Wrote and presented reports to current and prospective equity investors; produced country economic reports.

➪   Handled international journalist inquiries relating to all aspects of capital markets.

➪   Contributing and economics editor, *NASDAQ International Magazine*, read by over 2,000 institutional investors, CEOs and CFOs.

Research Analyst, Economic Research and Strategic Planning, Washington, D.C.   8/03-6/05
Conducted research to improve market quality, such as spreads and volatility.

➪   Monitored market information for Securities and Exchange Commission filings.

➪   Served as NASDAQ contact for the FIBY JASDAQ and Tokyo Stock Exchange.

➪   Responded to data requests and information inquiries from the Media Relations Department.

➪   Represented NASDAQ at numerous academic conferences, including the Journal of Finance conference.

Research Associate   9/02-8/03
Researched and analyzed studies related to the securities markets.

➪   *Team Leader*, produced a monthly NASDAQ statistics manual for executive management.

TRT/FTC Communications, Washington, D.C.   2000-2002
Financial/Revenue Analyst   4/00-9/02
Analyzed and modified proposed customer agreements with investments up to $50,000 per contract for this $400 million telecommunications firm.

➪   Negotiated customer agreement discount structures and investments with regional managers.

➪   Processed commission discounts for each account and salesperson on a quarterly basis.

➪   Hired as Financial Analyst, 8/90-4/91.

The Aries Corporation, Arlington, VA   2000
Research Assistant
Assisted this management consulting firm and the Big 8 accounting firms with proposal preparation for World Bank, Asian Development Bank and the Agency for International Development projects.

EDUCATION: George Washington University, Washington, D.C.
                 Master of Business Administration
                 Concentration: International Finance

                 University of Maryland, College Park, MD
                 Bachelor of Arts Degree: Finance

Used one resume as requested for an interview through a headhunter; declined the job offer.

James T. Wannamaker

77732 Club Court
Plymouth, MI 48170
734/555-9355   Wanna@maker.com

EXECUTIVE MANAGEMENT: MARKETING - SALES - TECHNOLOGY

PROFILE:

- Comprehensive corporate management experience, including marketing and sales development, organizational/infrastructure development, financial planning and the development of staff and managers.

- Skilled in market development through effective business plan development, "selling" the product, market share acquisition and profitability.

- Demonstrated practice of challenging the paradigms of normalcy; committed to longevity, aggressive strategies, results-oriented management teams and unequaled customer relations.

- Strong background in "taking the product to market" by developing product exposure and recognition, distribution and sales channel development, product/company image and product flow logistics; well versed in Japanese and Matrix management methods.

- Prior experience in product design, development and manufacturing processes.

ACHIEVEMENT SUMMARY:

Optrex LCD Corporation. U.S. Operations: Successful in taking this company from sales of $29 million to $252 million over seven years. Created infrastructure from the ground up; increased market share from 7% to 22% and profitability from negative to a robust condition, 2001-2009. Motivated management team to create "family" culture internally and a philosophy of "relationship" selling towards the customer.

Hitachi LCD/CRT Division: Joined this division in 1998, with the mission of penetrating computer industry leaders. Created a special task force to improve harmony and create a competitive spirit. Increased sales from $17 million to $27 million by 2001.

Hitachi Semiconductor Division: Core objective was to grow "Micro-Computer Sales" while developing national application engineering infrastructure, customer strategy and a team-oriented culture.

EXPERIENCE:

Elia America, Inc., Division of Ali Glass, the world's largest LCD manufacturer.

Director: Sales/Marketing Operations   2002-Present

Directly responsible for all sales and marketing activity in North and South America, MIS, Purchasing, and material operations.

Directed a highly focused, expert management team of five senior managers.

* Team achieved a six-year period of 50% annual growth.
* Increased market penetration from 7% to 22%.
* Implemented a "culture" of relationship selling.
* Bridged a strong understanding/relation between American and Japanese staff; virtually eliminated culture barriers and created a single team.

* Implemented an MBO structure and bonus reward system in a results-oriented management team.
* Developed a U.S.-based, value-added production operation to:
    1. Reduce dependency on financial support from the parent company.
    2. Establish an unmatched market advantage.
    3. Set up a U.S.-based "design center."

<u>Hitachi America,</u> Chicago, IL   1998-2002

Division Engineering Manager - Electronic Display Division

Managed up to 17 sales/technical staff and managers, as well as all aspects of technical marketing and application engineering.

Created a special task force and regained this division's market position.

Realigned market focus, narrowed the customer base and focused on major OEMs.

* Achieved 60% budget growth for this division over three years.
* Planned and implemented current U.S. sales and engineering structures.
* Supervised a design center and QC laboratory.
* Implemented a more effective distribution program in conjunction with sister divisions.
* Created a QC tracking and early warning system.
* Developed a technical service center for this division.
* Initiated the use of satellites for a worldwide design center communications program.

Hitachi Semiconductor Division responsibilities:

National Application Engineering Manager - San Jose, CA   1996-1998

Directed tactical field activity for this division's strategic account base.

Acted as liaison to a Japan-based design center.

Involved in LSI Architectural development for a four- and eight-bit product family.

* Indirectly responsible for custom/semi-custom LSI sales budget of $8 million/month.
* Developed a national engineering program and centralized management functions.
* Created a technical training program and MBO career development programs.
* Developed a strategic business plan for a new 16-bit microfamily through beta level.

Regional Engineering Manager - Dearborn, MI   1995-1996

Responsible for all aspects of regional sales engineering, including objectives, budgets, personnel planning, bonus structures and territory assignments.

* Established strategies for a custom LSI growth plan and achieved budget expansion from $2.5 million to $3.5 million/month.

Application Engineering Specialist - Dearborn, MI   1994-1995

Designated microprocessor application specialist to GM, Ford and Chrysler corporations.

<u>Prior Experience</u>

<u>Ford Motor Company,</u> Electronics Division, Dearborn, MI

Product Design Engineer - Electronic Instrumentation

Senior Test Engineer - Electronic Systems Engineering

Product Development Engineer

Product Design Engineer

EDUCATION:

<u>Oklahoma State University,</u> Stillwater, OK

B.S. Degree: Electronics Engineering

Sent 70; received 15 interviews.

Arnold Jabber

5467 Whiteside Drive
Hanover Park, IL 60103

630/555-5456
lord@world.net

MATERIALS MANAGEMENT

PROFILE:
- ➤ Profit-building skills in logistics and materials planning, including full P&L responsibility for special projects and Distribution Requirements Planning (DRP) in manufacturing environments.
- ➤ Coordinate new product introductions and design/implement custom MRP, inventory and forecasting systems.
- ➤ Effectively hire, train and supervise staff and management in freight routing, distribution, inventory control and warehouse operations.

EXPERIENCE: Apex Photo Film USA, Inc., Snapper, IL

Materials Planning and Logistics   2002-Present

Manage more than 8,000 SKUs and virtually all MRP and logistics, including sales forecasting and DRP with production staff.

In charge of multiple complex projects; negotiate contracts with vendors and suppliers, including all major freight carriers.

Perform cost-effective purchasing of OEM products, packing materials and capital equipment.

Coordinate new product introductions with manufacturing managers.

Conduct group and individual training of staff and supervisors in logistics and company procedures.

Authorize purchase agreements with numerous vendors.

Utilize Windows applications, including MS Word, Excel, PowerPoint and a custom inventory system.

- → Increased inventory turns by 400% and reduced months-on-hand from 2.7 to 1.5.
- → Reduced monthly inventory from $30 million/month to $20 million, while sales grew 22%.
- → Instrumental in developing and implementing a custom MRP and forecasting system.

Inventory Control Manager for Distribution   1999-2001

Trained and supervised staff in a warehouse management system, including physical inventories and freight claim processing.

Distribution Supervisor   1996-1999

Supervised a team of four and wrote/expedited freight bills.

Gained excellent experience in distribution operations.

EDUCATION: WR Harper College, Palatine, IL
A.A. Degree in Business
Certificate in Materials Management

MEMBERSHIP: **APICS: Association of Production and Inventory Control Society** since 1995.

Sent 30; received four interviews and a new job.

SINATRA FRANCIS

5634 Passer Drive   710/555-5303
San Pedro, CA 90732   Swinger@alumedu.net

Management Consulting: Business/Technology

A position where analytical and quantitative abilities in team building, communications, organization and strategic planning would be of value.

PROFILE:

- Skilled in project supervision, multimedia presentations, information technology, report preparation, technical research and team leadership.
- Coordinate a wide variety of team projects, including database management and the formulation of quantitative/analytical engineering models for applications in the medical, space and aircraft design industries.
- Plan and conduct technical presentations in a professional manner for executive audiences; research and produce articles and reports for publication.
- Consistently recognized by executive management and colleagues for cross-discipline talents in needs analysis, troubleshooting and problem resolution in high-pressure, technical environments.

TECHNICAL:

- Knowledge of Windows 7/NT, UNIX, Pascal, HTML, MS Office, FrameMaker and Internet applications.
- Familiar with AutoCAD, Pro/ENGINEER, I-DEAS, Maple, Mathematica and programming with MATLAB (SIMULINK, Nonlinear Identification Toolkit, Image Processing Toolbox).
- Currently hold an Engineer-in-Training license #XE093436 through the California Department of Consumer Affairs since 1994.

EXPERIENCE: Bolton Hospital, Boston, MA   2006-2008

Bioengineering Research Assistant

Responsible for project consulting with an interdisciplinary team, tasked with studying applications between mechanical engineering and cardiopulmonary physiology.

Worked closely with doctoral biomedical engineers, medical staff and physicists in data collection, analysis and solution generation.

- Supervised a team in the development of new methodologies to analyze a variety of medical data related to Positron Emission Tomography (PET) applications.
- Personally drove a project to develop a mathematical model to analyze PET data; quantitatively tracked gas exchange in lungs using PET medical images.
- Partnered with team members in over 72 full-day PET experiments, while producing collaboratory protocols and procedures.
- Key participant in 10 major bioengineering projects; author of two papers presented during conferences of the American Thoracic Society and Biomedical Engineering Society from 2007-2008.
- Submitted original research for publication in four different biomedical engineering and medical journals.

Rockwell Space Systems Division, Downey, CA   2005-2006
Technical Assistant

Interfaced with senior engineers in the dynamic/structural analyses of current and advanced versions of Space Shuttle payloads during on-orbit flight.

Served as a co-author for many detailed in-house reports to track and monitor project activity.

→ Revised and updated spreadsheet programs for quantifying and summarizing on-orbit loads for U.S. shuttle missions with the Russian Space Station Mir.

C&D Interiors, Inc., Huntington Beach, CA   2004-2005
Intern

Conducted a case study involving the testing of miniature, honeycomb-panel sandwich structures for mechanical strength and flammability properties for aircraft applications.

→ Recommended numerous modifications to select better materials, meet specifications and enhance redesign efforts.

→ Created and updated a searchable database to collate and analyze test results.

EDUCATION: Massachusetts Institute of Technology, Cambridge, MA   2003
M.S. Degree in Mechanical Engineering; GPA: 4.2/5.0.

→ Researched and wrote a thesis in bioengineering titled, "Quantification of Regional Perfusion, Shunt Fraction and Ventilation Using Positron Emission Tomography: A Nonlinear Tracer Kinetics Model."

→ Vice President of Young Alumni with the MIT Club of Southern California.

Loyola Marymount University, Los Angeles, CA   2001
B.S. Degree in Mechanical Engineering; Cum Laude, GPA: 3.7/4.0; Dean's List five of eight semesters.

→ Completed several engineering projects involving mechanical and automotive applications.

→ Recognized as 2001 LMU Outstanding Graduate in Mechanical Engineering, 2000 LMU Senior Mechanical Engineering Student of the Year and 2000 LMU Junior Mechanical Engineering Student of the Year.

→ Member of several key honorary societies, such as Tau Beta Pi, and listed in *Who's Who Among Students in American Universities and Colleges.*

ASSOCIATIONS: American Society of Mechanical Engineers.
                   Society of Automotive Engineers.

Sent 200 through email only; received 10 interviews and a new job.

Mohammed Fighter
23899 Blue Ocean
Columbia, MD 21045

ali@hotmail.com   443/555-5267

PRODUCTION OPERATIONS / MANAGEMENT

PROFILE:

➢ Skilled in a wide range of production operations, including full responsibility for production line setup and streamlining, quality control, staffing and budgets.

➢ Strong knowledge of ISO 9002, MRP, JIT, TQM, planning and logistics; coordinate job schedules and vendor relations; handle cost-effective purchasing and inventory control.

➢ Utilize Excel for spreadsheet development, graphs, charts and data diagrams; coordinate budgets and forecasts, and compile/present status reports for senior-level personnel.

➢ Effectively hire, train and supervise technical staff and production teams, including job scheduling, performance reviews and motivation.

EMPLOYMENT: Sumner Computer Corporation, Inc., Baltimore, MD   2008-Present
Production / Technical Manager
Responsible for the setup and operation of complete, turnkey production lines for the manufacture of high-end personal computer systems sold by major national accounts.
Utilize state-of-the-art systems and procedures for product assembly, testing and packaging.
In charge of ISO-9002 certification for all activities.
Effectively manage all production activities for the cost-effective assembly of more than 250 PCs per day, ranging from simple desktop systems to complex servers.
Manage various production supervisors, engineers, technicians and line teams.
Supervise in-house development and training programs for all categories of production staff.
Plan and prepare concise, detailed production schedules.
Develop master schedules to establish sequence and lead times for each operation and meet strict shipping dates, according to sales forecasts and customer orders.
Establish sequence of assembly, installation and other manufacturing operations to guide production teams.
Expedite operations to cut delays and constantly update schedules to meet unforeseen conditions.

→ Daily production turnover has increased from $50,000 to $300,000.
→ This is the largest national manufacturer of whitebox computers for major national accounts, such as Lockheed Martin.   .

→ Constantly analyze production specifications and plant capacity data to determine manufacturing processes, tools and human resource requirements.

→ Plan and schedule workflow for various divisions according to established manufacturing and lead times.

→ Prepare budgets and production/accounting reports.

→ Maintain excellent quality and quantity of products at minimal cost.

→ Effectively led the production team to meet initiatives in quality and cycle time.

<u>Ace Computer Systems Limited,</u> Kaduna, Nigeria   2005-2008
Technical / Plant Manager

Planned and established a complete, state-of-the-art production line for manufacturing personal computers.

Managed all assembly processes for more than 50 PCs per day.

Trained and supervised a successful team of technicians and assemblers.

→ Managed technical staff providing support in the Customer Service department.

→ Improved productivity by 100% over a period of six months through more effective management.

<u>Construction + Engineering Contract, AG,</u> Wiesbaden, Germany
Hardware Engineer   2004-2005

Updated and maintained all the computer hardware for the company's subsidiary: Dentate & Sawoe Construction company in Nigeria.

Diagnosed and repaired all types of hardware and software related problems for over 800 PCs.

→ Trained numerous technicians in preventive maintenance processes.

<u>Lilleker Brothers Limited,</u> Belfast, Northern Ireland
Electrical Engineer   2003-2004

Supervised electrical and telecommunication installation works in various projects executed by Lilleker Brothers Limited in Nigeria.

EDUCATION: <u>Ahmadu Bello University,</u> Zaria, Nigeria
Bachelor of Engineering   2003
Major: Electrical Engineering
Specialization: Electronics and Communication

<u>University of London,</u> London, England
General Certificate of Education   2000
Extensive training in:
Network Cabling Systems, NT administration, Advanced PC Maintenance, C-programming, Visual Basic Programming and MS Office.

Sent about 200 via mail and email; received 20 interviews.

Lester E. Square

7771 Ashfield Court		Res: 630/555-0279
Bloomingdale, IL 60108	mer@aol.com	Cell: 630/555-0724

CONSULTING / MANUFACTURING

PROFILE:

➤ Executive talents in high-tech manufacturing and turnaround operations, including full P&L responsibility for product development from concept to international marketing.

➤ Perform detailed business analysis for acquisitions and high-tech system streamlining; utilize TQM, ISO 9000 and Six Sigma concepts.

➤ Skilled in long- and short-term strategic planning, budgeting, forecasting, product sourcing and pricing with extensive contacts worldwide, especially Thailand; knowledge of the Thai language and Asian business customs.

➤ Effectively hire, train and supervise technical staff and management in product design, retooling, production, quality control, marketing and sales.

➤ Conduct top-level presentations and negotiate contracts in a professional manner.

EXPERIENCE: Top Die Casting, Ltd., Bangkok, Thailand   2008-Present
Director of Engineering
Responsible for the turnaround of this company, a major supplier to Scagate Technology, with $40 million in sales.
Conduct in-depth research to locate and transfer technologies used by 2300 employees producing die castings, including actuators and base plates.
Directly supervise a team of 80.
Utilize a solid background in procedures, including precision machining, composite insert molding and metallurgy.
Work closely with design engineers in the development of prototypes.
Directed and improved all sales and marketing efforts as the number one advisor to the company principal.

* Expanded the key client base from one to four through research and sales efforts, thus saving this company from closure.

* Utilized an extensive knowledge of Seagate Technology products and business techniques developed with that company, 2000-2004.

* Directed all retooling and production line setup, from vendor sourcing and cost-effective purchasing of parts and machinery to staff and management training.

* Refocused efforts from micro-management to highly successful teamwork, motivation and job ownership, from line workers to managers.

<u>Concise Industries,</u> Elk Grove Village, IL   2005-2008
Director of R&D/Sales and Operations Manager
In charge of research and development of cellular manufacturing in support of a turnkey program for Caterpillar.
Directed total manufacturing operations for sheet metal assemblies and climate controlled enclosures for the telecommunications industry.
* Managed a wide range of business interests for the company owner, including cash transactions and contract negotiations.
* This was a privately owned company with several business interests.

<u>Seagate Technology,</u> Scotts Valley, CA   2000-2005
Senior Materials Manager / Vendor Quality
Conducted extensive research of vendors and suppliers, including their prices, operations and capacity.
Worked directly with design engineers to ensure profitable, large-scale production.
Trained suppliers in effective communications to meet Seagate requirements and improve speed and profitability.
* Established systems to better respond to critical supply issues worldwide.

<u>MDA Thailand, Ltd.,</u> Bangkok, Thailand   Contract: 3/00-8/00
Managing Director
In charge of the Thailand facility of a U.S.-based company, producing machined castings and fine-blanked components for the disk drive industry.
Directed a team of five managers, while creating and implementing training for 150 production personnel.
Trained office staff in communications with foreign suppliers.
* Analyzed and improved procurement procedures.
* Greatly reduced monetary waste while leveling spending to match sales volume.

<u>Precision Founders, Inc.,</u> San Leandro, CA   1998-2000
International Market and Finished Parts Manager
Managed an entire offshore program for this manufacturer of aerospace equipment, computer peripherals and high-tech investment castings with gross annual sales of $32 million.
* Increased output of international sector from $2.8 million to $10 million in 18 months.

PRIOR EXPERIENCE: **Sales Representative:** Sold high-tech equipment and tools to various industries.
Tool and Patternmaker: Created wood and metal patterns from drawings.

EDUCATION: <u>Indiana University, Purdue University at Indianapolis,</u> Indianapolis, IN
Completed 12 hours in Effective Business courses.

Metals Engineering Institute, Indianapolis, IN
Completed 30 hours in Metallurgy.

Sent 40 and received 10 interviews.

SALLY M. BOND

2266 Metto Court
Naperville, IL 60540
007@gte.net

630/555-4880

MARKETING / PRODUCT DEVELOPMENT AND MANAGEMENT

PROFILE:

- Effectively manage product marketing to commercial customers with full P&L responsibility; plan annual marketing strategies and implement programs, including advertising and sales promotion components to build distributor and end-user sales.
- Conduct primary market research and surveys; perform data analysis and assess customer specifications and requirements; prepare sales proposals and executive presentations for clients and staff.
- Create sales materials and coordinate trade shows; work effectively with advertising agencies and develop direct mail programs targeting end-user markets.
- Manage communications with the sales force and act as marketing liaison between field sales and corporate staff. Assist with formal sales training.
- Knowledge of various Windows and Apple systems, including MS Word, ACT!, Lotus 1-2-3, Freelance and PowerPoint.

EMPLOYMENT: Breamer Marketing, Oakbrook Terrace, IL   1/09-Present
Account Executive

Personally market and promote the *Target Trak* and *Volume Trak* market reporting service to foodservice manufacturers through direct sales.

Provide support in client service and verify foodservice distributor cost data and product information.

→ Developed a strong knowledge of competing food and non-food products, used in creating new sales and marketing strategies.

Elmhurst Management Service, Elmhurst, IL   1/02-1/09
Contract Associate

As an Independent Market Consultant, performed in-depth professional interviews, data analysis and primary research for organizations marketing to industrial/commercial customers, including assessing client customer product quality requirements.

Kellogg Sales Company, Franklin Park, IL   4/99-11/01
Foodservice Division Product Manager

Managed the marketing of Kellogg's Eggo Waffles and Mrs. Smith's Pies to commercial customers, with P&L responsibility.

Planned annual marketing strategy and implemented marketing programs, including advertising and sales promotion components.

Built incremental distributor and end-user sales and a strong repeat business. Researched and developed tactical and strategic market plans and conducted sales training.

Managed market communications and acted as liaison between field sales and corporate staff regarding marketing programs, sales issues and customer service.

Piggybacked on the successful retail Special-K Waffle market and targeted the school/healthcare commercial/institutional market segments where low fat content is significant.

Worked with the American Dietetic Association to gain professional approval of the low-fat designation.

Developed a consumer preference brochure to market consumer category Eggos to institutional and commercial foodservice operators.

Designed direct mail campaigns targeted towards healthcare and commercial/institutional market segments.

→ Developed the *Eggo School Backpack* promotion for school foodservice.

→ Achieved 20% sales growth through targeted promotions; secured improved awareness in brand target markets.

→ Responsible for winning a state-awarded bid for 24,000 cases.

Orval Kent Food Company, Wheeling, IL

Marketing Manager, New Products   11/98-4/01
Assistant Marketing Manager   7/97-11/98

Productively managed, planned and implemented new product introductions of refrigerated prepared salads and entrees. Facilitated new product development and influenced decisions on pricing, packaging and logistics. Effected in-house media buying, planning and expenditure tracking; coordinated packaging graphics development and administered a multi-account budget. Implemented packaging changes for company's 100+ product line, including branded, private-label and distributor-label products, marketed to commercial end-users and consumers.

Alyn Darnav Productions, Inc., Chicago, IL   7/96-7/97
Marketing Consultant

Developed strategic marketing plans through compilation and analysis of primary and secondary research data; researched consumer groups.

Mandabach & Simms, Inc., Chicago, IL   8/94-8/96
Assistant Media Planner

Implemented media buying and planning for 13 national marketing organizations at this advertising and public relations firm. Supervised media cost estimating staff.

EDUCATION: Northwestern University, Evanston, IL   Graduated 1994
Master of Science in Advertising

University of Illinois, Urbana, IL
Bachelor of Science in Advertising   Graduated 1992
Earned 51 hours toward undeclared second major in **Modern German Studies**.

In the first week, sent 20 to recruiting firms; received one interview and compliments on the resume.

Darlene D. Mitchell
997 Stratford #27
Bloomingdale, IL 60108

Yeow@aol.com   630/555-1216

MANAGEMENT / OPERATIONS

PROFILE:

➤ Perform all aspects of executive business development and team leadership, including P&L responsibility for new startups, procedures and operations.

➤ Skilled in the direction of creative marketing, advertising and sales; handle product sourcing, vendor relations and competitive analysis to meet rapidly changing trends in U.S. and Canadian markets.

➤ Proficient in change management, including staff and management hiring, training and supervision in sales, direct customer service and product lines; strong knowledge of HR procedures and regulations.

➤ Proven ability to greatly increase sales through team motivation and leadership at multiple locations; oversee budgets, forecasts, purchasing and inventories.

➤ Plan and conduct written and oral presentations for senior-level staff and management on topics including Franklin Time Management and new sales/customer service techniques.

CAREER BACKGROUND: Zachary Studio, Inc., U.S. and Canadian locations

District Manager - Chicago, IL   2007-Present

Responsible for five middle managers and all aspects of market expansion, staffing, procedures and operations streamlining.

Current project includes site selection/acquisition and a major venture with Venture Corporation.

Closely analyze profit potential of new locations, including sales figures of previous vendors.

Utilize a knowledge of Canadian and U.S. laws related to new startups, taxes and licensing and human resources issues.

Manage 20 portrait studios throughout Illinois, Wisconsin and Iowa, including hiring and indirectly supervising a team of 100.

Coordinate creative functions and distribution for promotions and advertising, including direct mail.

Constantly analyze and control operating costs through vendor negotiations and effective purchasing.

♦ Effectively train and develop managers in sales, photographic and acquisition departments.

♦ Handle a wide range of public relations issues.

♦ Managed the opening of a new division: "Pix Venture Portrait Studios." Opened 28 new portrait studios in Venture stores; performed detailed market and demographic research to ensure high profitability.

♦ Responsible for successfully "selling" the idea of a price increase for portrait services to senior executives.

♦ Instrumental in eliminating non-profitable telemarketing operations, resulting in major cost savings.

Area Manager, Burlington, Ontario, Canada   2005-2007
Supervised two managers and the entire Canadian division of this company, including 24 studios in Ontario.
Indirectly managed six to eight employees at each location, including interpretation of HR regulations and issues.

♦ Directed all aspects of business development for photographic sales and marketing departments at the studio level.

Regional Sales Director - Special Project   2006-2007
Implemented a new portrait product, including profitable pricing structures.
Developed sales techniques and trained floor staff in them through professional meetings and presentations in Canada, New England, Pittsburgh and the Midwest.

District Marketing Supervisor, Burlington, Canada   2004-2005
Performed general management, including staff hiring and training in all telemarketing procedures.
Researched and implemented a new telemarketing system in marketing units in Canada and New York State, including scripts, dialing procedures and personal communications with potential customers.

Area Marketing Supervisor, Chatham and Burton, Canada   2001-2004
Managed 14-20 telephone sales rooms, including all staff training and development in sales and supervision.

♦ Met or exceeded quotas on a regular basis.

♦ Achieved a 54% increase in Club Plan sales in 1991 over 1990, and reduced the cost per unit sold by $4.93.

Area Appointment Supervisor, Chatham, Canada   2000-2001
In charge of training, developing and supervising outbound appointment and customer service offices in 20 stores throughout Ontario.

Photographer and Photographic Trainer, Chatham, Ontario   1998-2000
Promoted from Studio Photographer to Photographic Trainer.

♦ Became a Certified Photographic Trainer in the first year.

Certified to conduct 12 management sessions through the Zenger-Miller program.

Sent 10 resumes; received four interviews; eventually hired for a new position.

Robert Stavis

8 SW 20th Street		Res: (206) 555-4482
Normandy Park, WA 98166	vish@hotmail.com	Cell: (206) 555-6939

Supply Chain Management – Director / Senior Manager

PROFILE:

➢ Comprehensive experience in strategic planning and supply chain management, including sourcing and support for manufacturing with a focus on supplier quality engineering and business management for various system integration projects.

➢ Perform logistics and business process re-engineering in highly competitive global and multicultural markets.

➢ Skilled in project and process management, team leadership and Supplier Risk Management processes and practices.

➢ Proficient in Lean Enterprise techniques, TQM, Total Cost of Ownership and competitive benchmarking applications to reduce costs and add value through the use of cutting-edge processes and practices.

➢ Familiar with Kaizen, Six Sigma and PQMI quality methodologies, as well as multiple ERP and MRP systems, including Oracle Financials, MFGPRO and Fourth Shift; trained in statistical improvement and control techniques.

➢ Certified Project Management Professional and ASQ Quality Engineer; utilize Windows systems and MS Office, including Word, Excel, Access and PowerPoint, as well as Matrix One.

EXPERIENCE: Big Dude Wireless / Netro Corporation / Lucent / NCR, Chicago, IL

2000-Present

Promoted through various positions and locations during tenure and sale of companies, most recent first:

Commodity Manager – Supply Management, Redmond, WA   8/11-Present

Establishing a number of new benchmarking and RFP processes to reduce costs in procuring consumer electronic handsets, with annual spending of $2 billion.

→ Realized more than $60 million in savings during the first quarter against the product portfolio.

→ Migrated the RFP process for cell phone handset procurement to other product areas and to enterprise-wide devices such as PDAs, smart phones and PC modem cards.

→ Served as primary liaison between the Procurement Strategy Council and AT&T.

→ Developed supplier performance scorecards for the IT procurement and handset procurement groups.

→ Currently developing a supplier qualification and selection process.

→ Creating a freight benchmarking process to reduce costs.

Manager Supply Chain Operations

Fixed Wireless Services - Netro, Redmond, WA   2002-2011

Established procurement processes for both MRO and Production order placement. Hired, trained and managed a support team of five buyers, Supply Line Engineers, Materials and Receiving & Shipping Managers.

→ Managed the integration project of a new procurement MRP system platform (Fourth Shift).

→ Directed the identification and selection of a Contract Manufacturing partner.

→ Received Netro peer bonus for meeting accelerated objectives.

Manager - Special Projects and Processes, Supply Management

AT&T Wireless Services, Redmond, WA   1999-2002

Served as a member of the Supply Management Leadership Team, establishing organizational strategy, value and mission objectives.

Managed the integration of newly acquired markets' processes and resources for LA Cellular and Wireless One in Florida.

Directed the deployment phase of key supplier order management processes.

Developed and maintained ongoing measurement of key Supply Chain Management success metrics.

Developed and tracked target costs for primary product lines.

→ Saved $10 million in 1 year through the implementation of Supplier Quality/Engineering initiatives.

→ Supported the New Product Introduction process through supplier and component risk management methodologies.

→ Released six product platforms in an 18-month period.

→ Executed and maintained the supplier/component quality management processes.

→ Provided functional support to the selection, development and release of an enterprise-wide PDM system (Matrix One).

→ Utilized Six Sigma low cost sourcing, benchmarking and RFP processes.

Manager - Global Procurement, Supply Management Center

Lucent, Allentown, PA   1996-1999

Staffed and managed the IS team responsible for local data warehousing and information management.

Supported the $1.3 billion competitive analysis for annual semiconductor negotiations.

→ Released Printed Circuit Boards and Power Systems commodity cost models.

→ Supported the Printed Circuit Board and Backplane team responsible for commercial supplier management totaling $200 million in annual purchases.

→ Assisted in negotiating the $1.2 billion supply agreement for selling the Interconnect Business Unit.

→ Authored the supplier performance metric section of the supply contract and provided technical and quality expertise.

Technical Staff Member - AT&T Bell Labs, Interconnect Center of Excellence
NCR Corporation / AT&T, Columbia, SC   1994-1996
Tracked and benchmarked AT&T suppliers' competitive position relative to the printed circuit board industry.

→ Spearheaded the supplier evaluation training session for the AT&T Asia Pacific and China regional supplier management teams.

Principal Engineer - Printed Circuit Board Supply Line Management
Center   1992-1994
Managed the supplier development program for core printed circuit board suppliers.

→ Developed and released the Printed Circuit Board Design Tradeoff Cost Model.

Supplier Management Engineer - Supply Line Management, Ithaca, NY
                                                                    1990-1992
Implemented the Supplier Certification processes for component commodities.

AFFILIATIONS: American Society for Quality and the Project Management Institute

EDUCATION: **Rochester Institute of Technology,** Rochester, NY
                 M.S. Degree - Materials Science and Engineering
                 B.S. Degree - Chemistry

                 Project Management Institute
                 Certified Project Management Professional

                 American Society for Quality
                 Certified Quality Engineer

Used only one resume; received interview and accepted a new position.

Morris G. Father
3302 Keys Road
Elgin, IL 60120

630/555-0061   Mordude@ymail.com

MORTGAGE BANKING

PROFILE:
♦ Profit-building skills in new business development, including responsibility for special promotions, marketing and strategic planning.

♦ Skilled in diversification and the development of broker and/or correspondence relationships in multiple states, with a proven ability to increase volume and profits.

♦ Effectively hire, train and supervise staff in account acquisition, primarily through networking and personal relationships.

♦ Determine systems, controls and credit criteria, while ensuring compliance; coordinate underwriting and reporting procedures.

CAREER BACKGROUND:

<u>Just Stuff - Division of Western Bank,</u> Irvine, CA
Regional Sales Manager - Elgin, IL   2/08-Present
In charge of hiring and supervising up to 22 account executives, primarily acquiring broker-originated B&C product.
Personally train and coordinate sales staff in multiple states in accordance with business plans and volume goals.
Constantly analyze competitors' rates, products, services and marketing techniques.
Maintain a high degree of speed, accuracy and service between brokers and underwriting personnel.
Provide recommendations to update our programs to expand profits while minimizing risk.
Involved in all phases of program development and reporting on market status, including competitors' services.
Coordinate underwriting and reporting procedures, as well as broker selection.
♦ Currently on target to meet staffing and volume goals by end of the first quarter.
♦ Developing an extensive network of correspondent flow product.

<u>Access Financial Corporation,</u> St. Louis Park, MN
National Sales Manager   5/07-1/08
Trained and supervised sales teams and planned and implemented strategies to diversify in broker and retail products.
♦ Promoted to this position from:

Account Executive   5/04-5/07
Fully responsible for business development in the midwest region, as this company's first Account Executive.
Constantly exceeded all goals for monthly volume and new account acquisition.
Developed loans from correspondent sources comprised of forward commitments, bulks and flow product.
♦ Developed $450 million in new loans, 2007.

<u>Household Bank,</u> Prospect Heights, IL

Vice President: Consumer Division   1999-5/04

Successfully developed a national home improvement financing program for contractors.

Involved in all phases of implementing the home improvement financing program.

Ensured compliance and established underwriting criteria, forms and contractor selection criteria.

Responsible for hiring, training, scheduling and directing all sales personnel in account prospecting, sales presentations and customer service.

Designed and implemented a national financing program for mortgage brokers.

Involved in all phases of program development, including the analysis and reporting on market status, competitor's rates, products, services and marketing strategies.

Maintained a high degree of speed, accuracy and service between brokers and underwriting personnel.

Provided recommendations to update our programs to expand profits while minimizing risk.

- ♦ Programs were initiated in Illinois and eventually expanded nationwide.
- ♦ Responsible for originating the purchase of mini bulks up to $25 million.
- ♦ Programs were implemented in less than 10 months and well under budget.
- ♦ Volume goals were exceeded in the first year, and this division turned profitable in the first eight months.
- ♦ Personally earned the maximum bonuses available in the first year: 80 percent of base salary.

<u>Dartmouth Plan,</u> Garden City, NY

Vice President: Secondary Marketing   1994-1999

Effectively developed and maintained strong working relationships with financial institutions seeking to purchase bulk portfolios of home improvement or home equity loans.

- ♦ Developed new sources who committed between $1 million and $15 million in monthly funding.

Prior Experience

<u>Insured Credit Services,</u> Division of Republic Insurance Company, Chicago, IL

Senior Vice President and Director of Underwriting

In charge of all underwriting and business development, including supervision of up to 20 underwriters.

This company specialized in providing credit loss insurance to financial institutions.

EDUCATION: <u>Southern Illinois University</u> and

<u>Elmhurst College:</u> Various business courses.

<u>American Banker's Association:</u> Completed various courses in banking.

Member of the National Home Equity Mortgage Association and numerous state Mortgage Broker/Banker Associations. Member: National Remodeler's Association.

Sent four; received two interviews.

Irving Texan

444 W 844 Temple Drive
Medinah, TX 60157
gbbs@ameritech.net   Res.: 630/555-4041   Message and Fax: 630/555-9312

NETWORK ENGINEERING

PROFILE:

→ Technical and team leadership experience in network design, installation and troubleshooting, including full responsibility for special projects and team supervision.

→ **Certified Netware Engineer;** manage research and development for customized systems; coordinate vendors and suppliers, negotiate contracts and oversee cost-effective hardware and software purchasing.

→ Skilled in Y2K troubleshooting; experience with data acquisition equipment, sales automation, national surveys, infrastructure, remote access and customized e-mail systems.

→ Perform detailed needs analysis and establish and implement hardware, software and platform standards. *Experience in a wide range of systems listed on page two.*

EXPERIENCE: <u>Capers Manufacturing, Inc.,</u> Chicago, IL   10/05-Present
Director of Desktop Technologies

Responsible for full project management and all network duties for a 700-node, 45-server LAN environment, including full system research, configuration and installation.

Train and supervise a team of four, while overseeing network operations in 10 countries.

Install and configure all OEM and specialty software packages.

Supervise the group responsible for research and determine desktop hardware and software standards for the global enterprise network, including but not limited to: laptop and desktop computers, palm top computers, printers, plotters, scanners, digitizers, LCD monitors, LCD projectors, faxes and combination technologies.

Perform network backups and maintain NDS tree design and a bindery database.

Supply third-level technical support for the help desk and Capers' product support centers.

⇨ Developed and implemented a Sales Automation system using laptop computers, including infrastructure design and remote access; this was a highly successful $250,000 project, outlined below.

⇨ Act as Project Manager for various enterprise-wide software and hardware upgrades.

⇨ Effectively research, set up and maintain industry specific hardware and software for data acquisition processes.

⇨ Supervise teams in desktop technology, R&D and Capers customer technical support, as well as the entire R&D center.

⇨ Promoted to this position from Help Desk Technician.

Sales Automation Project: Laptop Infrastructure

Upgraded the entire laptop infrastructure, including extensive research, analysis and purchasing of systems used worldwide.

Increased systems from 55 to 200; connectivity now includes remote e-mail, full network and remote access to all application software.

Developed a network of support for end-users and supervised two employees.

Conducted extensive research of numerous brands and established all procedures for ordering, repairing, upgrading and refurbishing laptops.

Personally developed the standard base software package and hardware specifications, which now includes full remote access to network resources, including printing, files, e-mail and shared directory services.

⇨ With a budget of $250,000, this project was completed on time at a cost of only $220,000, spread through several different departments and general lcdgcrs.

⇨ Expanded global coverage of the Capers sales force by more than 50%.

⇨ Stabilized and standardized the system in place to order, maintain, support and expand the laptop base owned by Capers.

⇨ Developed a strong, committed vendor/customer relationship between Fujitsu and Capers; became a full global business partner with Fujitsu, placed on a PO system for all service, sales and support, resulting in a direct, yet global support structure.

PC Products and Services, Inc., Roselle, IL   9/01-10/05

Senior Supervising Technician promoted from **Bench Technician**

Bench technician repairing and troubleshooting printers, monitors and PCs. Software troubleshooting and technical support both via telephone and in person. Order and maintain general and specialty supply inventory, product analysis, product usage decisions, personnel scheduling and training for six technicians, warranty paper work for IBM, Compaq, Panasonic, Okidata, Citizen and Star.

Radio Shack / Tandy Corporation, Inc., Elgin, IL   7/98-8/01

Assistant Manager promoted from **Sale Associate**

District resource person for general electronics technical support, general sales, order, inventory and P&L refinement.

MEMBERSHIPS: MCP, CNE, CNA, ICSA, NUI (Novell Users International), Membership IBM Warranty repair certified for laptops and PCs through the Aptiva line; Compaq Warranty repair Certified A 4- Certified Windows 7; Certified Full CNE - track course completed.

Hardware setup and maintenance experience:

Exabyte Tape robot.

Hewlett-Packard Netservers E, Net pro, LC3, LH and LX series servers.

HP Jet Direct cards and boxes.

HP DeskJets all model series.

HP LaserJet 2 through 4L, 4000, 6000, 5si and 5 Color; Hewlett-Packard

Design Jet all series plotters.

Motorola bit surfer ISDN modems.

NEC, Fujitsu, Toshiba, IBM, Compaq laptops.

Compaq; Dell; IBM; Gateway 2000; and clone PCs.

Nematron Data acquisition modules, General Electric Data acquisition modules.

Network topologies and hardware:

Ethernet, 10Base-T UTP, 10 and 100 megabit hubs, Intelligent Hubs, switches:
NICS from 3COM, Intel, Xircom, Linksys, Madge, Boca and D-Link.

Operating systems:

Windows XP and 7; UNIX and Windows NT Workstation.

NOS:

Novell Netware and Intranetware - Install and Configure Microsoft Networking
Microsoft Windows NT Server 3.51, 4.0 - Basic knowledge of LANtastic NOS.

Network and groupware:

Exchange client; MS Mail client; Castell Faxpress hardware and software; IBM emulation
software using Rumba; WRQ Terminal Emulator Reflection 1, versions 4, 5, 5.1 and
5.21; Symantec antivirus for Netware and Windows NT; Support Magic Enterprise
edition V4.00.0; Seagate Software Winstall; Bitshare modem pool software; Arcserve
V6.0; Softrack Software tracking; Adaptées Smart CD writer; Hewlett-Packard's Sure
Store CD writer.

OEM and specialty applications

Stairs Financial tracking and reporting system.

Dun & Bradstreet financial tracking and reporting system.

Shot Scope data acquisition software.

Mattek data acquisition software.

Production Process and OPM data acquisition software.

Demand Solutions for Windows.

Data Streams MP2 Maintenance tracking software Enterprise edition and Access edition.

Sent about 50; received seven interviews.

LANSING D. CIRCUIT
2281 Papa Court
Carol Stream, IL 60188

kessel@flash.net   630/555-9432

NETWORK ADMINISTRATION

PROFILE:
> Provide high-impact, executive leadership in full system design, network administration and operations, including installation, troubleshooting and management.
> Effectively configure, install and maintain cutting-edge LANS and Windows NT systems, including full documentation; oversee the building, installation and troubleshooting of PCs and peripherals, including printers, as well as cabling and routing.
> Train and supervise technical and service staff; handle customer relations and written/oral presentations in a professional manner.
> Well versed in TCP/IP; utilize Windows XP, 7, NT, LANtastic, ISDN, TokenRing NICs; MS Word and Excel; familiar with Novell 3.12. LANS: TCP, SPX and NetWare.

EMPLOYMENT:
Toptronic, Inc., Chicago, IL   8/07-Present
Field Service Technician - Midwest
Determine specific client needs and install, repair and maintain reflow ovens and automated rework stations for printed circuit boards.
Interface with representatives from key accounts such as Motorola, 3Com and Visteon.
Conduct group and individual training for internal staff and end-users.
Involved in escalation from Tier-1 support; work closely with managers, field engineers and application engineers regarding customer issues.
Responsible for a wide range of technical functions, including the setup of Windows XP as a Peer to Peer NOS; perform software upgrades and install and configure operating systems, including Windows XP / 7 and Windows NT.
Effectively design, develop and maintain test platforms, including building test networks and evaluating test procedures and equipment.
→ Offered a Service Manager's position after only one year.
→ Specially selected for trade show presentations and to maintain all software and control systems for Visteon's new prototype oven.
→ Document system installation, configuration and optimization.
→ Determine reliability of single-level piece parts, including testing, verifying, approving and determining which vendors to utilize.

Medical Equipment & Imaging Services, Carol Stream, IL   2/05-Present (PT)
and:
Computer Hardware Engineering, West Chicago, IL   2/03-8/05
Consultant / Technician
Responsible for the setup and operation of these consulting companies, including all procedures, marketing and personal client relations.

Handle component-level troubleshooting of systems ranging from X-ray and therapy equipment to IBM mainframes.

Plan and conduct full system configurations, installations/de-installations and upgrades.

Acted as broker for used IBM equipment and repaired, upgraded and assembled PCs throughout the U.S., Europe, the Middle East and the Pacific Rim.

→ Install small networks and repaired printers and other peripherals.

→ Sell and market all services, including new business development and promotions.

→ Gained proficiency in LAN inter-working, routing protocols, TCP/IP configuration, modem technology, routers, ISDN and LANtastic.

→ Accurately diagnose failures and analyze/solve PCB, ICT and system-level problems.

Datanon, Ltd., Carol Stream, IL   3/95-2/03
Contract Maintenance

Relocated to the U.S. and performed service contract administration and maintenance at Leggett & Piatt, Carthage, MO.

Planned and managed the relocation of L&P's data center, including all daily maintenance and the repair of IBM data processing equipment.

Provided full technical support and trained service engineers on mainframes and peripherals.

→ Upon transfer to Chicago in 1986, directly involved in research and development for upgrade paths on the IBM 3080 series of mainframe computers.

→ Performed upgrades at major corporations throughout the U.S., Europe, the Middle East, Africa and the Pacific Rim, primarily on IBM ES9001 and 9121 mainframes.

IBM Corporation, Johannesburg, South Africa   10/91-3/95
Senior Computer Engineer promoted from **Computer Engineer / Trainee**

In charge of all equipment repairs and upgrades for the full line of IBM computers and peripherals.

→ Responsible for all hardware in the data centers at South African Airways and the University of Witwatersrand at Johannesburg.

Gilbarco, Alberton, South Africa   2/91-10/91
Field Service Representative

Responsible for timely repair of the first computerized fuel pumps in South Africa. Assisted in organizing parts repair workshops and field repair service kits.

EDUCATION: Vaal Triangle Technikon, Van Der Bijl Park, South Africa   1990
                   Successful completion of two years of courses in electronics.
                   * Currently studying for MCSE Certification.

PERSONAL: Enjoy SCUBA diving, outdoor sports, woodworking and home projects.

Sent 68 resumes; received four interviews.

SATHER C. ROLL
478 Swell Road, #204
Marietta, GA 30062

Res: 770/555-1290   cinnamon@pobox.com   Cell: 770/555-0243

EXECUTIVE MANAGEMENT / OPERATIONS / CONSULTING

PROFILE:

♦ Proven leadership talents in new business development, turnarounds and senior-level operations for multiple locations, including detailed analysis, consulting and the effective management of projects and revenue.

♦ Skilled in conceptual problem-solving in matters related to finance, budgets, revenue management, team building, hands-on leadership and computer system development.

♦ Plan and execute comprehensive plans for successful turnarounds in fast-paced industries; proficient in budget planning, forecasting, detailed performance modeling and financial analysis encompassing performance factors for individual business units.

♦ Human resource experience includes staff and management hiring, training, supervision and motivation; reorganize staff and management into cohesive, motivated teams, including assessment of management structures.

♦ Skilled in spreadsheet development, data processing and major corporate computer system upgrades; utilize Windows XP and 7, Lotus, Excel, Access, PowerPoint, Outlook, Smartstream and MS Word; familiar with Novell networks.

EXPERIENCE: Major Car Rental, East Coast Division, Atlanta, GA   11/06-Present
Senior Director of Operations

Promoted as part of a company restructuring and to improve the P&L of a poorly performing division with more than $200 million in revenues.

Directly manage a staff of 11, indirectly responsible for 1,100; provide training in all aspects of operations management, with a focus on how to manage branches to meet business plan goals.

Design and implement detailed plans to cease operations with a minimum of disruption, including a system to safeguard and redistribute company assets once operations had ceased.

Monitor pricing, reservations and utilization of automobiles to maintain effective fleet levels.

Travel 80% to establish, implement and conduct monthly operational review meetings with all branch managers.

♦ Successfully turned around 2006 divisional losses of more than $10 million to a 2008 profit of more than $10 million; 2008 was the first year this region ever showed a profit and the first time the division exceeded business plan.

♦ Created and directed a corporate task force to limit salvage losses nationwide; directed closing activities for 30 unprofitable locations.

♦ Through April 2009, company salvage losses are on a pace to be $7 million below 2008 losses of $35 million.

- Worked closely with each location to develop and oversee the implementation of customized, city-targeted business plans to improve bottom-line performance.
- Developed a profitability model used to determine an optimum business paradigm for any location, based on location-specific factors.
- Responsible for divisional P&L and daily operations, including the design and implementation of strategic and tactical plans to improve all areas of performance.
- Devised and implemented yield strategies with the corporate revenue management group to support profitable revenue growth.
- Created margin analysis models to determine optimal fleet mix in all locations.
- Planned and executed fleet acquisitions and disposals to maximize profitability.
- Devised and implemented a new management training program to increase the effectiveness of field management.
- Created and directed a corporate task force on limiting salvage losses.
- Implemented a division-wide field management restructuring process, which included determining staffing needs in all branches, assessing all management staff and the final disposition of all salaried staff in the branches.
- Team leader for Automotive Rental Group Odyssey team responsible for coordinating development of enhanced computerized rental system, revenue tracking and analysis of safety and security issues.

General Manager of Operations, Jacksonville, FL   11/05-10/06
Responsible for P&L, daily management and operational functions for an operation with annual revenues of $7 million, a fleet of 750 vehicles and a staff of 35.
Location's monthly profitability exceeded prior year in 11 of 12 months, even with volume below prior year in most months.
Introduced a new marketing plan for a park-and-fly operation and increased revenues by 50 percent.
- Location exceeded profit budget all 12 months.
- Location exceeded customer service standard all 12 months.

Divisional Incremental Sales Manager
South Division, Fort Lauderdale, FL   5/05-10/05
Effective in supporting local management efforts in incremental sales in 45 locations in Florida, Texas and the Southeast.
Trained field management in incremental sales (fuel, insurance and upselling to larger cars).
- Determined branch sales budgets and monitored performance.
- Assisted branch management in day-to-day implementation of strategies to improve incremental sales and customer service.

Corporate Manager

Incremental Sales, Operations Planning, Fort Lauderdale, FL   10/03-4/05

Conceived and implemented programs to improve incremental sales performance in all locations.

Produced forecasts and budgeted incremental sales; closely monitored performance of strategies.

♦ Acted as Project Leader in a significant upgrade of a company-wide computerized rental system to improve performance.

Incremental Sales Manager, Seattle Rental Station, WA   6/02-9/03

Responsible for managing rental counter operations in a location with 40 rental agents.

♦ Devised and implemented a training program that increased performance and decreased turnover.

Time Critical Freight, Laurel, MD   6/00-12/01
President

Established and managed this distribution company, specializing in next day delivery services in the Washington and Baltimore area.

Performed all marketing, sales and business development.

Coordinated budgets, forecasting and finance functions.

♦ Selected and installed the company computer system for order entry, tracking, billing, manifests and bills of lading.

♦ Managed up to 50 employees and sold the company at a profit.

Michael's Courier Service, Chevy Chase, MD   I/91-5/00

Positions of increasing responsibility included:

General Manager, Sales Manager, Salesman, Dispatcher, Messenger

Eventually responsible for a team of 125 in all activities.

♦ Hired a computer programmer; instrumental in developing an online delivery tracking system using a Novell LAN.

EDUCATION: American Management Institute, Washington, D.C.   1999
Successful completion of a week-long class in Financial Analysis.

Client Development Institute, Reston, VA   1993
Successful completion of courses in Professional Sales.

George Washington University, Washington, D.C.
M.A. Degree: English Literature   1990
B.A. Degree: English Literature   1989

Sent six targeted resumes; received four interviews and a new job.

Jackson Michaels
223 East View Drive
Bartlett, IL 60103

Res: 630/555-9223 Jack@netcom.com   Cellular: 630/555-8805

TECHNICAL SERVICE OUTSOURCING / OPERATIONS

PROFILE:

➢ Executive talents in new business development and IT outsourcing, including full responsibility for program planning, staffing and highly profitable sales organizations.

➢ Well versed in LAN and WAN systems, including SNA, frame relay and routed network architectures; coordinate budgets, systems, procedures and technical staff to quickly respond to new technologies.

➢ Effectively hire, train and supervise multiple, high-impact sales teams in account acquisition and management.

➢ Skilled in market research, strategic planning and technical product development; handle market penetration and determine and meet specific client needs for technical product lines.

➢ Oversee P&L, successful turnarounds, long-term business growth and high product and service quality standards.

EMPLOYMENT: All Technology, Inc., Lisle, IL   4/08-Present
National Team Manager
In charge of the sale and implementation of IT management software and solutions for system, data and application management, primarily for productivity enhancement and cost reduction programs to major national accounts such as Sears, IBM and Accenture. Personally recruit and motivate product specialists, including all interviewing and training.
Train and supervise a sales team in lead development, custom sales proposals, presentations and key account management.
Work directly with sales staff and clients to closely analyze their business procedures and create customized programs to lower cost and transaction time while expanding profitability.

♦ Projected to exceed annual sales quota of $4.3 million; currently 80% of 2009 quota.

♦ Exceeded 2008 sales quota in the first five months by 86%.

IBE, Schaumburg, IL   8/04-4/08
Project Executive
Directed all P&L and WAN outsourcing operations, primarily using SNA, frame relay and routed network systems.
Performed total project management, including full coordination of technical and sales teams.
Oversaw a team of 97 in sales, product configuration, installations, documentation and troubleshooting.
Developed and supervised delivery teams and prepared environments for ongoing operations.

♦ Specialized in account turnarounds, including detailed needs analysis and custom sales proposals and presentations.

- Accurately measured/tracked customer satisfaction and profitability.
- Designed and delivered mission-critical systems for operations at Sears, Zurich Insurance and Allstate.
- Responsible for an IBM business segment valued at $476 million at Allstate.

<u>Digital Equipment Corporation,</u> St. Louis, MO   1997-7/04
Sales Executive   2001-7/04

Performed extensive account acquisition and sales, as well as project management for large, complex computer system installations.

Produced sales leads through strategic analysis of markets and industry trends; created and implemented custom sales proposals.

Established contacts and worked directly with top executives at major utilities.

- Reached 193% of targeted budget for FY 2003; exceeded 2004 goal by 200%.
- Designed production systems and custom integration programs to meet critical business needs.
- Earned the Circle of Excellence award in 2002; achieved 800% growth in six months in a single account.

Senior Sales Representative   1997-2001

As Account Manager for the Caterpillar Engine Division, planned and implemented sales campaigns in office automation, analytical analysis, CAD/CAM, quality systems, systems integration and customer services.

Directly involved in strategic committees; gained a detailed knowledge of corporate goals to formulate new applications for goods and services.

Produced highly effective sales campaigns for the engine division.

- Expanded market share from 30% to 65% and revenue growth from $2.8 to $8.1 million per year, FY 1996 vs. 2000.
- Increased consumption of goods and services by more than 50% for three out of four years, 1997-2001.
- Promoted to Sales Executive for strong performance, 2001.

<u>Xerox Corporation,</u> Peoria, IL   1990-1997
Senior Marketing Executive

Personally managed the Caterpillar account for Illinois, working directly with plants to target business opportunities and negotiate agreements.

Directly or indirectly increased sales for 85% of all product lines.

- Consistently promoted for strong sales performance; increases exceeded 140% each year.
- Member of Xerox's PAR/President's Club, 1986-1990.

EDUCATION: <u>Eureka College,</u> Eureka, IL
                    B.A. Degree: Business and Economics   1990
                    Concentrations in Speech, Theater and Sociology.
                    President: College Alumni Board: 1982-1983; Elected Class President, 1986-1989.

                    <u>Babson College,</u> Wellesley, MA   2001
                    Advanced Consultant Training - Executive Education Program.

PERSONAL: Current board member of the Twinbrook YMCA.
                    Fundraiser for The United Way, The Salvation Army and Eureka College.

Sent 50; received 12 interviews.

JUAN VELDEZ
554 Hunter Court
Roselle, IL 60172

coffeeman@mailcity.com   630/555-2845

MANUFACTURING / PLANT MANAGEMENT

PROFILE:

➤ Comprehensive experience in total plant management, including full P&L responsibility for staffing, materials and state-of-the art production line setup and streamlining.

➤ Skilled in controlling materials, plant safety, inventories, the latest assembly methods and quality assurance for components and finished products.

➤ APICS Certified in MRP I and II; experience with ISO-9001, QS 9000, and SPC; constantly analyze production efficiency and reduce downtime.

➤ Effectively hire, train and supervise staff and management teams; design and implement cross training, operational sequencing, labor reporting, and corrective action procedures.

➤ Fluent in Spanish, with a proven ability to reduce overhead and consistently meet deadline and production requirements.

EXPERIENCE: Real Heavy Truck Products, Chicago, IL   12/08-3/09

Plant Manager promoted from **Manufacturing Operations Manager**

Responsible for all plant operations, including the management of up to 140 employees and seven supervisors.

Directed the setup and operation of production lines for truck parts, including vendor relations, job scheduling, tool maintenance and quality control.

Communicated with customers, vendors, suppliers and production staff in Spanish and English as required.

Oversaw a wide range of duties in shipping/receiving, manufacturing engineering and tooling, as well as in the sewing, trim, rock guard, shield and Tonneau Cover departments.

➤ Achieved 96% on-time shipping of products.

➤ Established a successful continuous improvement program.

➤ Created a preventive maintenance program and accepted oversight for plant safety.

Producers Financial Services, Hanover Park, IL   7/07-12/08

Loan Officer and Telemarketing Manager

Responsible for staff training and supervision to establish loans.

In charge of quality control, staff performance reviews and disciplinary measures.

Personally processed loans to successful conclusion.

➤ Acted as this company's radio and TV spokesperson.

Merkle & Korff, Des Plaines, IL   Freelance/temporary: 3/07-6/07

Manufacturing Consultant

On a consulting basis, conducted basic and motion/time studies.

Analyzed and incorporated more effective manufacturing processes; implemented procedures and trained personnel.

<u>Admiral Tool and Manufacturing,</u> Chicago, IL   3/06-2/07
Manufacturing Operations Supervisor
Effectively managed a first-shift metal stamping operation with a team of 35 union workers.
Conducted/oversaw quality inspections; ensured proper adherence to specifications and implemented adjustments as required.
Instructed staff in safety and daily procedures.
Trained hourly workers in conformance to QS-9001 standards, including translation from English and Spanish.

➤ As Chairperson for the Productivity Improvement team, created a $305,000 potential annual cost savings resulting from a six-month study.

<u>Olson International,</u> Lombard, IL   10/04-3/06
Manufacturing Operations Manager
Directed a two-shift manufacturing operation with 56 employees and additional temporaries.

➤ Increased profit by $100,000 by reworking non-conforming material.
➤ Effectively met 95% of production requirements.
➤ Chaired the Manufacturing and Process Improvement Committee.
➤ Established and implemented lockout/tagout procedures; trained workers in those procedures.
➤ Conducted monthly safety inspections.

<u>PSW Industries, Inc.,</u> Chicago, IL   2/03-10/04
Operations Manager - Pressroom
Managed a three-shift operation with 87 union workers for this independent lamination stamper, producing electrical parts for motors and transformers.
Member of the Quality Corrective Action Team & Safety Committee Chairperson.

➤ Met and exceeded press production goals within a 10-month period.
➤ Implemented successful press-operator training programs; greatly improved raw material processes, work-in progress, finished goods, quality and safety control.
➤ Reduced pressroom downtime and increased productivity.

<u>Hako Minuteman, Inc.,</u> Addison, IL   10/00-2/03
Operations Manager - Assembly
Managed six assembly lines and trained/supervised 35 union workers for this manufacturer of residential cleaning equipment.
Scheduled workers' hours and compiled production and efficiency reports.
Performed hiring, training, and staff performance reviews.

➤ Conducted safety and right-to-know training in compliance with OSHA standards; Chairman of the Safety Committee.
➤ Redesigned the assembly operation and increased efficiency by 40%, productivity by 7%, reduced manpower by 67%, and saved the company $250,000.
➤ Decreased downtime over 450 hours per month in 2000 and 10 hours per month by 2002.
➤ Completed the redesign and tooling of assembly operations $60,000 under budget.

<u>Midas International,</u> Bedford Park, IL   7/99-9/00
Manufacturing Superintendent
Managed four supervisors and up to 85 union employees using Mill, Eaton/Leonard
Benders and robotic, automatic and manual welding cells.
Coordinated workloads using a Mapics 36 system.
➤ Translated the entire quality procedures manual from English to Spanish.

Prior Experience:
Plant Manager: National Marketing Services, Mundelein, IL   1997-1999
➤ Converted a 28,000 s.f. warehouse to manufacturing use.
➤ Coordinated construction, material selection, permits and capital purchasing.
➤ Hired a trained union staff of 100; initiated manpower planning, policies and benefits.
➤ Established setup and sub-assembly operations; assisted in estimating and pricing.
➤ Prepared expense reports and capital budgets.
➤ Developed computerized scheduling/inventory and implemented successful labor
  improvement programs.

General Foreman: Parts Division, Deere & Company, Waterloo, IA,   1995-1997
Supervised up to 75 in sheet metal production using 200- to 600-ton hydraulic presses.
➤ Maintained a 93% incentive average within an 89% plant goal environment.

EDUCATION: <u>Truman College,</u> Chicago, IL
                   Associate in Applied Science Degree

**ADDITIONAL
TRAINING:**   Completed several Deere Employee Education Programs, college-level courses in:
                   Decision Processing, Data Processing/Control, MRP Concepts, Blueprint Reading,
                   Group Communications, Production/Inventory Control, Labor Improvement, Wage
                   Administration, Effective Interviewing, Supervisory Skills, Affirmative Action I and II,
                   and Safety Training.

                   Acquired a **Manufacturing Engineering Degree** through the Deere Employee
                   Education Program and completed 60 hours of MANMAN Manufacturing and repetitive
                   VAX training from ASK Computer Systems, Inc.

                   Perform Geometric Dimensioning and Tolerancing, SPC, Gage Repeatability and
                   Reproducibility from the American Supplier Institute, Inc., and Black & Decker.
                   ➤ Trained in TQM and Windows 7 through Northern Illinois University, DeKalb, IL.
                   ➤ Trained in Lotus through Elmhurst College, IL.

Sent 25; received 10 interviews; accepted five interviews.

Thomas Jefferson
2256 Scott Drive #238
Roselle, IL 60172

630/555-7221   Tommie@now.net

EXECUTIVE LEADERSHIP: PRODUCT DEVELOPMENT

A position using proven, creative talents and highly developed organization skills to bring to market new, successful products.

PROFILE:

> Comprehensive experience in multiple aspects of creative, new product design and development, including conceptualization, prototyping, project management and strategic marketing.

> Proven ability to handle multiple tasks and achieve specific goals; spearhead projects and work effectively in team environments; ensure follow-up and attention to detail to complete projects on time and under budget.

> Skilled in conceptualizing new item designs, including features, look and appeal; actively seek new challenges and pursue specific objectives.

> Coordinate brainstorming sessions, artwork, marketing/promotion development, prototyping and the production processes; visit foreign facilities to lead and improve new and existing product development.

> Proficient in Windows Office, as well as production management on an IBM iSeries to track the status of prototypes and items in production.

EXPERIENCE: Pottle Corporation, Itasca, IL

Senior Project Manager   2007-Present
Responsible for all aspects of new product and line development, including conceptualization, scheduling, art direction and production for this large consumer giftware producer.
Interfaced with overseas manufacturers to communicate item specifications, materials requirements, production schedules and prototyping.
Inspected prototypes and final product to ensure complete compliance with design and quality requirements.
Supplied manufacturing department with packaging specs, artwork, copyright and legal information.

→ Directed development of the company's third most successful line – eventually promoted to collectable status.
→ Effectively worked with a variety of departments to launch successful products.
→ Recognized for team building skills, leading to excellence in all finished products.

Project Manager, New Product Development   2004-2007

Coordinated the design and production processes of more than 30 licensed and in-house direct mail programs, with revenues exceeding $39 million annually. Directed total project management, including brainstorming, line development, product critiques and production coordination for 10 core product lines. Worked closely with licensed and freelance artists in the design of new lines and products.

→ Visited Asian manufacturing facilities to gain understanding of production processes and work with site representatives on prototypes, new product ideas and production requirements.

Project Manager, Licensing   2000-2004

Established licensing, international distribution rights and contracts, including administration and management.

Maintained extensive contact with international subsidiaries and legal department staff to track contract and negotiation status.

Processed contracts, amendments and financial agreements with licensed artists.

Acted as primary liaison between Enesco and their international subsidiaries and with the client base for copyright/trademark information.

→ Maintained accurate contract files, including copyright/trademark and royalty payments/financial commitment updates.
→ Promoted to this position from Licensing Administrator.

Cheshire Company, Mundelein, IL   1999-2000
Administrative

Responsible for coordinating the receipt of incoming equipment orders, as well as inventory control and trade show support.

Worked with District Sales Managers in distributing sales leads, planning sales meetings and preparing presentations for new dealers.

AWARDS AND DISTINCTIONS: *Outstanding Creative Support Person of the Year,* Enesco Corporation, 2002

Above and Beyond Award, The Greater O'Hare Association, 2007

One of only four interviewed for a job that received 2,000+ resumes; hired for the position.

HAROLD FIXIT
3248 Somerset Drive
New Orleans, LA 70131

504/555-3557   Fixme@done.com

R&D / PRODUCT DEVELOPMENT
Willing to Travel or Relocate

PROFILE:

➢ Provide full executive leadership for advanced R&D projects and new product development processes from concept to completion, including risk analysis, change management and cross-functional team performance.

➢ Skilled in product specification determination, concurrent design, quality control, budget administration and value analysis/re-engineering; read and interpret blueprints/schematics.

➢ Proficient in strategic planning, market research, sales management, lead development, new product introduction and high-quality client relations.

➢ Knowledge of intercultural business customs and practices; work closely with manufacturers and government agencies in the U.S., Canada and Mexico on supplier agreements and legal matters.

➢ Well versed in Apple and Windows systems, including AutoCAD 12.0, Excel, and Quick Books Pro; read and interpret blueprints/schematics; knowledge of production and inventory systems, including MRP, JIT and SPC.

EXPERIENCE:

Cleary Laboratories Inc., San Diego, CA   2002-Present (as required)
Consultant
Provide business management and technical assistance consulting services to this growing genetics testing laboratory in the Southwest.
→ Directly involved in restructuring the firm into a holding company, GenTest Laboratories, with three subsidiaries, from one centralized enterprise.
→ Develop and implement a strategic marketing plan to expand the human identification service, and a specific market penetration strategy for the newly created tissue typing department.
→ Interviewed consulting firms to create a new bar code chain-of-custody system.

Super-Damp, Inc., New Orleans, LA
A manufacturer of surge suppressors for the rail industry; in the process of becoming an ASTM AAR quality certified firm.
Operations Manager   12/02-Present
Perform planning, direction and administration of daily manufacturing and office management operations, including production scheduling, shipping/receiving, procurement and materials management, AP/AR and customer/supplier relations.
Hire, train and supervise a five-person staff, including three sales representatives; supervise two machinists utilizing standard digital readout lathes and in adherence to customer specifications and design requirements.
→ Renegotiated supplier pricing terms, resulting in a 7% cost reduction.

→ Reduced lead time for custom parts from eight weeks to two days by using JIT.

→ Currently in charge of two new products in service trials: a ruptured disk assembly and unique bolt for high-pressure chlorine tank cars.

Sales and Marketing Manager   6/98-12/02

In charge of the planning, logistics and supervision of market research, product positioning and introduction, publicity and sales management.

Hired, trained and supervised a five-person staff, including two independent manufacturer's representatives; negotiated the outsourcing agreements.

Conducted surveys and primary market research, performed data analysis and assessed customer specifications and requirements.

Worked closely with advertising agencies on sales brochures/direct mail campaigns.

Coordinated participation in and introduced new products at trade shows, including the annual Hazardous Materials Trade Show in Dallas, Texas.

→ Created and implemented a two-prong strategic marketing approach to sell to manufacturers leasing tank cars and to firms constructing tank cars.

→ Directly acquired 175 major accounts, including chemical companies American Cyanamid, Dow Chemicals, IMC Fertilizer, Vulcan Chemicals, Noranda Chemicals and BSAF and tank car manufacturers Trinity Industries, ACF, Union Tank Car, Procor and GATX Corporation.

→ Presented the Hydro-Damp product line to the American Railroads Tank Car Committee for approval as a new rail safety device.

→ Achieved an 11% increase in sales of $1.5 million from zero within the first year of Canadian government approval.

New Products Supervisor   4/96-6/98

Set up and directed all aspects of product development/management for this new company, with full technical, budget and schedule performance responsibility from concept to delivery.

Selected and worked closely with patent attorneys to process international patent applications and streamline the product approval process.

Handled publicity activities, including national print advertisement placement, promotional brochure design and direct mail campaign supervision; contracted a marketing/advertising consultant.

→ Gained product approval by AAR (USDOT), with legislative support from U.S. Representative Bill Tuazin, and consequently, approval by the Mexican Department of Transportation.

R.W. Aviation, New Orleans, LA   1995-1996
Flight Instructor/Commercial Instrument Pilot

Graduated 10 students to private pilot license status; an additional 25 flew solo.

→ Hold single/multi-engine ratings and logged 1100 hours.

EDUCATION: University of New Orleans, New Orleans, LA   Graduated 2002
Master of Business Administration

Louisiana Tech University, New Orleans, LA   Graduated 1995
Bachelor of Science degree: Professional Aviation

Sent about 25 resumes to ads and contacts; received 12 interview offers; accepted six interviews and a new job. Lionel followed up on all resumes with notes or phone calls.

LIONEL HUTZ

626 Camera Lane

Bartlett, IL 60103

630/555-3362   Hutzville@mine.com

PRODUCT MANAGEMENT / PURCHASING

PROFILE:

➤ Executive talents in new business development, cost-effective purchasing and the profitable management of multimillion-dollar, technical product lines.

➤ Design and implement systems and procedures for shipping, receiving, warehousing, product tracking and prompt distribution to key accounts.

➤ Perform cost-effective product sourcing, networking, pricing and competitive analysis; handle strategic planning and long-term business development through personal client relations and strong contacts in the electronics industry.

➤ Coordinate and expedite purchasing with vendors, suppliers and sales/marketing staff to anticipate and meet specific client needs on time and under budget; familiar with MRPII, JIT, ISO 9001 and MS Office for status reporting.

➤ Plan and conduct staff training in sales, contract coordination and state-of-the art product lines.

CAREER BACKGROUND:

<u>Zoller Electronics</u>, Addison, IL   2007-2011

Promoted to various positions, most recent first:

Product Manager

Managed extensive vendor relations, purchasing and business development for more than half of $23 million in semiconductor revenue for this component distributor.

Performed product sourcing through a wide range of vendors and suppliers for the best possible price.

Produced accurate price estimates and quotes; negotiated contracts within strict P&L parameters.

Responsible for expedites, registrations, deliveries and debits, as well as account follow-up.

Planned and conducted presentations to internal sales staff and clients on marketing strategies, competitors and product lines.

→ Increased gross profit from 17% to 21% on all designated product lines.

→ Recognized for the turnaround of unprofitable projects and deals.

→ Determined the reasons for lost sales; logged more than 2000 quotes and bids.

→ Responsible for a wide range of suppliers, including Actel, Altera, Analog Devices, Benchmarq, Fairchild, Harris, ICS, IDT, Intel, Intel Mass, Level One and Xicor.

Project Manager
In charge of all business functions for a $20 million system account.
Recommended asset buying and negotiated pricing for field sales staff.
Worked closely with the corporate asset manager on forecasts, inventory turns
and bonded inventory issues.
→ Managed an order processing function for 12,000 personal computers;
  achieved 99% on time delivery, with DOAs of less than 1%.
→ Coordinated a margin enhancement program that increased margins from 3%
  to 17%.

Inside Sales / Marketing Representative
Developed and managed more than 50 OEM accounts, including contract
manufacturers.
Produced and utilized a real-time price quoting system.

California Microwave, Bloomingdale, IL   2004-2007
Buyer / Expeditor
Purchased and expedited electronic components for high-volume producer of
wireless communication systems.
Utilized MRP and JIT standards; gained familiarity with ISO 9001.
This company closed its doors in 2007.
→ Reduced stoppages by 95%; conducted and managed the daily shortage meeting.

Personalized Trucking Service, Chicago, IL   2002-2004
Sales Representative
Performed needs analysis and truck/transportation sales to Fortune 500 accounts.
→ Produced $250,000 in new business; maintained a $5 million base.

Motorola, Inc., Cellular Group, Arlington Heights, IL   2000-2002
Supervisor / Dock Operations
Managed traffic, daily workflow and outbound UPS shipments.

Fuji Photo Film USA, Inc., Itasca, IL   1991-2000
Product Control Manager
Performed cost-effective purchasing and managed/promoted industrial film
products.
→ Increased annual inventory turns from two to six.
→ Shipped 95% of orders complete and on time, up from only 70%.

Wells Lamont Corporation, Niles, IL   1986-1991
Regional Sales Administrator
Expanded sales through competitive analysis and interface with purchasing and
production staff.

EDUCATION: Valparaiso University, Valparaiso, IN
                  B.S. Degree: Business Administration   1986
                  Emphasis: Management and Marketing

Sent about 20; received 15 interviews.

JAMES HENSON
3230 North Pembroke Drive
South Elgin, IL 60177

847/555-6822   Puppetguy@strings.com

EXECUTIVE LEADERSHIP: Production Operations

PROFILE:
➤ Skilled in all aspects of high-profit production operations, including job scheduling, staff motivation, training, evaluation, reporting and system trouble-shooting for multiple locations.

➤ Extensive background in a wide range of plant operations; oversee machine set-up, quality assurance, production reporting, custom molding, forklift operations and conveyor system installation to ensure quality and greatly reduce downtime.

➤ Proven ability to troubleshoot and resolve problems quickly; oversee injection molding, inventory and shop floor control, JIT and RF; utilize IQMS systems, as well as Windows 7, MS Word and Excel for reporting and database updates.

EXPERIENCE: Maurice Makers, Morris, IL   5/98-Present
Supervisor / Lead Process Technician
Direct all production activities at this automated plant, including working with robotic and other automated systems; additional duties similar to Duraco, below. Oversee the commission and qualifying of injection molding machines.
Schedule orders and work directly with customers regarding product specifications. Communicate with vendors and suppliers to order new equipment and supplies.
→ Gaining experience with closed and open-loop plant-process water systems.

Duraco Products, Inc., Streamwood, IL   1987-5/98
Lead Process Technician
Responsible for all plant operations, including quality assurance, staff supervision, work coordination, troubleshooting, inventory control and system streamlining for this manufacturer of plastic consumer items.
Trained and evaluated employees in mold setting and injection mold troubleshooting. Supervised a team of process technicians and coordinated activities of mold setters.
→ Evaluated machine cycles and identified ways to improve productivity.
→ Performed job scheduling for up to 90 workers on machines, packing and shipping.
→ Worked with quality control personnel to resolve any quality issues.

EDUCATION: Elgin Community College, Elgin, IL
→ Successfully completed a range of technical classes including Heating and Refrigeration, Welding, Electrical Controls and Sheet Metal Working.
High School Graduate

TRAINING: Fred Pryor Schools, **How to Supervise People** (Certificate)

Sent about 60; received 20 interviews.

Ralph Wiggum
4465 Cat Tail
Carol Stream, IL 60188

630/555-0194   Bark@dogs.com

TECHNICAL PROJECT LEADERSHIP / ORACLE SYSTEMS

PROFILE:
➢ Comprehensive experience in the setup and management of complete ORACLE systems for MRP, including cost-effective procurement, inventory control and MRO expediting.

➢ Perform staff and management training and supervision in complete system integration, upgrades and utilization.

➢ Negotiate contracts with vendors and suppliers for reduced overhead and quick response; skilled in JIT, Y2K compliance, cycle time management and process improvement; coordinate production, purchasing and operations for multiple locations.

➢ Familiar with state tax regulations; coordinate budgets and procedures with programmers, technical staff and management.

➢ Handle full system documentation and the writing of manuals and procedures; skilled in Windows 7, Excel and Wings for spreadsheets and status reporting.

EXPERIENCE: <u>Village Office Equipment, Inc.</u>, Libertyville, IL
ORACLE System Administrator / Trainer   2003-2011

Effectively trained and motivated up to 10 employees monthly for six years in rules and procedures for purchasing.
Directly supervised three buyers and one clerk.
Researched and wrote an article for Motorola's procurement newsletter on FER.
Resident expert on special user tax issues with the State of Illinois.
Created and implemented numerous cost reduction methods and process improvements (documentation available) related to:

- Implementing autofax procedures and FER (Facility Engineering Requests) procedures.
- Payables, purchasing and problem-solving.
- American Express and Pro-Card.
- Return order procedures and further process procedures.
- Progressive payment.
- Saved more than $1.8 million with numerous suppliers through price negotiation and working with employees at cellular facilities in Illinois, Washington, Arizona, Florida and Texas.
- Chosen to debug and implement a complete ORACLE purchasing system for Brazil.

- Eliminated a costly, non-value procedure; worked with attorneys to develop an extensive, FER master contractor service agreement.
- Produced and updated a monthly and Y.T.D. cost-saving spreadsheet for management.
- Developed and maintained purchasing guidelines, rules and procedures for ORACLE requisition users.
- Established and maintained a detailed, preferred supplier list.
- Earned an award from the president of General Systems for outstanding achievement and cost reductions.

Production Buyer / MRO Buyer   1998-2002

Performed cost-effective purchasing of all commodities for specific end products, including the IMTS carrier phone.

Responsible for a wide range of special projects and monthly reports, including tracking of cost savings and variances.

Reported the status of shipping plans to management.

- Handled extensive vendor sourcing and relations, including securing bids and quotes.

Production Buyer   1995-1998

Purchased a wide range of commodities for cellular phones, including injection molded parts, die cast items, sheet metal stamped items and other mechanical parts.

MRO Purchasing / Developmental   1992-1994

Primarily responsible for engineering procurement and a wide range of special projects.

Production Control / Planner / Scheduling   1989-1992

Recognized for highly accurate forecasting, including reading, interpretation and use.

Tracked and reduced inventory spikes, greatly lowering total inventory costs.

PRIOR EXPERIENCE: U.S. Army, Medical Supply Specialist

Earned Bronze Star medal and other awards.

EDUCATION: WR Harper College, Palatine, IL

Material Management Certificate

Completed an additional 77 hours of business-related study.

Selectively sent two and received one interview; hired for the position.

BILLY BOXER
14 Jammer Street
Rowlett, TX 22488

Res: 972/555-6423   Double@cyberramp.net   Ofc: 972/555-4850

SOFTWARE DEVELOPMENT / INTEGRATION

PROFILE:

➢ Highly successful, executive experience in custom software design and quality control, including team leadership/motivation, and technical product development from schematics and CAD design to modeling and production.

➢ Familiar with ISO 9001 and complete quality control, as well as client relations, documentation and budget administration.

➢ Analyze and streamline configurations and coordinate software applications, database management and documentation updates; leverage a strong knowledge of materials and vendor relations.

➢ Skilled in CAD drafting and design and state-of-the-art applications including:

Software and Platforms:
UNIX, Windows NT, Pascal and Oracle.

Applications:
Autocad Rev 13, CV CADDS 6 and Parametric/Explicit, and CV CAMU VIEWLOGIC, Digital Equipment VAX 8800 and 11/780 Series Computers; PCs using Windows 7 and UNIX operating systems; Macintosh computers and application software packages.

EXPERIENCE: <u>Mavic Systems, Inc.</u> Garland, TX
Mavic is a $10 billion, Fortune 600 Corporation in the Software Development/System Integration industry.
Group Leader - Engineering Design Drafter   12/06-Present

Responsible for supervising a team of five in schematic capture, including all drafting, design, CAD work and production for defense reconnaissance systems. Perform extensive group and individual training, as well as job assignment and coordination with upper management and other technical staff.
Accountable for complete project quality and documentation for upper management. Act as liaison to the engineering group, providing support, development and drafting expertise on schematic diagrams, mechanical drawings and printed wiring board drawings from engineering models.

→ Conducted meetings on ISO 9001 and implemented improvements, of which four out of five were accepted by upper management.

→ One idea reduced labor hours for a specific procedure from 100 to 10.

→ Act as VIEWLOGIC and ISO 9001 quality control administrator.

→ Advanced to Group Leader from zero experience in only one year.

Senior Engineering CAD Specialist   5/01-12/06

Directed the design of a 3D Solid Modeling project using Computer Vision's Product Visualization application. Produced a virtual reality walk-through of various floor configurations.

Generated software interaction diagrams using the Software Through Pictures application on a Sun/UNIX workstation.

Updated and maintained a database of more than 150 AutoCad files and a 20,000-record database using Oracle.

Scheduled and documented database updates to meet quarterly publishing requirements.

→ Planned and conducted extensive AutoCad training for peers and managers.

→ Updated and modified manager's floor plans, equipment rack elevations and cable wire listings.

→ Supported baseline installation activities requiring overseas travel to sites such as Australia.

Engineering Drafter   9/93-5/01

Assisted in staff training and managed the revision of schematics, flow charts, block diagrams and printed circuit board layouts in accordance with strict military standards such as 275E.

Updated and maintained floor plans CV CADDS 3 and 4x computer systems using a CVD digitizer and graphics workstation.

→ Captured microwave Integrated circuits and produced silk-screen layouts on CV systems.

→ Maintained and prepared site floor plans for facility interface, control documents and evolution floor plans.

SECURITY ACCESS: Acquired Active Security Clearances following Special and Extended background investigations.

EDUCATION: Amber University, Dallas, TX

B.S. Degree   May 2009

Major: Management: Information Systems, GPA: 3.7/4.0

Eastfield College, Dallas, TX

Associates Degree   July, 2002

Major: Drafting and Design

Stephen F. Austin State University, Nacogdoches, TX

Major: Computer Science   Spring/Fall, 1992

Richland College, Dallas, TX

Major: Computer Science   1991, 1993-95, and 2003-04

• Total college credit hours completed: 156.

Sent 50; received 14 interviews and six job offers.

Saunders Zach

2250 Iris Avenue

Hanover Park, IL 60103

630/555-8951   Zakman@yep.com

SUPPLY CHAIN MANAGEMENT / PROCUREMENT

PROFILE:

➤ Comprehensive experience in cost-effective purchasing, including extensive supply chain management, material sourcing, price negotiations and distribution management.

➤ Develop domestic and offshore sources and control high-volume distribution operations, inter-modal transportation and multi-step production operations.

➤ Background in manufacturing environments, including purchasing of raw materials, operating supplies, capital equipment and outside/contract services.

➤ Knowledge of SPC, JIT and MRP, as well as formal quality control programs; proven ability to improve inventory turns and overall profitability.

➤ Familiar with MRP II (BPCS 4.02 system); Certified ISO/QS 9001 Auditor; assist in QS 9001 Certification.

EXPERIENCE: Jeffrey Duncan, Inc., Chicago, IL

Commodities Manager / Purchasing   2007-Present

Manage the sourcing and purchasing of $15 million in production materials, including steel, plastic resins, cold forgings, molded cloth, paper and rubber speaker components, as well as packaging materials.

Train and supervise one planner/buyer and a purchasing assistant.

Utilize MRPII (BPCS 4.02 system) for inventory management, shop floor control and prompt, accurate status reporting.

→ Through effective negotiations, achieved a $400,000 cost reduction in 2 1/2 years.

→ Trained in SPC and the automotive Production Part Approval Process (PPAP), as well as Failure Mode Effects Analysis (FMEA).

→ Chosen to travel to China and Taiwan to conduct audits of suppliers, 2007 and 2008.

→ Promoted to this position from:

Senior Buyer   2006-2007

TLK Industries, Palatine, IL   2004-2006

Project Coordinator

Established new, more effective procedures and supervised concurrent projects, including ISO 9001 certification.

Directed the corporate quality management process, system documentation and virtually all internal communications.

Trained, supervised and scheduled two employees in the quality department.

→ Revised and updated virtually all purchasing procedures.
→ Researched, updated and re-wrote procedures for the quality manual to ISO 9001 specifications.
→ Updated bills of materials and organized material safety data sheets.
→ Documented the emergency response system.
→ Acted as Senior Advisor to management on process systems, redundancy elimination, hazardous materials and preventive maintenance techniques.

Zitti, Inc., Reedsburg, WI   1993-2004
Purchasing Manager
Directed virtually all corporate purchasing, including the cost-effective buying of capital equipment, raw materials, components, packaging, supplies and outside services.
Performed vendor sourcing, bid preparation, price/discount negotiation and the review of vendor performance.
Worked closely with domestic and offshore sources; coordinated procurement planning and operations with manufacturing, engineering, finance and marketing managers.

→ Played a key role in creating and implementing a quality management program.
→ Established and maintained a sophisticated cataloging system detailing product and vendor history.
→ Negotiated single-purchase contracts valued up to $80,000 for die cast molds and tooling.
→ Managed a major inventory and implemented JIT and MRP systems.
→ Joined this company as Production Control Specialist; gained experience in scheduling manufacturing and assembly operations and advanced to management of shipping and receiving before promotion to Purchasing Manager.

EDUCATION: WR Harper College, Palatine, IL
Certificate in Materials and Logistics Management, 2006.
Expected completion of Associate's Degree in Management, 2011.

Triton College, River Grove, IL
Completed training in Excel 5.0 and MS Word 2007.

Sent or emailed about 200; received 25 interviews.

SANTO PROVENZANO

2201 Calib Avenue, #302   310/555-6459
Santa Monica, CA 90403   E-mail gath@aol.com

PRODUCT MANAGEMENT

A leadership position utilizing hands-on abilities in communications, project supervision, client relations and business administration.

PROFILE:

- Executive talents in new product development and introduction, process re-engineering, strategic planning, target marketing, distribution operations and team leadership in international markets.

- Manage product sales, key account maintenance, competitive analysis, pricing, market surveys, contract negotiation, quality control, inventory and report preparation.

- Successfully develop and implement innovative programs to increase market share, profit margins and cost savings in rapidly shifting markets.

- Train and supervise staff in a wide range of industrial chemicals; participate on cross-division teams involved in business expansion and market identification.

- Extensive experience with international business practices and protocols, particularly in Europe and the Pacific Rim; fluent in English, German, Chinese (Mandarin), Filipino, Spanish, and French.

EXPERIENCE: Uncle Chemical Group Inc., Dallas, TX

Senior Sales Representative - West Coast   2005-Present

Responsible for sales, account maintenance, order processing and product management for a $13.8 million territory in California and the Rockies and part of the $108 million West Region.

Successfully maintain and upgrade major account sales volume in a highly competitive and decreasing market.

→ Oversaw cross-functional groups in identifying and accommodating logistical requirements to ensure timely delivery and client satisfaction.

→ Consistently recognized by management and clients for excellent skills in troubleshooting and problem resolution in high-pressure situations.

Financial Analyst   1996-2005

Provided extensive market and financial analysis to enhance long-term marketing and customer satisfaction strategies for the entire company.

→ Personally improved methods for generation of Slope and Scatter diagrams and analyses, which are now used company-wide.

→ Assisted in developing three marketing strategies, leading to increased earnings of almost $6 million for two separate divisions.

→ Served on a seven-man Customer Satisfaction Implementation team that used Malcolm Baldridge Assessment skills gained in an intensive training program.

Product Supervisor   1995

Coordinated production activities for VA/Acetyls and Formaldehyde at six plants in the U.S., Mexico and Canada, including the largest acetic acid facility in the world in Clear Lake, TX.

→ Recognized by management for achieving a complete and profitable plant turnaround in only 34 days.

→ Resolved a recurrent problem to better manage storage and production planning.

→ Finished cross-training in sales techniques and product orientation, as well as Purchasing, Legal Liaison, Transportation and Credit.

Uncle AG, Frankfurt, Germany   1991-1994

Product Manager

Coordinated new business development, marketing, order processing and international client relations for up to $20 million in annual volume.

→ Worked with a full range of products, including Acetaldehyde, Acetic Acid, Carboxylic Acids and NPG and Butyraldehyde.

→ Expanded the internal client base through extensive market surveys and analysis for the Organic intermediates group.

Uncle Singapore Pte., Ltd., Singapore   1987-1991

Management Assistant   1990-1991

Provided effective support to executives involved in contract negotiations, new office operations and product development in Asian marketplaces.

Maintained close contact with Board of Directors and ZDA corporate planning group in Frankfurt, Germany, along with legal liaison and site inspections.

→ Coordinated all construction activity and new business start-up for the regional technical center and rebottling/refilling facility.

Senior Sales Executive   1988-1990

In charge of chemical sales to a highly diverse clientele, including refrigeration, pharmaceutical and fire-fighting firms.

→ Personally developed and introduced Frigen refrigerants into a completely new market; also managed a small-scale CFC mixing/filling facility and tank farm.

EDUCATION: Singapore Institute of Management   1988
Diploma in Marketing Management

National University of Singapore   1985
B.Sc. Degree in Chemistry

* Received an ASEAN Merit Scholarship from 1982-1985.

Sent about 100; received six interviews; education removed, as he did not finish high school or college.

Ted E. Williams
5520 East Crystal Avenue
Crystal Lake, IL 60014

Res.: 815/555-8945   410@mc.net   Fax: 815/555-8984

EXECUTIVE PURCHASING / MANUFACTURING

PROFILE:
> Comprehensive experience in production operations and cost-effective purchasing, including full responsibility for manufacturing, quality and successful turnarounds.

> Skilled in quality control and highly profitable operations at multiple locations; manage production line setup, analysis and streamlining.

> Proficient in supply chain operations, vendor relations, product/component sourcing and inventory control for domestic and foreign locations.

> Familiar with TQM, JIT, continuous flow manufacturing and focused/cell manufacturing; accurately measure and reduce scrap, re-work, lost time and inventories.

> Train and supervise teams of engineers, supervisors, line workers and support staff at all levels of experience.

EXPERIENCE: Golfers, Inc., Crystal Lake, IL   2006-Present
Director of Manufacturing
In charge of virtually all operations at four plants, including cost-effective purchasing, inventory control, cost-reduction and profit/loss.
Effectively train and supervise all plant managers and purchasing staff in purchasing, MRP and quality control for high-volume production of electrical products.

→ Purchase up to $20 million per year, including all price/contract negotiations with vendors and suppliers worldwide.
→ Save up to $800,000 per year in purchases through detailed planning, charting and status reporting of all production operations.
→ Provide detailed documentation of production output to constantly compare and improve techniques, processes and procedures.

Eaton Corporation, various locations
Corporate Quality / Supplier Management - Carol Stream, IL   2004-2006
Personally developed a solid base of North American commodity suppliers for the Appliance, Automotive and Lectron Divisions.
Established preferred supplier status and on-time deliveries.

Effectively interfaced with all department supervisors and purchasing staff.
→ Created, implemented and met strict quality standards for 17 manufacturing facilities and eight purchasing departments.
→ Reduced suppliers from 15,000 to 8,000.

Plant Manager - Athens, AL   2003-2004

Effectively trained and supervised a team of seven in engineering, accounting, human resources and quality management.

Products included hot and cold controls for various appliances.

Annual sales exceeded $20 million, with 350 employees in all major departments.

→ Through detailed research and negotiations, reduced inventory by $1.2 million and eliminated the need for - and use of - a 60,000 sq. ft. off-site warehouse.

→ Implemented continuous flow manufacturing

→ Developed - and trained supervisors in - a very effective Focus on Quality operating system.

General Manager - Melbourne, Australia   2002-2003

Researched and documented all primary plant operations, including output, overhead, staffing and quality.

Developed and implemented new Quality Operating systems.

Established quality improvement teams with customers.

Supervised six staff and managers to successfully implement all procedures.

This plant has a total of 150 employees and annual sales of $25 million, producing timers for washing machines, switches, automobile horns and thermostats.

Focused on field failures and cost improvement, resulting in:

→ Greatly increased quality and profits, with reduced downtime and a letter of commendation from top executives of the Email Laundry Group Division.

Plant Manager - Wauwatosa, WI   2001-2002

Implemented quality operating systems, with a focus on reduction of defects shipped to customers, thereby regaining their confidence.

Greatly reduced scrap, re-work, customer returns and unfavorable labor variance.

Employees: 350, with annual sales of $28 million.

→ Reduced defects from 27,800 ppm to 1000 ppm in just over a year.

Plant Manager - St. Thomas, Ontario, Canada   1999-2001

Developed and utilized a Quality Operating system with a focus on scrap, rework and labor reduction.

Products included drier receivers and accumulators for automotive applications; 550 employees and $32 million (CDN) in sales.

→ Turned around the operation from a $3.5 million loss to break even in nine months; on target to a $1 million profit within six months.

→ Lowered part defects from 22,500 ppm to 140 ppm over 14 months.

→ Earned the Ford Q1 Award for excellence.

Plant Manager - Crystal Lake, IL   1980-1999

Implemented major quality improvements and reduced costs, while increasing production from 6,000 motors to more than 50,000 daily.

→ Cost improvements offset 19 years of materials and labor cost increases.

Sent 38; received 10 interviews; accepted new position through a personal contact.

George B. Strait

221 Sheridan Drive
Joplin, MI 34801

Res: 452/555-6154
E-mail: Geo@teraworld.net

EXECUTIVE LEADERSHIP: Quality / Engineering / Plant Management

Executive experience in plant management and operations, with P&L responsibility for total quality systems and process engineering, in consumer and light industrial markets.

➢ Advise fellow executives on emerging industry standards; formulate strategic quality management policies to achieve financial goals; effectively communicate ideas and technical information at all levels for a high-performance environment.

➢ Recruit and direct cross-functional teams to meet strict engineering, production and customer requirements; skilled in needs assessment, competitive analysis and full product development.

➢ Oversee benchmarking, supplier relations, facility layout, concurrent engineering, contract negotiations and budget administration.

Technical:

➢ Well versed in lean manufacturing processes, including cellular manufacturing, TQM/SPC, JIT, PPAP, APQP, line balancing and Design of Experiments; working knowledge of J.D. Edwards production control software; registered ISO 9000 auditor.

➢ Technical knowledge includes grey/ductile iron casting, plastic molding, die casting, stampings, metal removal, heat treating, forging, sheet metal forming, painting and product assembly; expert in metrology and metalography.

EXPERIENCE: The Appliance Company, Outdoor Cooking Division, Neosho, MI   2007-Present
Quality Manager   1/07 to 11/07
In charge of strategic and daily quality management functions for this $400 million plant manufacturing gas, electric and charcoal barbecue grills, with 1,250 employees in peak production season.

⇨ Planned and launched a total quality management program to meet ISO 9000 requirements and customer-defined product specifications.

⇨ Initiated a program to reduce critical defects by 50% in the 1998 production year and to zero defects in 1999; decreased customer complaints to the Call Center by 30%.

⇨ Served as 1999-2000 ASQ local chapter Program, Education and National Quality Month Chair.

⇨ Redesigned the facility layout to accommodate an outsourcing contract to manufacture PowerMate/Coleman consumer generators in unanticipated high demand.

Production Manager   3/07-11/07
Directed all manufacturing operations, including product fabrication, finishing, assembly and packaging, with responsibility for line balancing, daily production schedules and quality craftsmanship in sheet metal forming, powder paint, porcelain coating, wire grid fabrication and silk-screen printing.

⇨ Increased production volume from 7,000 ($IMM) units per day to a record 14,600 ($2.17MM) units per day, while reducing direct labor workforce by 200 employees.

⇨ Improved productivity from 40% to over 90% in actual vs. earned direct labor hours.

The Thermos Company, Freeport, IL   2005-2007
Director of Quality Assurance and R&D
Managed quality systems functions for North American operations, including the Consumer Customer Service group and Return Materials Department, of this Nippon Sanso $250 million subsidiary manufacturing gas barbecue grills, steel and glass vacuum insulated food containers, ice chests and jugs and school lunch kits.
Acquired the R&D group in December 1995.

⇨   Standardized engineering change order procedures, decreasing the turnaround time from 30 to 10 days.

⇨   Introduced a fastener standardization program and generated a savings of $300,000 on implementation.

⇨   Redesigned the Thermos barbecue grill line for a $2.9 million cost savings.

⇨   Commercialized several houseware products, including Steel Commuter Travel Mug, 56-Quart Split Lid Cooler, and the TAZ Lunch Kit, to achieve $3 million in additional sales revenues.

The American Tool Companies, Inc., DeWitt, NE   2000-2005
Director of Product Standards   1/04-11/05
Set up and managed external/internal product reliability testing facilities serving plants in the U.S., Europe and Brazil for this $300 million privately held manufacturer of hand tools and power tool accessories for the do-it-yourself and industrial markets.

⇨   Produced corporate quality manuals, detailing procedures for quality system documentation, product quality planning, quality data retention and warranty returns.

⇨   Member of various corporate teams, including the New Product Development Committee and ISO 9000 implementation; contributed to the rollout of 14 new products.

⇨   Developed testing policies, procedures and methods for new and manufactured product lines, including Vise Grip Locking Pliers, Quick Grip Bar Clamps, Marathon Saw Blades, Prosnip Metal Shears, Unibit Step Drills, Chesco Hex Keys, Turbo Max Drills, Hanson Drills and Taps, Straight Line Chalk Boxes, Irwin Auger and Speedbor Flat Bits.

⇨   Designed and implemented a supplier certification process to meet ISO 9000 requirements.

⇨   Promoted from Director of Quality Assurance, 11/00-1/04.

Prior Positions/Employers:
Senior Quality Control Engineer, Quality Control Engineer, Compressor Assembly, Quality Control Engineer, Purchasing for Parts and Process Control Die Cast, The Trane Company, Tyler, TX
Assistant Plant Metallurgist, Republic Steel Corporation, Union Drawn Division, Gary, IN
Management Trainee, Metallurgical Department, Republic Steel Corporation, Action, OH

TRAINING: Numerous seminars completed include:
Lead Auditor Training/RAB ISO 9000 Certification.
ASQC Stepping Toward Quality.
Juran - The Last World Tour.
Quality Management by Deming.

EDUCATION: University of Cincinnati, Cincinnati, OH
B.S. Degree in Metallurgical Engineering

Sent 50; received 15 interviews.

Mary T. Zidek

4405 Sword Place #45

Bloomingdale, IL 60108

630/555-4397 Bigmar@aol.com

OPERATIONS / MANAGEMENT

PROFILE:

➤ Executive talents leading customer service, sales and business development, including staffing, procedures and cost-reduction for multimillion-dollar operations.

➤ Coordinate inventories, promotions and status reporting for multiple locations; handle internal audits and analytical problem-solving in fast-paced situations.

➤ Familiar with international business practices; handle top-level presentations in a professional manner; conversant in French.

➤ Analyze and reduce payroll and capital expenses; reduce shortages and negotiate with vendors and suppliers; utilize Windows 7, Lotus 1-2-3, MS Word, GroupWise and MS Publisher for sales reports and correspondence.

➤ Effectively hire, train, supervise and motivate staff and management teams; well versed in human resource issues and regulations.

EMPLOYMENT: <u>Lores & Tony,</u> Schaumburg and Oak Brook, IL

Operations Manager   2007-Present

In charge of virtually all operations for this $30 million location, including the hiring, training and/or supervision of 250 staff and managers.

Manage all aspects of housekeeping, stocking and inventory control; oversee detailed audits of all products and sales records.

Coordinate functions of the cash office, as well as alterations and the purchase of all supplies.

Ensure maintenance and repair of numerous POS registers, telephones and computer systems.

Oversee petty cash and constantly track and reduce expenses.

In charge of maintenance issues related to facilities, such as landscaping and interior lighting for maximum promotional effect.

→ Increased gift certificate sales by 5% for FY 08.

→ Earned $25,000 in corporate credits for reducing chargeback claims to zero.

→ Reduced general workers' hours by 23% for FY 08; ranked #19: up from #72 of 73 stores.

→ Physical inventory: achieved provision of 2% for three consecutive seasons.

→ In charge of all store hiring; achieved a major reduction in payroll.

→ Exceeded goals for new accounts in the last three seasons.

→ Plan all vacations and schedules for 250 workers.

→ Resolve all customer service problems as Senior Executive Representative.

Regional Control Manager   2005-2007
Central Shortage Control, Manhattan, NY
Regions: Chicago, Dallas, Houston and New Orleans   2005-2006
Regions: New Jersey, New York and Connecticut   2005

→ Trained two successful Regional Control Managers.
→ Trained an entire region in the Physical Inventory Process.
→ During inventory reconciliations, worked closely with staff and managers in loss prevention, profit improvement, price management and buying office procedures.

Successfully reduced shortages in six target stores.
Inventory Control Representative for four seasons.
Internal Auditor: Responsible for the cash office, safe room, sign placement, pricing and reduction of losses, as well as for receiving.
Completed formal corporate training in a wide range of issues.

Manager of Support Services, Woodfield, Schaumburg, IL   2004-2005
Directed housekeeping, stocking, supply expense reduction and inventories for annual sales volume of $25 million.
Assisted operations managers in all duties, including staffing issues and the flow of merchandise in and out of the building (averaged three trucks per week and 500 receipts per truck).

→ Assisted in the liquidation process; converted the old Woodfield store to a virtually new location; worked with numerous truck lines and contractors.

Area Sales Manager, Woodfield, Schaumburg, IL   2002-2004
Developed a sales volume of $2.5 million in men's furnishings, clothing, intimate apparel, hosiery and children's wear.

→ Increased sales growth over plan for six consecutive seasons.
→ Achieved passing shortage and pricing audit scores.
→ Conducted accurate, quality physical inventories within merchandise areas.

EDUCATION: Illinois State University, Bloomington/Normal, IL
Bachelor of Science Degree   2001
Major: International Business; Minor: Management
GPA: 3.0/4.0
Member: Alpha Delta Pi Sorority.
Panhellenic Delegate and Treasurer.

Bristol Polytechnic University, Bristol, England   Spring, 2000
Completed courses in International Business
GPA: 4.0

Sent about 24; received eight interviews and a new job.

DANIEL BURKE

231 Rosati Road   580/555-5101
Enid, OK 73703   E-mail: pizza@ionet.net

COMMERCIAL INFORMATION SYSTEMS / QUALITY MANAGEMENT

PROFILE:

➤ Skilled in the senior-level direction of corporate commercial information systems and quality assurance functions, with P&L responsibility for technology policies, standards and budgets in deregulated environments.

➤ Perform or coordinate strategic planning, policy formulation, product development, risk analysis, change management, implementation logistics and budget administration; proven ability to lead organizations through restructuring and process re-engineering.

➤ Hire, train and supervise project teams and independent contractors in quality and federal/state regulatory compliance; nearly certified PMI project manager and BSI Lead ISO Auditor; well versed in ISO 9002, JIT/EDI and continuous improvement processes.

TECHNICAL:

➤ *Software:* Windows/Apple and mid-range turnkey and company-developed accounting, office productivity and dispatch/freight forwarding systems.

➤ *Network/Communication Software and Languages*: Novell, TCP/IP, NFS, leased line T-l and Frame Relay WAN.

➤ *Hardware*: IBM iSeries, SCO UNIX servers, Novell and Qualcomm two-way truck satellite communication systems.

CAREER BACKGROUND:

<u>Nolan Transport, Inc.</u>, Enid, OK   1997-Present
A $101 million privately held, tractor/trailer over-the-road bulk trucking firm.
Vice President, Information Systems and Quality   7/04-Present
In charge of planning and directing information systems and quality assurance functions, including all telephone and communication systems, with full P&L responsibility.
Hire, train and supervise 10 direct staff and four managers, with oversight management of 12 project team members, on $100,000 to $750,000 projects.
Administer a $1.4 million annual operating budget, with capital acquisition determination and approval authority.

→ Analyze, interpret and apply lane/market data and emerging trends to demand forecasts.

→ Modernized the company technologically from a high-cost job shop environment to low-cost, standardized operations; completely replaced every application with networked, online systems and methods.

→ Acquired and transformed the Quality Department into a driving force for cost containment and avoidance, focusing on costs of quality and ISO certification.

→ Initiated and developed a middle management training program; involved in staff training and the setup and opening of all new offices.

→ Orchestrated the ISO 9002 certification process in 50 offices nationally; certified 12 locations and corporate headquarters by 2005.

Director, Information Systems   8/02-7/04

Responsible for all aspects of daily company-wide information systems operations, with a budget of $1 million; supervised three data processing managers.

Determined and managed technology capital acquisitions, installations and maintenance.

→ Upgraded the IBM AS/400 system to an iSeries, interfacing with AR/AP, general ledger and payroll staff for the first time in the history of the company.

Manager, Communication Systems   5/87-8/92

Directed multiple projects to support AT&T UNIX communication systems for order entry applications, including software development and post-installation troubleshooting, working closely with clients to assess and adhere to project specifications, requirements, schedules and budgets.

→ Purchased over 50 UNIX-based computers, networked with home office computers, for field dispatchers to place orders and monitor equipment resources.

Prior Experience

Computer Applications Ltd., Oklahoma City, OK

Software Development Project Leader

Managed a team of system analysts/programmers in order entry system development and maintenance for clients of this privately held, Sperry value-added reseller.

→ Provided direct sales force with technical evaluations of clients.

→ Negotiated consulting/development contracts with companies ranging in gross revenues from $3 million to $12 million.

→ Management liquidated the company as of the Sperry/Burroughs merger.

TRAINING: Seminars completed include:

Project Management, Project Management Institute

ISO/Quality Management, British Standards Institute

EDUCATION: Oklahoma State University, Stillwater, OK

B.S. degree in computing and informational sciences

Sent about 40; received four interviews and numerous inquiries from Internet distribution.

ROBERT SIMPSON

2253 Sofar Court   630/555-1276
Bartlett, IL 60103   E-mail: Whale@cdnet.edu

EXECUTIVE TRAINING / DEVELOPMENT

PROFILE:

➤ Comprehensive experience in corporate training and communications, including program planning, administration and human resource development.

➤ Skilled in creative public relations and promotions; effectively plan, implement, and track the performance of market research, strategies and community outreach.

➤ Utilize Internet resources, databases and various software for such applications as Web site development, job market analysis, applicant testing, career matching and the publication of findings.

➤ Detailed experience in staff hiring, training, supervision and motivation; handle performance reviews and all key aspects of employer/employee relations.

➤ Perform group and individual counseling for virtually all ages; determine aptitudes and career goals and define methods to reach those goals.

EXPERIENCE: <u>Peterson College,</u> Gilberts, IL   1999-Present
Career Services Manager
Responsible for all major career services at this community college, the largest in Illinois, with more than 20,000 students.
Personally hire, train and supervise a team of three office staff and five student aides in program creation/administration, media relations, student testing and job placement assistance.
Through research and analysis, provide and interpret data on the local employment outlook and on future staffing needs of national and global industries.
Plan and conduct seven to 10 presentations for up to 400 at-risk students per week to encourage further education and skill development to meet changing employer needs.
Handle extensive public and media relations to promote COD educational and career services to the public at large.

* Developed a highly successful, $60,000 computerized job matching system called AIMS: the Automated Industry Matching System. This is now linked to more than 20,000 employers and matches more than 2,000 students per week. AIMS was eventually adopted by four other community colleges.
* Compiled data on local, national and global job trends and wrote/published *Jobs and the Economy*.
* Designed a Web site featuring COD career services, classes and special programs.

* Recently co-chaired a conference of the Midwest Association of Colleges and Employers, with a guest list including John Callaway, Lynn Martin and numerous CEOs.

Elgin Community College, Elgin, IL   1994-1999
Admissions and Registration Supervisor
Directed all admissions and registration activities at ECC to increase enrollment and improve service to full- and part-time students.
Worked closely with the Dean of Student Services and acted as liaison to foreign students.

* Responsible for writing and implementing a script for touch-tone registration, resulting in greater enrollment.
* Chaired the Nursing Selection Committee and updated/maintained entrance records for all nursing candidates.

Illinois Technical College, Chicago, IL   1992-1994
Admissions Counselor
Provided advice and assistance to students in the selection of academic programs to meet their needs.
Counseled and worked with students throughout the enrollment process.
Evaluated high school transcripts, administered entrance exams and assisted students in applying for all types of financial aid.

* Edited and wrote articles for the school newspaper: Tech Talk.

PRIOR EXPERIENCE:
Chrysler Learning Service Center, Detroit, MI
Intake Specialist
Administered interest inventories and job skill ability tests to people who had been incarcerated or institutionalized or who had experienced long-term unemployment.
Tested candidates and recommended training programs based on findings.
Updated and maintained weekly progress reports on all clients.

EDUCATION: DePaul University, Chicago, IL
Pursuing a Master's Degree in Career Counseling
Expected graduation: 12/02

University of Illinois at Chicago, Chicago, IL
Bachelor of Arts Degree: Psychology

MEMBERSHIPS: Member of Two Boards of Directors:
The Naperville Community Career Center for Downsized Executives.
DKIN: Disabled Kids In Need.

* Affiliated with ACE: The Midwest Association of Colleges and Employers.

Sent about 50; received 10 interviews.

WILLIAM TAYLOR

452 Cedar Court
Dunwoody, GA 30350

Res: 770/555-9797   TaylorA@aol.com   Ofc: 770/555-3513

EXECUTIVE PROJECT MANAGEMENT

PROFILE

➤ Comprehensive experience in staff training, supervision and operations management, including full responsibility for team leadership, customer service and quality control.

➤ Trained in project management, system setup and administration; consistently track call center volume and measure needs and capacity for effective staff scheduling.

➤ Experience in sales support and troubleshooting, including pricing, contract negotiations, budgeting and forecasting.

➤ Communicate with customers, vendors, suppliers and fellow workers with professional yet personal written and oral communication skills.

➤ Utilize Windows 7 and MS Office, including Word, Excel, Access and Outlook, as well as Netscape PC for spreadsheets and correspondence.

EXPERIENCE: Computers By George, formerly All Electronics Corporation, Alpharetta, GA

Call Center Supervisor   9/03-Present

Effectively train and supervise a team of 15 in call center operations and the dispatch of service technicians to client locations nationwide.

Work closely with district managers and staff in telecommunications, including call routing and the analysis/streamlining of service calls, including routing and logging of calls to engineers.

Assist in staff hiring and the constant updating and support of this 24 x 7 call center with top management.

Interface with contractors and ensure quality of work; compile and present monthly reports on contractor quality.

Utilize a relational database to register, profile and track customer and call status; maintain four different screens/nodes.

Provide mission-critical support for desktop hardware and applications, UNIX, VMS, premium services, Windows NT, server teams and Internet/multivendor support.

➔ Earned Trail Blazer award for three years due to highly professional, personal involvement in ensuring excellent service delivery and a positive attitude.

Contract Administration   5/00-9/03

Handled established accounts for upgrades, renewals and contract changes.

Sold supplemental services, including upgrades and add-ons; negotiated prices with customers.

→ Maintained a large database of major accounts, sales leads and multivendor relations.

→ Instrumental in conversions, updates, renewals, warranties and supplemental services.

Service Delivery   9/98-5/00

Worked extensively with major accounts to track performance measures and responses.

Coordinated/allocated vendor resources and subcontractors for quick problem resolution.

→ Implemented action plans by effectively managing installations and outages.

Office Manager, Chicago, IL   6/95-9/98

Effectively planned and implemented office procedures for internal support, including work order expediting.

Closely tracked and reported expenses and inventories.

→ Performed group and individual cross-training of technical staff in general reception, customer relations and office procedures.

Receptionist, Chicago, IL   3/92-6/95

Managed a wide range of tasks for complete administrative support, including call answering and expediting.

Communicated with customers and staff in a professional manner.

Handled a variety of general office procedures and paperwork.

EDUCATION: Harry S. Truman College, Chicago, IL
Successful completion of courses in Business.

New Horizons Learning Institute, Atlanta, GA
Completed courses in various Microsoft applications.

Sent five; received two interviews.

Pamela L. Elfin

2225 E. Madison Street
Chicago, IL 60661

Pamie@aol.com   312/555-4557

EXECUTIVE TRAINING / DEVELOPMENT: FINANCE

PROFILE:

➢ Plan and conduct executive training programs and seminars, including full responsibility for written and oral presentations to groups and individuals.

➢ Experience in promotions, public relations, special events and meetings to train and motivate staff, management and potential customers.

➢ Skilled in the research and writing of newsletters, brochures and instructional aids; familiar with various desktop publishing software, including Microsoft PowerPoint for promotions and creative correspondence.

➢ Strong knowledge of financial products, including stocks, bonds and mutual funds; utilize Excel for spreadsheets, graphs and charts.

EXPERIENCE: Old Tabby Investments, Chicago, IL   2007-Present
Investment Executive
Responsible for new business development by presenting seminars, networking and conducting informational programs to the general public.
Conduct interviews of potential clients and create custom investment programs for people in a wide range of situations.
Analyze individual portfolios to determine asset allocation, employing stocks, bonds, mutual funds and annuities for personal and retirement accounts.
Work closely with clients to determine and meet their specific investment goals.
Perform product research, spreadsheet development and status reporting on stocks and business development.

→ Utilize research skills and a strong knowledge of investment instruments and tax codes related to personal investing.
→ Winner of a free trip for Outstanding Contribution to Sales.

Smith Barney, Chicago, IL   2002-2006
Financial Consultant
Planned and conducted numerous presentations on investment topics for investment clubs and community groups.
Acted as consultant for fee-based, money management programs.
Conducted training on such topics as risk tolerance, needs, asset allocation and rollovers for retirees.
Assisted in strategic planning, defining investment goals and building investment portfolios.

→ Responsible for more than 300 accounts.

→ Additional topics included projecting financial needs for retirement, funding college education and maximizing retirement plans.

Gruntal & Company, New York, NY   2000-2002

Account Executive / Assistant to a Certified Financial Planner

Performed customer service and problem-resolution on a daily basis.

Assisted clients in retirement planning.

→ Advised and monitored investments for a small, personal group of clients.

→ Assisted in producing a quarterly newsletter with an emphasis on investment strategies.

Woodlawn Foundation, New York, NY   1998-2000

Fundraising Coordinator

Involved in designing a successful volunteer program to raise capital for an educational foundation.

Recruited, trained and motivated up to 75 volunteers involved in networking and fundraising.

Produced and constantly updated donor lists.

→ Monitored and computerized records.

> Chief writer, producer and editor of a quarterly newsletter.

Dean Witter, WI and IL   1991-1998

Account Executive

Responsible for selling and marketing investment services to a wide range of clients.

→ Promoted from various positions, including:

Branch Manager's Assistant, Registered Sales Assistant and Account Executive.

Prior Experience as:

Secretary to the president of a business consulting firm.

Secondary English teacher.

LICENSES: Series 7, Series 63, and N.A.S.D. Registration (1982).
                   Series 65 (1992).

EDUCATION: Boston College, Boston, MA
                   Bachelor of Arts Degree
                   * Graduated Cum Laude.
                   * Major: English; Minor: Secondary Education.

Job Search Resources

Following are some books, listings and online resources I've found to be valuable to my clients. Of course, what works best for you will depend on your current situation. As always, don't depend on any one resource—instead, always try to build and expand your network of personal industry contacts.

Websites, Books, Listings and Catalogs

Many of the books listed here cross-reference companies by industry and provide insight on company size and products, as well as names of human resource personnel and key managers.

Check the resources and support materials on these sites:

- **Execareers.com.** Free resume analysis by me or my staff; send your resume to Careers@Execareers.com or call toll-free: 877-610-6810. Optional: Custom career coaching for networking or interviewing, or targeted resume distribution to hundreds or thousands of recruiters, locally or nationwide, including their names and phone numbers so you can follow up.

- **6figurejobs.com** or **hundredK.com**

- **Careerpath.com.** Run by CareerBuilder.

- **Dice.com.** Especially for technical positions.

- **Indeed.com** or **SimplyHired.com**

- **Monster.com** or **CareerBuilder.com**

Aggregators and engines:

- **EmploymentCrossing.com.** They call themselves "job aggregators" and search for jobs across multiple platforms, including employer career web pages and Internet job boards.

- **StartWire.com.** Provides free, automatic updates on your job applications from more than 2,100 employers via email and text message. They can also provide recommendations on where to apply and friends who can help, as well as status indicators of your chances of getting a call based on your application date, the age of the job and industry benchmarks.

- **Hound.com.** Claims "unique access" to positions advertised on company sites.

- **Jobdig.com** and **Linkup.com.** Job search engines.

- **TheFeng.org** Financial Executives Networking Group or **Mengonline.com.** A network of top marketing executives.

- **TheLadders.com.** Good for six-figure positions; not recommended for resume writing.

- **Futurestep.com.** Outsourced recruitment; a Korn/Ferry Company.

- **Bluesteps.com.** Contacts with search firms.

- **Ritesite.com.** Contacts with hundreds of retained executive search firms.

Information:

- **ReferenceUSA.com.** Track down and research companies, locally or nationwide. There's a cost to register, but your library should have a subscription, and you might be able to log in at home with your library card.

- **CareerMag.com**

- **Employmentguide.com**

Job Agents

If you have a job and are looking for a better one, try a site that has a job agent. A job agent is a program that shops for jobs for you. These sites protect your confidentiality, search for your dream job and send you a private email based on the profile you provide. You can set up job search agents on sites and be notified automatically by email when new job postings match the criteria you listed. Many employer websites also allow job seekers to set up search agents to send new jobs as they're listed. A job search agent can also be set up to send listings to your cell phone or instant message account. Pretty cool.

When placing your credentials before a World Wide Web audience, be sure to use the text, online, digital format explained earlier, unless otherwise directed to use MS Word, PDF or other formats designated by the receiver.

Remember that using the Internet is not a substitute for traditional job-hunting techniques. Only a small percentage of jobs are filled through the big, public job boards (Monster, CareerBuilder, and so on), which should supplement, not replace, targeted emailing and networking. Of course, everything you post on the Internet is a public document, so keep it clean, honest and not too personal.

Networking Resources

There are entire books devoted to networking and career marketing; here are a few we've come across:

- *Guerrilla Networking: A Proven Battle Plan to Attract the Very People You Want to Meet* (AuthorHouse, 2009) by Jay Conrad Levinson and Monroe Mann

- *In Search of the Perfect Job* (McGraw-Hill, 2007) by Clyde C. Lowstuter

- *In Transition: From the Harvard Business School Club of New York's Career Management Seminar* (Harper Paperbacks, 1992) by Mary Lindley Burton and Richard A. Wedemeyer

- *Make Your Contacts Count: Networking Know-how for Business and Career Success* (AMACOM, 2007) by Anne Baber and Lynne Waymon

- *Network Your Way to Your Next Job...Fast* (McGraw-Hill, 1994) by Clyde C. Lowstuter and David P. Robertson

- *Never Eat Alone: And Other Secrets to Success, One Relationship at a Time* (Doubleday, 2005) by Keith Ferrazzi and Tahl Raz

- *The Networking Survival Guide, Second Edition: Practical Advice to Help You Gain Confidence, Approach People, and Get the Success You Want* (McGraw-Hill, 2010) by Diane Darling

- *Seven Days to Online Networking: Make Connections to Advance Your Career and Business Quickly* (JIST Works, 2008) by Ellen Sautter and Diane Crompton

Additional Job Search Resources

- *Rites of Passage at $100,000+ to $1 Million+* (Viceroy Press, 2001) by John Lucht. Lucht maps out a career marketing strategy that may work for you. Covers the recruitment business and how to make it work, personal and non-personal networking, direct mailings, interviewing and more.

- *America's Corporate Families, Vol. J and America's Corporate Families and International Affiliates, Vol. II* by Dun's Marketing Services. Two hardcover volumes updated annually. Information on more than 11,000 U.S. parent companies and their 60,000 subsidiaries and divisions.

- *Commerce Register's Geographical Directories of Manufacturers.* Numerous directories for specific regions. Organized by city, this book provides information on manufacturers with more than five employees in the state or region, including addresses, telephone numbers, products and sales figures.

- *Corporate 1000 Yellow Book, International Corporate 1000 Yellow Book, and Over-the-Counter 1000 Yellow Book.* By Monitor Publishing Co. Each lists names, titles, and many direct-dial numbers for officers, plus outside board members and their companies.

- *Directories in Print.* By Gale Research, Inc. Published every two years. Companies are organized by industry. Describes the contents of 10,000 publications, including directories, professional and scientific rosters and other lists and guides.

- *Directory of Corporate Affiliations.* By National Register Publishing Company, Inc. Subtitled *Who Owns Whom.* Lists 40,000 divisions/subsidiaries of more than 4,000 U.S. public and private companies. Gives assets, liabilities, net worth, income/earnings and approximate sales. Indexed by geography (state and city), S.I.C. (Standard Industry Code) and professionals affiliated with the company, with a cross-reference index of divisions, subsidiaries and affiliates. Also summarizes recent mergers, acquisitions and name changes.

- *Directory of Executive Recruiters.* Kennedy Publishing. Updated each year, lists thousands of executive recruiters. Indexed by industry specialties, with information on recruitment industry methods. The book and its lists of recruiters are also available on disc for an extra fee.

- *Dun's Europa.* By Dun's Marketing Services. Profiles top 35,000 European manufacturing, distribution, financial and service companies. Listings in both English and indigenous language.

- *Employment Agencies.* By American Business Directories. Lists thousands of employment agencies around the country.

- *Encyclopedia of Associations.* By Gale Research, Inc. Four volumes in three books, with detailed information on more than 22,000 U.S.-headquartered nonprofit associations and organizations of all kinds.

- *Encyclopedia of Business Information Sources.* By Gale Research, Inc. More than 20,000 information sources on 1,280 highly specific subjects ranging from abrasives to zinc. Lists encyclopedias, dictionaries, handbooks, manuals, bibliographies, associations, societies and so on.

- *Guide to American Directories.* By B. Klein Publications. Updated every two years. Describes content, frequency and cost (if any) of 7,500 directories in a variety of fields (more than 300 classifications) with phone numbers.

- *International Directory of Company Histories.* By St. James; available from Gale Research, Inc. Gives basic information and histories for about 1,250 companies in the United States, Canada, the U.K., Europe and Japan.

- *International Directory of Corporate Affiliations.* National Register Publishing Company, Inc., Vol. 1: Non-U.S. holdings of U.S. parent companies; Vol. 2: U.S. and worldwide holdings of foreign enterprises.

- *Job Hunter's Resource Guide.* By Gale Research, Inc. Annual, one volume. Lists reference materials for 150 specific professions/occupations. Also has a "how to" section.

- *Job Seeker's Guide to Public and Private Companies.* By Gale Research, Inc. Information on more than 25,000 companies, including corporate overviews, specific job titles, estimated number of openings for each, hiring practices, personnel contacts, employee benefits, application procedures and recruitment activities.

- *Million Dollar Directory Series.* Dun's Marketing Services. A five-volume series listing 160,000 public and private U.S. companies. Includes facts on decision makers, company size and lines of business. This may be hard to find, considering its $1,250 annual lease fee.

- *Million Dollar Directory of Top 50,000 Companies.* Dun's Marketing Services. Covers the top 50,000 companies from the *Million Dollar Directory* series.

- *Moody's Industrial Manual and News Reports.* By Moody's Investors Service. Annual, two volumes. Provides full financial and operating data on every industrial corporation on the NYSE and ASE, plus more than 500 on regional exchanges. Twice-weekly news reports update developments.

- *Moody's International Manual and New Reports.* Moody's Investors Service. Full financial data on more than 5,000 international corporations. Twice-weekly news reports update developments.

- *The National Directory of Addresses and Telephone Numbers.* By General Information, Inc. Great for your mailing list. Provides addresses and phone numbers for U.S. corporations, both alphabetically and by S.I.C. category.

- *Standard & Poor's Register of Corporations, Directors and Executives.* Three volumes with just about everything on major U.S. and Canadian companies and those who run them.

- *Standard Directory of Advertisers.* National Register Publishing Company, Inc. More than 25,000 U.S. advertiser companies with addresses, phone numbers, sales, number of employees and primary businesses.

- *Thomas Register of American Manufacturers.* Thomas Publishing Company. Annual profile of 150,000 manufacturers and their major products and services. Includes 12,000 pages of catalog material and 112,000 registered trade/brand names.

- *Ward's Business Directory of U.S. Private and Public Companies.* By Gale Research, Inc. Annual, four volumes. Provides demographic and financial business data on more than 85,000 companies. Includes alphabetical and ZIP code listings.

■ *Who's Who in America* or *Who's Who in Finance & Industry.* By Marquis Who's Who, Inc. These books profile thousands of leaders and innovators from fields including business, government, art, law, science, medicine and education.

Here's a sheet we give to our customers:

10 Strategies for Planning and Executing the Job Hunt

1. **Write/get a professional resume and solid base of operations.** When your resume is perfect, consult books on interviewing and get access to an answering machine, computer and high-quality printer for custom cover letters.

2. **Develop a "big world" outlook.** Enhance your peripheral vision. Look at any and every opportunity to get your foot in the door. If you're going after a select few companies and agencies, you face tremendous competition. Broaden your search and *network, network, network.*

3. **Target your audience.** Make your target group as large as possible, but remember the 80/20 rule: Focus most of your efforts on the 20 percent of your target group of greatest interest. Customize/personalize correspondence and, when possible, tailor your resume to the job.

4. **Be strategic.** Create a marketing plan for your job hunt. You're the product. Share the plan with those you meet. Refine the plan as you go along.

5. **Adjust your search to the market.** Concentrate your search on high-growth markets. Make yourself available for freelance or contract work.

6. **Don't be afraid to phone first.** Be assertive, yet considerate of the other's time. Persistence pays. Your goal is to get your name into the employer's head, to extract information and/or schedule an information interview. Thrive on rejection. Stay positive no matter what happens. Things change—sometimes quickly.

7. **Develop outside interests, but put in regular hours for your search.** If your life is well balanced, finding your next position is less stressful. You'll need endurance. Eat smart, get your sleep and get plenty of exercise.

8. **Be realistic.** It can take up to one month for every $10,000 in salary to find a job. Be prepared to start at a lower-paying position if required to supplement your income.

9. **Get attention.** Expand your network by joining a chamber of commerce or professional groups in your industry. Attend luncheons, seminars, dinners and after-hour meetings when possible. Meet new people and develop a network of contacts.

10. **Enjoy the hunt.** Job hunting can be a complex, challenging game with great payoffs for those with drive and stamina. Finding a job is probably the toughest job you'll ever have—and you don't even get paid for it—but you will become stronger for the experience.

Index

Free Resume Review

The career experts at ECS & DTP, Inc. have written thousands of resumes and performed career coaching or recruiter networking for clients in all 50 states and worldwide.

For a free, confidential review of your resume materials (outdated or recent) by the author or his staff, send to the email below in Microsoft Word or text format. You may also call our offices between 9 a.m. and 6 p.m. Central Time, Monday through Friday, or between 10 a.m. and 4 p.m. most Saturdays.

Email: Careers@Execareers.com

Author Direct: Execareers@aol.com

Toll Free: 877-610-6810 or 630-289-6222

Site: www.Execareers.com